The

Vital Touch

. . . .

HOW INTIMATE CONTACT

WITH YOUR BABY

LEADS TO HAPPIER,

HEALTHIER

DEVELOPMENT

Sharon Heller, Ph.D.

A Holt Paperback

HENRY HOLT AND COMPANY

NEW YORK

Holt Paperbacks
Henry Holt and Company, LLC
Publishers since 1866
175 Fifth Avenue
New York, New York 10010
www.henryholt.com

Library of Congress Cataloging-in-Publication Data
Heller, Sharon.
The vital touch: how intimate contact with your baby
leads to happier, healthier development / Sharon Heller.
p.   cm.
"A Holt Paperback"
Includes index.
ISBN-13: 978-0-8050-5354-8
ISBN-10: 0-8050-5354-9
1. Infants—Care. 2. Parent and infant. 3. Parenting—
United States. 4. Infants—Development. I. Title.
HQ774.H435   1997
649'.122—dc21   97-9434

Henry Holt books are available for special promotions and
premiums. For details contact: Director, Special Markets.

First Holt Paperbacks Edition 1997

Designed by Victoria Hartman

Printed in the United States of America

D 20 19 18 17 16

In memory of my father,
Seymour Heller (1921–1996)
and his tender touches

So the child learns life within human arms.
It learns to eat . . . to laugh, to play, to listen,
to watch, to dance, to feel frightened
or relaxed, in human arms.

—Margaret Mead, on Balinese childrearing practices

Contents

Part 3: Getting in Touch

Acknowledgments

$\mathscr{I}$ thank colleagues Gene Anderson, Ronald Barr, Angie Clausen, Virginia Colin, Daniel Freedman, Tiffany Field, Marshall Klaus, Steven Halpern, James McKenna, John Money, and Edward Tronick for their invaluable input in various parts of the book. I greatly appreciate the perceptive suggestions of friends Ileana Basquez, Hilary Liebowitz, and Marilyn Stephan, who each read different drafts of the manuscript. Special thanks to friend and colleague Cheryl Mroz for ongoing feedback and support throughout this project.

I am enormously grateful to my editors at Holt, Theresa Burns and her assistant Amy Rosenthal, for leading me in the right direction and helping me to pull it all together. And I thank my agent, Sherry Bykofsky.

Thank you Ashley Montagu, whose landmark book *Touching* inspired and informed this project, and whose encouragement, friendship, wit, and cheerful postcards carried me through its five-year evolution.

Last, I want to thank Patricia Crittenden for her profoundly illuminating theories on attachment and our many long conversations during which she taught me how to better understand what underlies human relationships. Had I not been touched by her brilliance, this book never could have evolved.

The Vital Touch

Introduction

$\mathcal{W}$hen I was four, I had my tonsils removed. More than forty years later, the experience reels back to me, scene by scene, like a home movie—a bad one.

I am lying alone in a hospital crib, crying. No one comforts me. I am taken on a long, lonely trip down a stark white corridor. Lying on my back on a cold, stiff cart, I peer in panic at the bright walls and white coats above me. Doctors and nurses hover over me. A doctor puts an ether mask on my face. "Count to ten backwards," he says.

I am then at home, sitting on my bed and crying frantically. My mother and grandmother are trying to force an aspirin down my throat. The harder they try, the harder I cry and push them away. From beginning to end, the experience was one of terror and loneliness. It's obvious why: Missing from the script was gentle, soothing touch.

Years later, again waiting to go under the knife for something quite minor, I felt a reverberation of the early panic. But now I had a better scriptwriter. Out of nowhere appeared two Filipino nurses by my side. "It's time to go to the operating room," one whispered with a gentle smile, as she tenderly caressed my cheek. Down that long, cold corridor they rolled me—all the while softly stroking my cheek, my brow, my forehead, and gently repeating, "It's okay, Sherry, it's okay." I no longer felt afraid. Why should I? I was a baby, safely back in my mother's arms.

I think it telling that the two nurses who nurtured me en route to surgery were from the Philippines. In the East, societies tend to fall on the high-touch end. This comfort with close contact starts in infancy, with mother and infant together most of the day. Here in the United States, which is a low-touch society, mothers and babies are apart most of the day, a fact that ranks our infants among the *least* held on this earth.

In nature's nativity scene, mother's arms have always been baby's bed, breakfast, transportation, even entertainment, and, for most of the world's babies, they still are. For more than a million years, mothers have carried their infants almost continuously, slept with them at night, nursed them frequently the first two to four years of life, and offered immediate comfort.

But in a blink of evolutionary time, we've altered the way humans have always lived on this earth, straying far from the intimate connectedness firmly rooted in forces of natural selection. Rather than keeping our babies on our bodies, we cache them in a container, transport them in buggies, breastfeed for a short period, if at all, and often sleep in separate rooms. When they cry, our first reaction is frequently to offer a pacifier or shake their buggies before picking them up. Many of us return to work before our babies complete the infancy period.

With our babies more often in a container than in our arms, our infants are "at odds with their evolution," as anthropologist James McKenna put it. This is no small problem. We may live in the Cyberspace Age, but our brains remain grounded in the Stone Age, the way humans have lived for 99 percent of our existence on this earth. Our brain, particularly the old mammalian part called the limbic system, which governs our emotions, is ancient. *"Darwinian Man, though well-behaved, / At best is only a monkey shaved,"* says a W. S. Gilbert song; scientists are now confirming this tongue-in-cheek lyric. So old is our brain that humans are 98.4 percent genetically identical to chimps and early humans. This means that nearly all our biochemistry and physiology are fine-tuned to conditions of life that existed when we were hunters and gatherers. And in that lifestyle, babies were kept on or near their mothers, their source of safety. After eons of such behavior, the baby's brain evolved through natural selection to *expect* life to be "a womb with a view," as Ashley Montagu phrased it in *Touching*, with the mother's brain hard-wired to provide that closeness.

The need to stay in touch hasn't changed: At the sight of our babies, our fingers itch to cuddle, stroke, and fondle them. What *has* changed is our environment. We opt for the buggy rather than the Snuglie, the crib rather than the parental bed, the swing rather than the rocking chair, because cultural values and customs discourage us from freely following our natural maternal feelings for intimacy and from responding fully to our baby's signals for closeness.

The first cultural shift to discourage closeness is equating touch, and therefore intimacy, with sexuality. *Touch* has become a dirty word. Because of our disturbingly high rate of childhood sexual abuse in this country (current figures estimate that 32 percent of children are affected) and the backlash that accompanies it, innocent touch can be misconstrued. As a result, parents who mistrust each other are more careful of acts that might presume impropriety. Nudity, co-sleeping, co-bathing, kissing on the lips, hugging, and holding unclothed children—all are often done, if at all, with some hesitancy, even with the very young child.

And then there's the issue of dependency. Obsessed with self-reliance, we demand early independence of our infants from our bodies and supreme independence for ourselves. In this way, we feel that we ensure that our infants don't get drunk with desire for hugs and later refuse to let go and we prevent our own cups from running dry.

Of course, there are those brave enough to transgress our culture's tacit law against holding babies too much—carrying their infants in slings, sleeping with their babies, refusing to wean early. But to do so they must fly under the radar of the touch police, who arch their brow, point their finger, and warn, "You'll spoil that baby!" Sorry, we need to tell them, our baby's genes beg to differ. Babies were meant to be held for hours, for days, and especially for nights. Touch is not an emotional fringe benefit for infants. It's as necessary as the air they breathe.

Our silent and most potent language, touch is the medium through which parent and infant communicate and become attached, each tender touch strengthening the bond between them. It nurtures our infants' psychological growth; stimulates their physical and mental growth; assures smoothness of physiological functions like breathing, heart rate, and digestion; enhances their self-concept, body awareness, and sexual identity; boosts their immune system; and even enhances the grace and stability of their movement. Experiments done with infant rats, cats, and monkeys show that, if cuddled, stroked, and licked, these animals grow up more gentle, peaceful, smarter, bigger, and healthier; if deprived of gentle touch, they grow up antisocial, miserable, sicker, smaller, less able to remember, less able to cope, and less able to mother. We've reason to believe humans are no different.

In fact, touch is literally a baby's lifeline. Able to thrive without hearing, without vision, and without smell, infants lacking affectionate touch literally perish from a syndrome called, appropriately, failure-to-thrive.

And touch never loses its force. Encompassing the gamut of human emotions, it guides us through life's emotional maze and unleashes emotional blockades: We can hide our feelings when spoken to or looked at, but when touched, feelings gush out. Nor does touch lie. Not to babies, who arch their backs to protest or stiffen up when touched by awkward hands, nor to us, for whom uneasy hands feel clawlike, making our skin taut, while loathesome hands make our skin crawl.

Nor does touch wane as we age, as do vision, taste, smell, and hearing. Rather, it continues to communicate caring, pleasure, love—even healing—all our lives. And we know why: The deep solace of our mother's embrace—that "oceanic feeling" as Freud called it—remains buried deep in our psyche, leaving us with a raw need for touch. When experiencing sorrow especially, a primitive longing for our mother can emerge. Witness Tolstoy, old and disconsolate:

> Felt dull and sad all day. . . . I wanted, as when I was a child, to nestle against some tender and compassionate being and weep with love and be consoled . . . become a tiny boy, close to my mother, the way I imagine her. Yes, yes, my Maman, whom I was never able to call that because I did not know how to talk when she died. . . . Maman, hold me, baby me!

When another's arms are unavailable, we hug ourselves, stroke our pets, and somehow cope. But it's never the same. In the embrace of another, we reclaim our wholeness.

"The need to touch someone can be so great at times that it's as close to madness as I ever hope to come," lamented poet Rod McKuen. And while few of us would express such extreme sentiments, touch's power to mellow us when agitated, reconnect us when isolated, and renew our spirit when forlorn leaves most of us clamoring for more.

We cannot—nor would we want to—return to our primeval past and hold our babies all day, which would exhaust and bore the average parent. Nor do we need to. Few babies demand round-the-clock contact, and no longer do we fear, if we put them down, that they will be eaten by predators. Furthermore, humans are marvelously flexible and adaptable to a broad range of parenting styles.

But this flexibility is constrained by the patterns stamped into our DNA. For though culture modifies instinctual patterns, it doesn't remove them: We can vary our behavior from these original patterns, but we can't alter our basic human nature. Carrying our babies to the car in a container, out of the car in a container, through the mall in a container, into the restaurant in a container, back to the car in a container, and home to a container, so that objects define our baby's existence more so than our body, is not just a step away from tradition. It is a cataclysmic change *far* out of step with the rhythmic pas de deux to which our babies' minds and bodies were choreographed. True, every culture plays out evolution's composition in a slightly different tune, but by disregarding the biological and natural conditions in which our infants were designed to adapt, our society is piercingly discordant.

No species in a hundred years or so can turn the time-tested mother-baby relationship on its head without consequences. In the short term, diminished contact makes babies fussier than they need be and mothers more conflicted than they need be. Though the long-term consequences are less easily identified, our isolationism, our difficulties with intimacy, our adversarial relationship with our own bodies, all likely relate to a culture that promotes mother-baby disconnection from the beginning and pronounced reduction in close human contact that, even in the most affectionate parent-infant relationships, is still often a mere slice of an infant's day.

This book is not a parenting how-to. This book is about the continuous battle between our genes and our culture, between wanting intimacy with our babies and being discouraged from getting close, and how that friction stresses the very fabric that holds the mother-baby relationship together.

Since our biology has existed for about two million years longer than modern culture, it is not an equal fight. A mother's wish for intense intimacy with her child—the baby's key means of survival since the beginning of human history—is a part of our biological heritage that isn't going away. A culture that makes a mother feel guilty for this natural inclination (and therefore in doubt of her own maternal feelings) and that fails to provide necessary support systems to buttress the mother-infant relationship is out of sync with our basic human nature. It begs for change.

Part I of this book begins by explaining how the *power of touch* affects birthing practices, newborn stability, the quality of mother-infant attachment, how and how much sensory stimulation our babies receive, and even the speed at which they get up and crawl away from our arms. Part II discusses the cultural habits that put us *out of touch* with our infants: all the containers in which we nest our babies; our prudish sense of our body, which leads to a withholding of affection, unsuccessful nursing, and a distortion of normal sexual development; our lack of support for the nursing mother; and our taboos against co-sleeping. Part III discusses how modern parents can compromise between nature's call for closeness to their babies and our culture's plea for distance.

A few caveats: When speaking of infants, I am speaking of infants in general. If you are a parent reading this book, your baby may or may not fit into behavioral generalizations. That's all right. Each baby demonstrates uniformity (our inherited biology) and individuality (our unique inheritance from our parents and from our culture). And, in order to avoid the gender problem inherent in our language, rather than calling a baby *it*, I interchange *he* and *she*.

PART *1*

The Power of Touch

Our days, our deeds, all we achieve or are,

Lay folded in our infancy . . .

—John T. Trowbridge

1

❧

Parenting in the Machine Age

Nature is already as good as it can be.
It cannot be improved upon.
He who tries to redesign it, spoils it.
He who tries to redirect it, misleads it.

—Lao-tzu

In the child development classes that I teach, I often ask my students to tell me in what position women have traditionally given birth. Lying down, they say. No, I tell them: squatting. Invariably, I get confused looks. The problem lies in the word *traditionally*. My class defines it as what most women in the United States have done in the last fifty years or so. I define it as what most women on this earth have done for millennia.

Independence vs. Interdependence

❧ To best understand our human nature, which will aid us in making parenting choices, we need to look first at our evolutionary roots.

From the beginning of human time, people have roamed this earth in small bands of thirty to one hundred, forming little villages that congregated around a water source. Social animals by nature, and team players, people lived not separated by concrete walls and locked doors but in huts and tents positioned close together: Either they cooperated and shared resources or they competed and killed one another.

The !Kung San Bushmen of the Kalahari Desert in Africa, a modern tribal culture studied intensely since the 1950s, were believed to be one of the few hunting-gathering tribes still left on earth. The structure of their culture reveals much about how humans lived before we ever wielded a hoe or shoveled coal.

Women all came from a "double-income" family, where both mother and father contributed to the family's welfare. Every few days, with their babies safe in slings on their hips, the women paraded in small groups into the bush to gather baobab fruit and other delectables. They left their older children at the village to romp with the other kids, under a grandmother's or aunt's supervision: Day care was free, entertainment was free, and playmates were everywhere. Returning to the village, the women sat on the ground with their babies in their arms or next to them, grooming each other's hair and chattering about what a good lunch they would have. Their older children galavanted nearby. Every three days or so, the men hunted an antelope, a sand grouse, or a giraffe.

Continuously surrounded by kin and community, mother was able to hand her baby over to the waiting arms of grandmother, sister, aunt, neighbor, or an older child when she was tired or wanted to swim in the river or escape into the bushes with her husband. With time to rest and revitalize, she could then eagerly take her baby back.

Though few hunting and gathering tribes are left, most people on this earth still live within the basic structure of extended family and close-knit communities where people, for the most part, rally to one another's side and where the community takes responsibility for the welfare of the children.

Most people, that is, except us. Inhabitants of islands unto ourselves, we live in an individualistic culture, where independence and self-reliance rule. Housed in nuclear families of mother, father, and a few children, we are relatively isolated from kin and live next door to people we rarely talk to. Our motto is every man for himself. When mother is tired, which is often, she stays tired. When she wants to soak in the tub, she places her baby on a blanket on the bathroom floor. When she needs to run to the store, she carts her baby along. When she desires time alone with her husband, she needs to pay a babysitter. As for time alone—what's that?

Stressed, frustrated, unsure, conflicted, and at times resentful from the pressure to assume almost full responsibility for their children's care, modern mothers have a lifestyle that seems "normal" and "traditional" but is in fact neither. Interdependence, not independence, sits best with our basic human nature.

Nor is this pattern going to change any time soon. Our brain's biochemistry and structure, having evolved over millions of years as an adaptation to life within small communities of close kinship, is unable to accommodate the supreme self-reliance and isolation of modern urban life. To ask us to conform to patterns so out of sync with our fundamental tendencies is, as anthropologist Lionel Tiger put it, "like trying to teach a very old animal some very new tricks, without taking into account the nature of the beast." The sounds of personal, familial, and social chaos in our anxious, malcontent, frenzied, and violent society attest to this. Jarring our nerves, our society's practices beg for tuning.

Technology's Isolating Influence

Our strong emphasis on independence came of age with the industrial revolution. Driven by the competition of the free market, upward mobility was the hallmark of our new technology, and self-reliance was the battle cry. The close emotional ties that had defined our species were suddenly discouraged. They were encumbering, we were told, a hindrance to moving up and out and therefore against the American grain of progress.

With the invention of the telephone and faster transportation, families spread out, and the nuclear family replaced the extended one, leaving mother almost single-handedly in charge of children and home. The sooner infants could soothe themselves, feed themselves, sleep and play by themselves, the easier for her.

And so began the denial of infancy as a time of deep dependency. The transition period into independent existence for some American babies, quipped Margaret Mead, "lasts less than a minute—until the umbilical cord is cut!"

Given this climate, American parents were ripe for behaviorism. Led by John Watson, the behaviorists believed we are born a blank slate, our habits and personality formed by rewarding good behavior and punishing the bad. Dependency was bad.

To "form" an independent child, we needed to nip infantile cravings in the bud, before the newborn had the chance to learn dependent habits. *Hold* your babies too much, mothers were warned, and later they will *hold on.* Let them cry it out, and they will become self-reliant, hardy, and able to tolerate frustration (of which there was no shortage!), the qualities necessary to succeed in a competitive market.

The following excerpt from Watson's book *The Psychological Care of Infant and Child,* written in 1928 and hailed by *Parents* magazine as necessary for "every intelligent mother's shelf," reveals the severity of the views that shaped our parents' and grandparents' upbringing:

> There is a sensible way of treating children. . . . Never hug and kiss
> them, never let them sit in your lap. If you must, kiss them once on
> the forehead when they say good night. Shake hands with them in the
> morning. Give them a pat on the head if they have made an extraordi-
> narily good job of a difficult task.

If Watson's advice doesn't make you shudder, consider that of Luther
Emmett Holt, Sr., the Dr. Spock of that generation. An inveterate anti-
baby toucher and a forceful influence on Watson, he dealt the coûp de
grace to loving and nurturant parenting. In *The Care and Feeding of Children*, the doctor recommended that a parent not spoil the baby by picking
it up, no matter how long it cried; to feed the baby on a strict, four-hour
schedule—bottle feeding considered as good as breastfeeding; and to abol-
ish the cradle, as rocking was an an "unnecessary" habit, "hard to break
and a very useless and sometimes injurious one."

In one fell swoop, these touch prohibitionists denounced the womb
comforts that had served babies from time immemorial. Deprived of sufficient holding, warmth, containment, rocking, and sucking, babies spent
long periods hungry and frustrated, and parents turned from being a source
of assured comfort to one of frequent frustration.

The influence of the behaviorists was powerful. For more than twenty
years, *Infant Care*, published by the U.S. Children's Bureau, warned mothers to avoid at all costs picking up baby between feedings, lest they teach
baby that "crying will get him what he wants," and create "a spoiled, fussy
baby, and a household tyrant whose continual demands make a slave of the
mother." Pressured by the "experts" and reassured that crying was necessary
to "exercise their baby's lungs," mothers for decades denied normal maternal feelings. Reluctantly, but dutifully, they withheld cuddling, kissing, and
rocking, delayed soothing, discouraged thumb-sucking, and bottle fed on a
strict four-hour feeding schedule.

This had profound repercussions on how our grandparents parented our
parents and how they, in turn, parented us. "It *killed* me to hear you cry,"
said a friend's mother to her, "but I thought I would do you harm if I picked
you up." Another mother cried along with her baby. By the time her
second child came, she decided this was senseless: "No one's home but me,
so no one will see if I pick him up."

Why did the American public buy into such harsh treatment of babies?
The behaviorists' philosophy fit into the American dream. If we are born a
blank slate and lack any biological influence on our behavior, we can shape
our babies into becoming anything we want them to become. "Give me a

dozen healthy infants," wrote John Watson, "well formed and my own specified world to bring them up in, and I'll guarantee to take any one at random and train him to become any type of specialist I might select— doctor, lawyer, artist, merchant-chief and, yes, even beggar-man and thief, regardless of his talents, penchants, tendencies, abilities, vocations, and race of his ancestors."

For countless parents, life is not that simple. By asserting that all behavior is learned and subject to unlimited malleability, the behaviorists ignored inborn tendencies. In so doing, they wrote their own epitaph.

Both our physical characteristics and our behavior are products of natural selection, fine-tuned over several million years to best assure the survival of our species. Our large brains, for instance, evolved as an adaptation to the large variations and unpredictability inherent in the environments in which we lived. Regardless of its adaptability in our modern high-tech society, our behavior remains guided by the survival mechanisms within our brain that served genetic self-interest in a time long past. Who we marry, the food we eat, and how we parent reflect in large part what solutions to problems succeeded in spurring our early ancestors' genes into the next generation.

Take the problem of what to do with the infant when mothers went foraging. The obvious solution was for mothers to carry their babies with them, since leaving a child unattended for even a moment could spell peril. Having lost our body hair so that our babies could no longer cling like monkeys, mothers developed rounded hips for their babies to straddle and a powerful desire to keep their baby close to them. That our cultural patterns have jumped far ahead of nature's original design for baby care is something that our brain doesn't give a hoot about. Since our maternal feelings and behavior were tested in the environment in which we evolved, these early patterns will remain a stubborn influence in modern life. In other words, though carrying babies around may be at times inconvenient and emotionally stifling, we will continue to have curved hips and, when separated from our infants, guilty feelings.

This does not mean we live in a biological straitjacket. Our behavior is neither wholly learned nor wholly inherited. Rather, heredity lays the foundation of our psychological house and, depending on the plan that best suits adaptation in any given environment, culture varies the style. In life-threatening environments, babies are kept continually close to their mothers during the first year of life. In environments where predators do not lurk, babies are often nested in cradles or cribs for part of the day, with mother nearby. Nevertheless, the underlying structure of the culture reflects nature's original blueprint—an intimate mother-baby relationship embedded in a close-knit community.

To uphold the integrity of this basic design, nature always seeks balance. Consequently, when a given culture varies too far from this basic design, threatening the stability of the mother-baby relationship, a self-righting system motivates us (as a group) to restructure our behavior to a closer ecological fit. It was thus only a matter of time before mothers united against an edict denying them their natural maternal feelings. Slowly, the empire of the anti-touchers began to crumble—though not without resistance.

Among the first people to help infuse nurturance back into our limp infant rearing system was Dr. Fritz Talbot, who discovered stirring proof of the power of tender loving touch while visiting the wards of a children's clinic in Dusseldorf, Germany, before World War I. Struck by the sight of a squat old woman carrying around a sick, feeble child, he inquired who she was. "Oh that is Old Anna. When we have done everything we can medically for a baby and it is still not doing well, we turn it over to Old Anna, and she is always successful." Upon his return to his hometown of Boston, Talbot introduced loving touch into our hospitals and institutions. By the late 1920s, Dr. J. Brenneman, a hospital pediatrician, introduced a rule in his hospital that every baby should be "picked up, carried around, and 'mothered' several times a day." Thanks to "mothering," by 1938 mortality rates for infants at Bellevue Hospital in New York City fell within one year from around 35 percent to less than 10 percent.

With a trend throughout the century moving increasingly in the direction of less harsh parenting, modern parents tend, in general, to be more nurturant than their parents were, who were more nurturant than *their* parents were. Nevertheless, there's still cause for concern: In spite of all our progress, the postmodern era is more container crazy then ever. Cribs, port-a-cribs, bassinets, cradles, plastic infant seats, bouncies, playpens, highchairs, swings, walkers, buggies, strollers—there's no limit to our use of containers. Of course, there's nothing wrong with using them as parenting supports. But we've gone beyond this: Too often they become parenting substitutes.

Overuse of these touch thieves dehumanizes parenting, creating a wedge between mothers and babies that robs infants of maternal warmth, comfort, and security and robs mothers of intimacy and the assurance that their baby is safe. Pushing babies into premature independence by forcing early self-regulation, rather than mutual regulation with mother, and instilling in infants a sense of disconnectedness from the human experience, a dependence on containers contributes to the social isolation that plagues modern society.

Why do parents use containers so much? Modern parents lack helping hands. What's more, though mothers are more nurturant today, conflict still abides. Even when maternal feelings seem right, a voice of doubt nags at us that too much love will create dependency in our infants. This worry infiltrates our child-care practices: From the beginning, there's a push to disconnect mother and baby.

It begins with a denial of the mother's dependent needs, with a disconnection between her feelings and her body. It begins with the way we give birth.

Our Technological Birth

Jessica just had a baby boy. "Oh how wonderful," I say. "Who's your doctor?"

"Isaiah Coopersmith."

"Which hospital?"

"Memorial."

"Did you deliver naturally?"

"Yes, but it was touch and go. I labored for so long, Coopersmith kept on suggesting a C-section."

"Did they give you pitocin to speed up labor?"

"Yes."

"Did you have an epidural for the pain?"

"Oh God, yes. The pain was unbearable."

"Did you have an episiotomy?"

"Yes, doesn't everyone?"

Hospital; male doctor; C-section; epidural; pitocin; episiotomy—outside the industrialized world, these terms would not suggest childbirth.

The twentieth-century machine age made hospital births rather than home births de rigueur. As a result, birth often takes place in a perfunctory, cold, overlighted, overstimulating delivery room that transforms birth from a natural event attended by supportive family into a depersonalized medical model of illness directed by machines and strangers in a strange environment.

Theoretically, hospital births are not all bad. In fact, they accord with the basic rule of evolution: survival. Giving birth is a time of maximum defenselessness: Should danger arise, the mother is unable to fight or flee.

To maximize survival, birth needs to take place where mother feels most safe and secure. In that modern medicine has all but eliminated childbirth as a life-threatening event for both mother and baby, this *should* have made childbirth less anxious, but it didn't. To feel safe, human beings need the comfort of others.

"In the imagery of our industrial society," wrote Margaret Mead, "the human body becomes a factory that manufactures human beings." Anthropologist Robbie Davis-Floyd extended Mead's metaphor further. The hospitalized birthing process, she said, operates like an "assembly line," with mother a "birthing machine" run by "skilled technicians working under semiflexible timetables to meet production and quality control demands." If the medical team was prepped but mother's labor slowed down, the medical team got the "show on the road" by giving the mother a shot of pitocin, a labor-inducing drug.

No sooner did mother enter the hospital than birth as a technological ritual began. Stripped, tagged, IV'd, shaved, monitored, and, before husband and other family were allowed in, lying all alone, the mother "was symbolically stripped of her individuality, her autonomy, and her sexuality." With the mother emotionally disconnected from her own body, birth lost its intimacy and set the stage for the disconnection between mother and newborn.

This split typified the tendency inherent in Western culture to divide the mind and the body as two separate entities. Later, the epidural—which by freezing the lower half of the body divides mind and body—made an interesting accomplice to the schism, points out Davis-Floyd. And it further reinforced the hospital's control over the mother's body.

All this impersonalization left the mother feeling alienated, passive, and anxious. As a result, her contractions suppressed, her pain escalated, and her labor was prolonged. Interestingly, though home births present greater risk for mothers and babies, the mother, surrounded by family and friends, feels less fearful.

These findings are not trivial. So profound is the effect of the mother's emotional state on childbirth that it even affects her baby's birth weight. In the days following birth, babies commonly lose weight, something we assume to be both normal and physiological. Since newborns initially receive colostrum (a yellowish milky substance that, though rich in protein and antibodies, has fewer calories than milk) from their mother's breast, its ingestion was presumed to be the reason. But in studying home births in France, Dr. Michel Odent discovered something quite extraordinary: One in three babies do not lose weight. Apparently, the intimacy of home birth, which relaxes the mother and creates serenity and exquisite closeness with her baby, allows her milk to flow more easily. As a result, her baby ingests more colostrum.

The orchestrator of the whole American birth process? For the first time in human history, it was a male. Most women, from the villages of India to the barrios of Guatemala, would be dismayed. In only two of 186 cultures studied by pediatrician Betsy Lozoff did a man partake in the delivery of the baby. In 81 percent of societies, men, unless they are the fathers, are not even allowed at births. In 96 percent of all cultures, a female companion (who has herself had a baby and who is usually trained in midwifery) is present during birthing. A comforting presence, midwives traditionally give advice and massages throughout the pregnancy; during delivery they nurture the mother with soothing words and comforting touch. Advice, massages, giving of herbs, even cooking, cleaning, and caring for the other children continues often for a month postpartum. What does it mean that our birth practices have traditionally excluded the presence of a comforting, nurturant woman? Far more than we realize.

Mothering the Mother

In the 1970s, pediatricians Marshall Klaus and John Kennell were observing the way mothers touched their babies following birth. They instructed their research assistants only to get approval for study participation from mothers in early labor and then leave, allowing the mother to go through the usual hospital routine. But one of the medical students failed to follow instructions and instead stayed with the mothers, giving emotional and physical support until they delivered.

At first, Klaus and Kennell were upset at this because they had to throw out part of their data. But when they looked at the charts of these mothers, they discovered something interesting. These women had unusually short labors. Three even delivered in bed. The "birth" of this mistake was the introduction of the doula—a Greek term for a woman caregiver of a birthing woman, into labor and delivery.

What is the difference between a nurse and a doula? While a nurse is assigned to the mother throughout labor, she is not trained to nurture the mother but rather to monitor the birthing process and to provide nursing care. A doula, by contrast, acts as a traditional midwife. She holds the laboring mother, strokes her gently, speaks to her softly, explains what is happening to her, follows the mother's pace, and remains by her side.

Her impact? Powerful!—a 50 percent reduction in C-sections; 25 percent reduction in length of labor; 40 percent reduction in use of oxytocin to increase contractions; 30 percent reduction in need of pain medication; 40 percent reduction in use of forceps; 60 percent reduction in requests for epidural and less pain during labor. In other words, the doula has an incredible ability to mitigate maternal stress and to influence the progress of labor. T. Berry Brazelton once witnessed this firsthand: While observing a birth among the Mayan Indians of Mexico, the midwife left while the woman was laboring. Labor stopped. Nothing Brazelton could do helped the labor along. When the midwife returned, labor spontaneously resumed and the woman had a normal birth.

The doula's power doesn't stop with birth. Mothers who had a doula feel better about their delivery, have far less postpartum blues, and show increased self-esteem six weeks postpartum.

Why don't we think to use a doula? It goes back to the mind/body dichotomy. When the mother gets distressed, our impulse is to treat her body and largely ignore her thoughts and feelings—to administer a drug to solve the problem. The doula does the opposite. Through touch, she taps into the mother's feelings, into her need for reassurance and for nurturance. And through touch she taps the mind's own drugstore, releasing endorphins—a natural painkiller—and raising the level of serotonin in the mother's bloodstream, relieving depression.

By providing, as Klaus says, "a holding environment for the mother . . . a strong metaphor for what the mother does to the baby," the doula allows the laboring mother to feel mothered. She in turn transfers that nurturance onto her infant. Thus, mothers who had a doula were more affectionate with their babies, spent less time away from them, and breastfed more. They also reported far fewer feeding problems in their infants—16 percent versus 63 percent in the no-doula group. This gives us hope that perhaps a mother who had been badly mothered herself has the opportunity for a more positive start with her baby. (For information about how to find a doula, see the Resource Guide.)

Does this mean father should be eliminated from the delivery room? Not at all. In fact, says Klaus, the presence of the doula helps reassure the often inexperienced and nervous father.

Don't Take It Lying Down

When the first male entered the delivery room in the seventeenth century, out went another time-honored tradition: giving birth upright.

The !Kung woman sits on the ground to give birth. The Native American woman leans against her husband. Woman has always given birth either standing, squatting, or sitting reclined against someone because it helps her use her thigh and abdominal muscles to push the baby out and down with the force of gravity. This increases her contractions and helps the cervix to dilate more efficiently, shortening labor by a third.

Why did no one tell the American mother? Off in the twilight zone, lying on her back with her feet in the air, a position used rarely in societies other than technological ones, she was forced to fight against gravity, thus prolonging her labor and reinforcing her loss of control to the hospital. Additionally, lying supine resulted in reduced blood flow to the fetus, which increased the frequency of fetal distress. It is further implicated in the routine use of the episiotomy—an incision into the tissues surrounding the opening of the vagina (perineum)—which is still employed in 50 to 90 percent of all American births. Used presumably to avoid extensive tearing of the perineum and to make delivery easier and speedier for the baby's safety, many claim it is used more for the doctor's convenience and is unnecessary.

Dr. Michel Odent, who heads a hospital in Pithiviers, France, devoted entirely to natural childbirth, would agree. At Pithiviers, where the mother enjoys maximum control over her delivery, most "choose" to give birth squatting, which makes episiotomy unnecessary. In fact, Odent has never observed a dangerous tear following delivery in the squatting position. Writes Dora Henschel, Principal of Midwifery Education at King's College Hospital in London, who witnessed a birth at Pithiviers in the early days:

> As she [the mother] started to push, the midwife showed her the progress of the head using a mirror. I was somewhat amazed to find the midwife at the side of the bed. . . . I thought this baby was going to fall out or there was going to be a tear. The only thing the midwife said was, do some more, do some more, there, we are all done. The head was born and the perineum just gave. . . .

In other words, severe tearing appears to be more a casualty of modern birthing methods than a biological given, which makes evolutionary sense. In hunting-and-gathering societies, the woman's role as gatherer was essential to the economy. Severe tears following childbirth would have prohibited a mother from mobility for a period of time, and thus from finding food for her family. The !Kung San woman gives birth alone in the bushes, cuts the umbilical cord, and then carries her baby back to the village. A few days later, she returns to foraging. Furthermore, when resources became sparse, villages were moved—about five to six times a year. A mother lacking mobility would have become a burden to the clan, as each member had to carry her children and all her belongings.

Use of episiotomy also furthers the medical model of childbirth by transforming even the most natural childbirths into a surgical procedure. What's more, along with the high rate of C-sections—currently 20 percent of American births—episiotomy converts the postpartum period into one of recuperation. This draws the mother's focus onto her healing body and away from nurturing her newborn. At Pithiviers, Henschel was surprised to see the mother take her newborn into her arms and walk to her room. In the United States, mothers, weary after an exhausting labor and an episiotomy, need rest and often willingly relinquish their baby to the care of the nursing staff.

American Birth Today

Societies, notes anthropologist Robin Fox, have their own endogenous healing powers, their own antibodies and autoimmune systems. Consequently, just as our anti-nurturing caregiving practices underwent a revolution in the last thirty years or so, so too did our birthing practices: Nature has been weaved back into the birthing room. The presence of father and family as a support system during the birth is now routine. Rooming-in is commonplace and comforting. Heavy anesthesia during delivery, which robbed mother of postpartum closeness, is essentially nonexistent. Women, given a choice in positioning during labor, are encouraged to "stand and deliver." And midwives are more common in low-risk pregnancies.

Nevertheless, though off the critical list, our birthing process has not fully recovered. Technological overkill still typifies births, and we continue to use procedures that seem to relate more to hospital convenience than to necessity. For instance, to expedite the transfer of the baby to a radiant heated table or crib for evaluation, many hospitals routinely clamp the umbilical cord and cut it immediately postbirth. With mother and baby no longer attached, one person can care for the newborn, cleaning, weighing, and so forth, while another can stitch up the mother following an episiotomy and give her pitocin to release the placenta and contract her uterus to normal size. When mother receives her baby, the newborn is all wrapped up, depriving both mother and baby of the intense intimacy of skin-to-skin contact.

But in traditional births, the naked, wet baby is put immediately on the mother's stomach and the umbilical cord not cut until it stops pulsing a few minutes after birth, since the baby continues to receive blood and oxygen from the placenta. The mother, who likely delivered in a squatting position, will probably need neither episiotomy nor stitching. Nor does she need pitocin to expel the afterbirth, which happens naturally if baby is put to breast. The baby's licking of the mother's nipples releases oxytocin, which causes contraction of her uterus, expulsion of the placenta, and inhibition of postpartum bleeding. Why change what doesn't need change?

Why aren't mothers more assertive in requesting traditional care? When they do, they're often in conflict with hospital policy and procedure. Furthermore, the overwhelming majority of mothers still put control in the doctor's hands. ("I wanted to use a birthing chair but my doctor was old-fashioned, and so there I was, flat on my back," one mother tells me.)

When mother gets home, the opposite occurs. Mothers are in complete charge—of everything and everyone!

Who's Minding Mother?

✻ "You look exhausted," I say to a Jamaican woman in my child development class. "Yes. I have a three-month-old at home and I'm up all night." She was unsuccessful at nursing and so the baby is bottle fed, she tells me, "but the nipple opening is too small and he's swallowing a lot of air." Fussy and constantly gassy, "he screams all night for food, and sleeps only twelve hours a day." She wants to sleep with him but her husband, who is American, has forbidden it, telling her she will make the baby "too dependent."

She asks for my advice on everything from finding a better nipple to calming him.

"Is anyone helping you at home?" I ask her. "No one," she says, "I'm all alone. A nurse was supposed to come and teach me the basics, but three months later I've yet to see one."

"If you were still in Jamaica, would you be having these problems?"

"Oh Lord, no," says she. "There would be people all around helping me."

Loss of Postpartum Confinement

In rural Jamaica, mother and baby go into seclusion for a minimum of nine days following birth. The midwife, grandmother, or nanny cooks, cleans, shops, does the chores, and takes care of the other children as well as the new mother. They bathe and massage her, teach her the best nursing positions and how to bathe her baby. And mother? She rests and takes care of her baby. In many households, the nanny stays to help care for the baby throughout infancy.

In southern Mexico, the Zinacanteco Indian mother and infant will be confined for one month, the infant swaddled in mother's arms or lying supine beside her. Baby grows. Mother rests. Farther south in Sao Paulo, Brazil, even the modern mother enjoys a month or so of pampering, as her own mother moves in to assume all the chores, care for the other children, and support and train the mother in baby care and personal hygiene. In southern Italy, mother, rarely left alone during the first months, is cared for by her mother-in-law who, in addition to the chores, prepares sumptuous meals for up to one month after birth. In Holland, mothers who deliver at home get ten days of help from a baby nurse. And in Australia, within days of the infant's birth, a trained nurse visits and takes care of all the baby's routine health needs and makes herself available by phone for all questions ranging from bathing to breastfeeding.

On the Japanese islands of Goto Archipelago, studied for many years by T. Berry Brazelton, new mothers stay in bed for one month after delivery, wrapped in their quilts with their new baby wrapped up next to them. As mother feeds her infant and rests, she is cared for like a child; grandmothers, aunts, and relatives take care of her, feed her, help her to the bathroom, and speak to her in baby talk to which she responds in a high-pitched voice. In Japanese cities, an urban mother travels to her own mother's home to give birth in a hospital in her hometown, surrounded by her relatives.

Indian mothers from the modern city of Bombay spend four to five days in the hospital and then stay with their mothers for up to two months after delivery; fathers visit as often as possible. Mother gets massaged for an hour every day for a month, as does her baby. Swedish mothers stay in the hospital until recuperated, able to care for their infants, and into the nursing groove.

Postpartum confinement exists for at least a week in 97 percent of the world's cultures, says pediatrician Betsy Lozoff of Case Western Reserve University. "In our own colonial past, women of the community took turns helping the mother for three to four weeks, so all she had to do was stay in bed and take care of the baby."

And today? In the United States, after one day in the hospital, mother and baby are expected to function more or less independently. With little if any outside help, mother returns home to nurture a new baby, a spouse, often other children, *and* to cook dinner, do dishes, wash clothes, make beds, go grocery shopping. With few supports, the new mother, physically exhausted, emotionally depleted, and, if a first-time mother, lacking experience in caring for an infant, finds the responsibility awesome and will become easily anxious and confused about doing what is "right." American writer Anne Tyler echoes such sentiments:

> I remember leaving the hospital . . . thinking, "Wait, are they going to let me just walk off with him? I don't know beans about babies! I don't have a license to do this. [We're] just amateurs."

When a family hires a nurse, the nurse takes primary care of the baby and mother takes primary care of the house, rather than the opposite. ("I felt as if I needed permission to change her diaper," said one mother.) Given the mother's meager preparation for parenting, her quick deference to a stranger is not surprising. Though mothers receive training in breastfeeding, bathing the baby, and other postpartum care before discharge from the hospital, because of her short hospital stay, training needs to be done the first day postpartum. But mothers are often in a fog during this time and unable to absorb all the information.

Little wonder many arrive home feeling overwhelmed. Our alarmingly high rate of postpartum blues in this country—from 50 to 85 percent—occurs, in part, from an ethos that says do it all yourself and learn instantly, without experience, with little training, and with little or no guidance, perhaps the most essential role you'll ever perform. Baby blues are so rare in more child-oriented societies, writes baby expert Penelope Leach, that the very concept is hard to communicate. Asked a puzzled West African woman: "Has this unhappy woman you tell me of not got her child?"

At Michel Odent's clinic in France, postpartum blues is rare. Mothers experience drug-free natural birth, a supportive environment, active participation in learning how to care for their infant, and rooming-in. There is no "nursery" at Pithiviers—and mothers go home when they feel ready. Moreover, because of the close contact, their newborns do not cry excessively. It makes a difference.

❧

2

Newborn Harmony

I stood in the hospital corridor the night after she was born.
Through a window, I could see all the crying newborn infants and
somewhere among them was mine. . . .

— Liv Ullmann, actress

*I*magine a mother from the African bush reading what Liv Ullmann wrote, or one from the mountains of Mexico. What would she think?
Stolen! Her baby must have been stolen and left alone to cry.

In technology's takeover of labor and delivery, mother lost ownership of
her body. With birth itself, she lost ownership of her baby. After nine
months in the womb, newborns were pulled out and then, before spending
nine minutes in their mother's arms, whisked away to slumber in plastic
containers behind a glass partition. Mother, by turns exhausted and ex-
alted, beguiled and bewildered, was sent to her room to recuperate, united
with her baby after six to eight hours and after that for twenty- to thirty-
minute feedings every four hours.

Was this separation of mother and infant wise? Not if we think of the
postnatal adaptation required of the newborn.

Bonding

❧ In the dark, warm, snug bath of the womb, life is perfect harmony, all
needs provided automatically, effortlessly. Then . . . *boom!* . . . cold,
humidity, discordant sounds, bright lights, gravity, and unbridled space
assault the newborn's brain, while probing, pulling, intruding, rubber hands
assault his as yet untouched body.

But when the baby is reconnected with the mother's body, hugs, warmth, and thumping are reinstated and the need to fight gravity is eliminated. The changes to which the newborn must adapt now minimized, the crying ceases. What power in the mother's touch! What's more, as Marshall Klaus and John Kennell discovered in the 1970s, postbirth is an opportune time for mother and baby to get in touch.

If mother was unmedicated during birth, newborns have an amazing forty-five minutes or so of wide-eyed, quiet alertness postbirth—longer than they will have for weeks. This is presumably due to the intense stimulation encountered in the four-inch trip through the birth canal. As the mother gazes into her newborn's eyes and glides her fingertips along his silky soft skin, her infant quiets and stares back at her. Nature could hardly have planned a better time for the newborn to seduce mother into undying selfless devotion.

And her newborn is beautifully primed to soak in all her mother's loving touches. Touch, the "mother of the senses," is the earliest sense to develop in the fetus. Over the first five days of birth, the newborn's sensitivity to touch increases. The newborn's face especially is highly innervated and exquisitely sensitive to touch. Nor does this change. Let the right person touch our cheek and we melt, a floodgate of emotions opening up.

Our lips are even more sensitive than our cheek, but nothing like the tip of our tongue, where the largest concentration of touch receptors lie. If a newborn feels pressure against his cheek, he reflexively roots—turns his head and opens his mouth, as if searching for the protruding nipple. When he finds it, he suckles with a fury.

Mothers given early contact show greater affection for their infants and are more likely to breastfeed and do so longer, discovered Klaus and Kennell. At age five, their children had higher IQ scores and more advanced language than a control group without this early contact.

Fathers, too, if permitted postpartum contact, get quickly absorbed in and preoccupied with their infant. Later, they will be less rigid in their parenting and more involved with their children. This jibes well with biological interests. Apparently, at some point in our evolutionary history, genes that inclined a man to love his offspring began to thrive over those genes that fostered distance. This enhanced the chance that the offspring of undevoted, unprotective fathers would perish.

The potential for this connection is so strong that, to stifle it, some cultures may deliberately prevent fathers from early contact. Observed Margaret Mead:

No developing society that needs men to leave home and do his "thing" for the society ever allows young men in to handle or touch their newborns. . . . [T]hey know somewhere that . . . the new fathers would become so "hooked" that they would never get out and do their "thing" properly.

With these encouraging benefits of postpartum contact, hospitals began to make it policy. "Bonding" was born. This humanized the birthing process. Nevertheless, mothers deprived of this experience—such as those of preterms, babies of adoptive parents, or those mothers who didn't feel instant infatuation (about 40 percent don't)—worried they wouldn't bond with their infants. But though postpartum contact appears to jump-start attachment, "good enough" mothers catch up. Human bonding does not occur in a single, magical moment in the delivery room—like falling in love, it is an ongoing process that matures over time.

Separation Anxieties

~⁊~ Postpartum contact was a positive step on the road to reinstate mother-baby closeness. But it didn't go far enough. Until the relatively recent acceptance of rooming-in, mother and newborn spent an hour together and then went their separate ways. It was as if society by turns encouraged profound initial intimacy between mother and newborn and then set up props to disconnect them, engendering ultimate loss for both.

Why, for so long, did we permit this separation? It relates to our cultural script of the neonate as an organism capable of a solo act. But from a biological perspective, this casting is incorrect: The highly immature newborn was made to perform in duet with his mother, not alone.

Born with only 25 percent of our adult brain size, we are the least mature of all mammals. The newborn foal takes a few steps on wobbly legs, and after three days, saunters after his mother. The elephant baby is ready to run with the herd shortly after birth. With the exception of the Aboriginal newborn and some African newborns, we can't even lift up our head. Our cousins, the apes, born with 45 percent of their brain and born our intellectual superior, quickly achieve a state of physical maturity that we do not reach until six to nine months of age, when we start crawling. The only mammal more dependent than us at birth are marsupials, but until maturity they live snugly in their mother's pouch—the ideal "womb with a view."

How is it the human infant came to be the least mature of all mammals?

It seems nature left us in a tight squeeze. The problem is both our small pelvic structure, which allows us to saunter upright on all fours, and our big brain. If human babies were born with a more mature brain, our heads would be too large to travel through the birth canal.

Nature's solution? Birth before we're ready and extension of fetal brain development into postnatal life. In other words, in a sense we're all born premature, not ready for life until eight or nine months of age, when we begin to crawl and venture forth on our own. At this time our level of maturity matches that of other mammals at birth and our physiological functions are far more autonomous. This indicates, says Ashley Montagu, that our gestation is truly eighteen months long—nine in the womb, and nine out.

Given our exterogestation, as Montagu named it, separation of our babies from our body *earlier* than any other mammal defies logic.

In the wild, infant monkeys—our closest relatives on the evolutionary ladder—are rarely apart from their mother in the first year of life, since separation is likely to spell sure death from a predator. Strongly protesting separation, they are inveterate clingers—having a "monkey on our back" means we can't get rid of something. Moreover, monkeys stay close to their mothers until four years of age, long after the need for maternal protection.

Separation is so traumatic for the infant monkey that their whole system rebels: They experience loss of body temperature, release of stress hormones (cortisol), cardiac arrhythmias, increased heart rate, agitation, sleep disturbances, and immunological compromises. And although hormones stabilize when they are reunited with their mothers, there are long-term effects—for instance, in sleep and immunological efficiency.

Mothers, too, appear strongly affected by separation. In fact, they show such a powerful attachment to their infants that they will carry a dead one for days. Were a primate mother to hold her infant as little as we do, she would be considered unfit and, if in a zoo, would have her baby removed.

Like the primate, the human infant arrives hard-wired to seek contact with the mother. Take the newborn's primitive reflexes. First, there is cuddling. When picked up and held, newborns mold their arms and legs into the cavity of our arms. Next there is clinging, the apparent purpose of which is to grasp mother and maintain contact. For instance, if you press your finger into the sole of your newborn's foot, she will curl her toes around it; if you press your finger into the palm of her hand, she will clench it. In fact, to ensure you don't walk away without her, she will clench so hard, she can hang in the air holding on to only your fingers! If she feels herself falling, she will throw out a Moro reflex: with a look of panic and a brief cry, her arms and legs automatically fling back as if to stop a fall, then, as if groping for an embrace, forcefully pull in.

Infants also have a crawling reflex, which gets played out in the most extraordinary drama. If placed on the mother's abdomen directly postbirth and if the mother has not had pain medication, newborns lie there quietly for thirty minutes and then begin to inch their way up to the mother's breast, find the nipple, latch on, and begin to suckle. During the Mexican earthquake of 1988, a mother was found knocked out with her newborn suckling her breast.

These primitive reflexes, along with our infant's greater immaturity, tells us that separation would likely be at least as stressful for the human newborn as for other mammals, if not more. We are, after all, more mammal than human. The newborn's cry, falsely viewed as normal and not harmful, is a window into this stress.

Newborn Cry

> . . . I see her in my sleep, my red, terrible girl.
> She is crying through the glass that separates us.
> She is crying, and she is furious.
> Her cries are hooks that catch and grate like cats.
> It is by these hooks she climbs to my notice.
> She is crying at the dark, or at the stars
> That at such a distance from us shine and whirl.
>
> I think her little head is carved in wood,
> A red, hard wood, eyes shut and mouth wide open.
> And from the open mouth issue sharp cries
> Scratching at my sleep, and entering my side.
> My daughter has no teeth. Her mouth is wide.
> It utters such dark sounds it cannot be good.
> —Sylvia Plath, *Three Women: A Poem in Three Voices*

Sylvia Plath was correct in thinking these "dark sounds" heard from the nursery are *not* good. They place stress on the baby's entire system. Gene Anderson of Case Western Reserve University in Cleveland, a leading researcher on the physiological effects of separation on the newborn, suggests that they may even slow the newborn's transition to life outside the womb and, perhaps, even compromise it.

The cry resembles the adult Valsalva maneuver—a deep breath taken and held against the glottis, as occurs in defecation, coughing, lifting, and other physical exertions, explains Anderson. This means that during each cry utterance, there's a second when newborns hold their breath. During that time, arterial oxygen falls, which means that the lungs get less oxygen and the body goes on the defense: white blood cell count rises and cortisol increases. Once the threat is removed and the crying stops, stress hormones can remain in the bloodstream for at least twenty minutes. In other words, even after crying ceases, a newborn remains stressed.

What's more, according to Anderson, long stretches of crying may reestablish fetal circulation. At birth, a valve closes to reroute the blood to the lungs rather than to the umbilical cord. This process takes a few days to complete. Excessive crying can interfere with this process for as long as four to five days of life.

Excessive crying, which drains energy reserves and burns up calories, may contribute as well to the weight loss that is common postbirth. Furthermore, exhausted from all the crying, the newborn may fall asleep when it's time to nurse, discouraging the mother's attempt to establish breastfeeding.

As for the popular notion that newborns need to cry to expand their lungs: "Not true," says Anderson. A newborn's lungs fill up after the first breath and are as fully expanded thirty minutes postbirth as they are at twenty-four hours.

All this stress, and for what? A friend of mine who had her baby at home held her infant for six straight hours after she was born. "She uttered barely a sound and took right to my breast," my friend said. There's little reason why hospital birthing mothers cannot enjoy the same closeness.

Newborns Are Ill-Designed for Autopilot

Throughout history, the newborn's traditional rite of passage has been from mother's womb to mother's arms, not to surrogate plastic container. And for good reason. The transition to the outside world is far smoother with mother in close touch.

Regular heartbeat and breathing, smooth, quiet body movements, body temperature control, ease of digestion—all are physiologically demanding for the newborn. While in contact with the mother, the infant's systems are kept at a regular tempo. But apart, the newborn must work doubly hard to maintain physiological harmony. Hence, they cry. "The behavioral equipment of the newborn is adaptive to the ecological situation," says newborn specialist Dr. Heinz Prechtl. And the natural ecological situation "is neither the crib nor the incubator." Furthermore, mother and baby mutually regulate each other. (The newborn suckling at the mother's breast, as we recall, completes the birth process for the mother.)

In the first hours postbirth, newborns who are left with their mothers and who are responded to quickly rarely cry, Anderson found. If hungry, they squirm, grunt, bring a hand to their mouth—all cueing mother that it's time to be fed before crying begins. In one study, newborns who were "mothered" in the first four hours postbirth cried for a mere two minutes. In the nursery, rows of newborns resounded in a Greek chorus of wails for an average of 38 minutes. Given the residual effect from crying, these figures tell us that newborns kept in the nursery postbirth may be stressed much of this time. Little wonder Anderson describes postbirth separation as a crisis for the infant, both "unhealthy" and "unsafe."

Additionally, the mothered infants stayed warmer than the nursery infants, had more stable breathing and pulse rates, and did not startle. At their first feed, they sucked more strongly, took in more liquid, and had much less difficulty swallowing, all of which supports mother and newborn's efforts to lock into nursing. The infants also had lower blood pressure, which correlates with lower levels of cortisol, our stress hormone.

A newborn in bed with the mother has a cortisol level even lower, and, as one might guess, cries even less. In a Swedish study, babies kept in skin-to-skin contact with mother stayed warmer than those in a cot and had higher blood glucose levels. The researcher concluded that keeping mother and baby skin-to-skin preserves energy, accelerates metabolic adaptation, and may increase the well-being of the newborn.

But what about mother? Since the rationale for separation at night has been to allow her to sleep better and recuperate faster, a practice lacking scientific evidence, Anderson and her team wondered if mothers *do* sleep better alone. Their findings? Despite less medication, mothers slept slightly better and slightly longer when their babies stayed *with* them. The notion that babies should be separated at night to aid the mother's sleep proved false, which makes good evolutionary logic. Since closeness to mother enhances the baby's chances for survival, separation and all the crying that goes with it was meant to alert the mother, motivating her to correct the distance. Further, mothers who keep their babies with them at night might also increase their chances of breastfeeding success. Prolactin, the hormone known to stimulate lactation and maternal behavior, is ten times as high at night.

Mother's Body as a Baby Thermostat

One reason newborns cry easily is that, vulnerable to heat loss, they get cold easily—especially when birth takes place in the cool hospital labor and delivery room. In danger of hypothermia in all but the warmest climates, some hospitals place newborns in incubators the first two to four hours postbirth to regulate body temperature and to register respiratory rhythm and fetal heartbeat. But is this necessary?

Perhaps we need to learn from the Eskimos. Before they became Americanized, they carried their babies naked inside their parkas and against their skin, keeping their infants warm through *the* best form of thermoregulation: body heat. At night, mother and baby curled up against each other under a caribou skin, the babies kept warmer by the mother's body than by any blanket.

Our first experience is the warmth of other bodies. The more skin-to-skin contact, the more pronounced the warmth and the better we feel as the other's heat exudes into our being, comforting us, soothing us, and healing our emotional wounds. In fact, the exquisite pleasure of the naked embrace comes in part because our skin sensitivity is greater when we're warm, activating that many more touch receptors in our skin.

And yet, few of us sleep naked with our babies. If we did, we would discover that nature designed the mother's body as a natural thermostat for the newborn. The human newborn fits into an atricial patterning of thermoregulation, meaning we are nonshivering and have a low or moderate capacity for thermoregulation. Other atricial mammal mothers build a nest and use their own body to warm their infants. In humans, the mother's body is the "maternal nest."

When a mother pulls her baby to her chest, the infant's abdomen, which contains little fat, readily accepts heat from the mother's belly and loses it more slowly. Researcher and midwife Judith Färdig discovered that, when separated from her, the healthy full-term newborn loses a whole degree of body heat, uncompensated for when placed under a radiant warmer for his postbirth exam, *even* if the temperature equals that of the mother's body. The apparent release of stress hormones, such as cortisol, during separation likely accounts for this. In other words, the newborn reacts to the separation as if in danger.

The earlier the infant receives skin-to-skin contact with the mother, the more easily he maintains a normal body temperature. Färdig compared three groups of newborns: one receiving immediate skin-to-skin contact and then transfer to a radiant warmer—typical hospital practice in those that permit immediate postpartum contact; one receiving continuous skin-to-skin contact, nursing care done with the baby on the mother's abdomen; and one receiving standard separation to a radiant-heated crib without contact with the mother. Upon transfer from the delivery room to the recovery room, the newborns with the continuous care had the smallest heat loss and the quickest recovery to a normal temperature. This tells us that it's not only unnecessary to separate newborn and mother for temperature regulation, it's less efficient and more stressful.

Moreover, in some hospitals, separation can reach ridiculous proportions. While working in a neonatal unit in a Chicago teaching hospital, I observed a naked newborn lying flat on his back under a radiant warmer, red-faced and screaming like a siren for twenty minutes. I asked one of the nurses why he was lying there.

"We watch them for the first hour following birth to make sure they are stable," she said. "Why is this necessary?" I asked.

"Because a few years ago a newborn alone with the mother went into cardiac arrest and the hospital was sued," she replied.

Has legal logic usurped our survival instincts? The notion that a hospital should observe newborn physiological stability by removing the newborn from his *source* of stability and allowing him to cry almost nonstop in an alien environment tells us how much we are out of touch with our newborn's needs and the mother's exquisite ability to meet those needs. What better example of the mother's power to do so than the preterm infant.

Kangaroo Care

In our society, preterm infants, too immature to regulate their own temperature, live isolated from their mothers in little glass booths (called Isolettes) that artificially regulate temperature for them.

But, in Bogotá, Colombia, hospitals too poor to provide incubators for all but the most unstable and tiniest "preemies," turned to Mother Nature to help them: a technique called kangaroo care. Infants up to two months premature but stable enough to breathe on their own were placed diaper-clad upright between their mother's breasts inside her clothing. In her "pouch," the infants suckled her breast in short, frequent bouts throughout the day.

Soon, nurses began to notice a difference in K-care infants. They grew faster, and their heart rates and body temperature stabilized more quickly. The reason why gives us astonishing insight into the innate sensitivity of the mothering system.

In an amazing feat of thermal synchrony, during K-care the mother's temperature fluctuates to maintain her baby in a thermoneutral range, found Susan Ludington of UCLA. If her baby is not warm enough, the mother's body warms. When her baby's temperature reaches the thermoneutral range, the mother's temperature returns to baseline. If her baby gets cold, the mother begins to warm up again.

Gene Anderson has been studying K-care for over ten years. Her work and others' has shown that K-care babies not only grow faster and stay warmer, but sleep deeper, stay alert longer, breathe better with fewer episodes of apnea (cessation of breathing) and bradycardia (slowed heart rate), gain weight faster, spend less days in an incubator, and go home sooner. Moreover, K-care benefits even tiny preemies who are hooked up to mechanical ventilation for breathing.

As one would predict, almost *no* crying occurs during kangaroo care. Even at six months of age, K-care babies cry less than their incubated counterparts. This is not surprising. Both the early close contact and the minimal crying helps mothers bond quickly to their infants and become more sensitive to their needs. Off to a good start, the mothers are more likely to breastfeed and do so for a longer time, and they feel more confident in monitoring their infant's health when they take them home, something that many mothers of preterms are at first reluctant to do. Fathers who engage in K-care also feel a special closeness to their infants.

European hospitals, especially in Scandinavia, have been using K-care for years, with fathers participating as well. In fact, K-care is now standard policy in Sweden and Finland, and approaching so in Denmark, Holland, and Norway. But in the United States, faith is placed more in technology than in natural ecosystems. Though all benefit—babies do better and go home earlier, the mothers feel less anxious and more attached, and the hospital saves money—this new tradition of preemie care has been considered risky here.

The resistance to K-care during hospitalization does not come from parents but, rather, from our hospitals' conservatism, which stems in large part from fear of that old nemesis of the medical profession, the lawsuit. Moreover, because their babies are fragile, parents of premature infants feel the hospital, not they, has control of their baby, and they defer easily to the wishes of the medical staff. And our hospitals are slow to warm to K-care, says Anderson, because we are not a breastfeeding culture.

Consequently, though K-care has been around for at least ten years, it has only recently caught on in the United States. Further, it is only done in what is called *late* K-care—beginning usually when the infant is relatively stable, breathing room air, and ready to go home, and with mothers staying with their hospitalized infants only part time.

Ideally, Anderson says, preemies should be put between their mother's breasts as early as possible. For most that means right after birth. This does not mean that, like the Colombians, mothers should take their two-pound infants home after a day or two in the hospital. But it does mean that mothers, under nursing supervision, should be allowed to engage in K-care with healthy preemies and, if it's safe, to do so right from the start.

Stabilization Takes Time

⚜ When I was doing developmental assessments on babies at risk, many of whom were preemies, I would often see mothers sitting in the waiting room with little two-month-olds in plastic containers. So tiny, so fragile. Why aren't they holding them? I would lament.

Physiological vulnerability eases up only gradually over the first year, suggesting that separation of mother and baby for any length of time may be undesirable for several months, especially with fragile and vulnerable infants. It takes six to nine months, for example, before the normal infant acquires the chemical responses necessary for proper functioning of the liver, kidneys, immune system, and digestive tract.

For several months, babies will, at times, gasp, choke, and stop breathing for what seems like an eternity; they may even turn blue before starting to breathe again. They will be unable to stay warm easily: Because of immature circulation, their lips quiver and turn blue at the first sign of cold and, for most of infancy, their hands and feet will remain cold. In fact, one study found that up to seven months of age, babies briefly separated from their mother *still* show a significant drop in temperature.

Initially infants will sleep only four hours at a stretch, working up gradually to a normal circadian rhythm of alert most of the day and asleep most of the night, which is not well set before around eight months of age. Their EEG waves are fast at first, as is their heart rate, which averages around 120 beats per minute.

Because their stomachs are underdeveloped, babies will have frequent digestive problems. Moreover, after living in a sterile environment, babies' stomachs must quickly cope with an onslaught of bacteria, particularly if bottle fed and thus not sharing mother's immunities. Even if an infant's immune system is protected by mother's breast milk, it is still not fully mature until around age four.

In other words, until around nine months or so, contact with the mother isn't just nice, it's needed for the baby's stability. It even relates to how tall babies will become.

Touch and Growth

❧ Mothers who used K-care found that there babies grew faster. One reason? Vital touch is a master switch for growth hormone.

Growth hormone emanates from the hypothalamus (located in the limbic system and part of our old mammalian brain). Touch sends a message to the pituitary gland to release growth hormone. Conversely, separation and touch deprivation block it. Saul Schanberg of Duke University discovered that in infant rats, it takes only 45 minutes of separation before growth hormones start to suppress.

Schanberg wondered exactly what released growth hormones in the rats. Was it mother's warmth? No. Her movements? No. Her milk? No. Her active stroking through tongue licking? Bull's-eye! So essential is this need for survival that, though rat babies prefer their mother's odor, they will prefer nonmaternal odor if it has been paired with touch.

In this country, as late as the beginning of the twentieth century, orphans received little caressing. Due to *marasmus*—a Greek word meaning wasting away without apparent medical cause—almost 100 percent died. Now called nonorganic failure-to-thrive, infants deprived of nurturant touch often fail to grow *even* if hospitalized and fed enough calories intravenously. Recent studies of infants from the Romanian orphanages found that those suffering from touch deprivation achieved only half the normal height for their age.

Preemies, isolated most of the day in an incubator, traditionally receive little normal touch. Would stroking also make them grow more quickly? Tiffany Field, a developmental psychologist and professor of pediatrics at the University of Miami, and colleague Frank Scafidi had a hunch it would.

They weren't disappointed.

For three fifteen-minute periods a day for ten consecutive days, they massaged and stretched the limbs of small preterm infants. Their findings? A whopping 47 percent increase in weight gain. As a result, the babies went home an average of six days earlier than the control infants—a savings of $3,000 per infant! The massaged babies were also better able to calm themselves, and less likely to cry one minute and fall asleep the next. At eight months of age, the stroked infants still showed advanced weight gain compared to babies who didn't receive the stroking, as well as better intellectual and motor development. In a study done in England, preemies given extra strokes in the neonatal intensive care unit were smarter at age seven. Be cautioned, though. Because preemies are easily overstimulated, especially tiny ones, infant massage should be done under the supervision of the medical staff.

Massage Is the Message

The results from this landmark study inspired Tiffany Field to develop the Touch Research Institute at the University of Miami. Field and her staff massage babies born cocaine addicted, babies born HIV positive, as well as physically and sexually abused infants, colicky infants, and those with depressed mothers. They also massage children with asthma, skin disorders, diabetes, burns, cystic fibrosis, juvenile rheumatoid arthritis, and bulimia.

The results so far indicate that Field truly may have found the Midas touch. Massaged babies often show greater weight gain, fewer postnatal complications, and decreased cortisol levels. They are more social, more alert, less fussy and restless, sleep better, and have smoother movements. They enjoy playing with their mothers, who, in turn, enjoy their babies more—even depressed mothers, who often behave intrusively with their infants.

After one month of fifteen-minute touch therapy sessions twice a week, preschool autistic children, who suffer from extreme touch aversion, were more willing to be touched, and showed less autistic behavior.

Massaging babies is nothing new. In Nigeria, babies' whole bodies are massaged from birth until they are twelve months of age. In Fiji, mothers massage their babies with coconut oil following a bath. In New Zealand, the Maoris have a saying:

> Massage the legs of your daughter,
> So she will walk with grace
> Across the plains of
> Poverty Bay.

In India, babies are massaged daily, from one to six months of age. In Malpe, India, where babies start out underweight by 500 grams, as compared to American newborns, 65 percent doubled their birthweight by three months. In the United States, where few babies are routinely massaged, babies tend to double their weight much later, at five months.

Why Massage Creates Magic

Everyone knows massage feels good, but only now are scientists figuring out why.

Our fingertips contain an incredible pharmacy. Slide them across the trunks of preterm infants and the pressure stimulates a branch of a cranial nerve called the vegetative vagus, which, in turn, stimulates the gastrointestinal tract, releasing hormones like glucose and insulin, explains Field. Aiding in gastrointestinal food absorption and enhancing digestion, this likely explains the dramatic weight gain of the massaged infants.

Massage stimulates circulation of the blood and lymph fluids, fuels the muscles with fresh oxygen and nutrients while flushing away metabolic waste products, releases physical tension and soothes the nerves by lowering the stress hormones cortisol and norepinephrine and by releasing endorphins in the brain. Little wonder that as the masseur irons out the wrinkles of tension in our body we feel at once achy and enervated.

Massage affects the immune system as well. Premature infants who were gently stroked had higher levels of secretory immunoglobulin A (SIgA), which protects against respiratory tract infections, than those not stroked.

In fact, how we were touched—or not touched—early in life may even impact on the immune system later on. Consider skin diseases. Carolyn S. Koblenzer, a dermatologist and a psychiatrist, estimates that 30 to 75 percent of the patients who show up in her office have an emotional component to their disease. The skin is both the visible physical boundary of the self and an immunological organ, with every type of immune cell presented in its grooves. This makes it a choice medium for psychosomatic expression. Psoriasis, eczema, warts, and chronic acne all are exacerbated by stress. Since the skin is so sensitive to bad vibes, Koblenzer believes that the way a new mother handles her infant influences skin sensitivity for life.

That early handling may have long-term effects on later stress is not a leap of imagination. Michael Meaney, a developmental psychologist at McGill University, looked at old rats handled during infancy and those not. The handled rats, he found, could learn and remember at levels similar to young rats. The nonhandled rats, in contrast, had trouble learning and remembering. Exposure to stress apparently kills brain cells—specifically those located in the hippocampus, which is part of the limbic system and important for memory storage. Handled rats are more capable of turning off the stress response, concluded Meaney. In other words, how we were handled in infancy may relate to how easily we later remember our grandchildren's names.

That the deep pressure touch experienced during massage mends, relaxes, and rejuvenates the baby is not something recently discovered in a twentieth-century laboratory. These benefits are built into the infant's natural sensory repertoire and begin in the womb, as the amniotic fluid swishes against the fetus's skin and as the mother's movements press the walls of the womb against the fetus. After the baby is born and the mother pulls her into the folds of her body, she recreates similar pressure against her baby's skin, as do her movements when ambling along with her baby in her arms. Periodically, she strokes a brow, pushes in a leg, kneads a thigh, rubs an arm. In other words, these advantages are the everyday experience of the babe-in-arms.

3

Holding Holds Babies Together

My mother groaned! my father wept.
Into the dangerous world I leapt:
Helpless, naked, piping loud:
Like a fiend hid in a cloud.

Struggling in my father's hands,
Striving against my swaddling bands.
Bound and weary I thought best
To sulk upon my mother's breast.
—William Blake, Songs of Innocence
and Experience: Infant Sorrow

*R*afael, three weeks old, is lying in his crib on his back, red-faced and screaming. His little hands clench and unclench, tremor, and punch the air, while his legs randomly fly out, quiver, and twitch. But when mother comes, picks him up, and pulls him to her body, his limbs become contained: the flailing stops, the punching stops, the crying stops, and his face turns to its normal baby pink.

Coming Apart

One primary reason newborns cry is that they lack the neuromuscular maturity to control their limbs against gravity—a task not accomplished on their own until two to three months of age. Unable to tell their arms and legs what to do, they become frightened and disturbed when their arms and legs fly out or when they startle, and so they start to cry. The crying causes more flailing, which feeds into a succession of crying and menacing movements. If this cyclic activity occurs near sleep, it keeps awakening the baby; if it occurs while awake, it prevents him from absorbing the surrounding world. In short, it keeps him fussy.

So disorganizing is uncontrolled activity that, until the baby's limbs are still, calming techniques like rocking, lulling sounds, or sucking a pacifier have little effect. In babies left lying on their backs in a buggy, this helps explain the frequency of their sudden crying jags.

The quickest way to contain infants' limbs and keep random movement at a minimum is, of course, to pick them up and hug them to our bodies, which restores the comforting embrace of the womb. The more babies are held, the less they are at the mercy of disorganizing movement. But our neonates, mostly in cribs, infant seats, or buggies, frequently lack this support. This is something that our culture tends to overlook.

Take bath time: Unaware of a young infant's need for containment, we frequently place them on their back for bathing, which creates fertile ground for insecurity and makes bath time often a tug-of-war. And, though special tubs for babies are not slippery, sinks and tubs are, causing the infant to squirm and flail in a frantic attempt to secure grounding.

Of course, mothers' bodies are not slippery. Lying on their mother's breasts, babies are naturally contained, which eliminates the struggle to maintain balance and fight gravity, while the hair on daddy's chest affords the opportunity to practice grasping. (A word of caution: While we may like a hot bath, babies, with their thinner more sensitive skin, prefer lukewarm to cool water.) Here, though, co-bathing is more occasional than common. In Japan, in contrast, bathing is a family affair that starts in infancy and often continues until children are around ten years of age.

Birth as Panic

We need to appreciate the young infant's need for containment, a need that begins with birth itself. In the closed chamber of the womb, the fetus floats weightless, much like an astronaut. Stretches, kicks, and turns are encumbered by the amniotic fluid and cushioned and stopped short by the uterine wall. Movement emerges as a slow-motion fetal dance, with twitches and startles hardly making more than a wave. By term the womb becomes tight quarters indeed, as space for movement steadily decreases, wrapping the fetus into a tight ball. Movement is an aborted push up against the mother's ripe belly.

When birth rudely catapults the baby from this cramped cavern into a brave new world of open space and gravity, it's a shock. If we immediately contain the newborn's limbs by placing the newborn on the mother's belly, we keep lack of support to a minimum. But in most hospital births, obstetricians traditionally pull the baby out and, supporting only trunk and head, hold up the newborn to the anxiously awaiting eyes (but not arms) of mother and father. All support momentarily lost, it's not uncommon to see the newborn's arms and legs begin to thrash in mass protest, and for the infant to start to cry furiously.

The crying and flailing continue as baby, handed over to the nurse, gets placed on his back on a resuscitation table. Should the baby's head drop backward even slightly on the trip from womb to warming table, this registers as falling, which results in a Moro reflex, and panic intensifies. Not so long ago, newborns were held upside down and slapped! This loss of physical support makes birth our first moment of panic, ushering in the fear of falling that remains our most primary terror.

But babies can have a gentler start. At Michel Odent's clinic in France, the newborn emerges from the squatting mother and is placed directly prone on the ground in front of her, leaving barely a second in which he feels loss of support. Then, with umbilical cord still attached, the mother pulls the baby to her body, and both feel the reassurance of intimate body contact. Not surprisingly, the newborn doesn't cry, something that really surprised Dora Henschel, who witnessed a birth in the early days at Pithiviers:

> The midwife came around and gently lifted the baby up into the mother's arms. The mother gave a shout of joy but there was not a cry from the baby. That was another shock to me because I was used to babies shouting their heads off.

French obstetrician Frederic Leboyer, well known for dark, quiet births where the baby is put immediately on the mother's abdomen, reports the same phenomenon. First the baby lets out a few yelps, welcomed heartily since it indicates the newborn has met its first challenge for survival. But then the baby is silent. Mothers, expecting howling, need reassurance their baby is alive!

Fetal Tuck

❧ When you stretch out an infant's legs, they snap back like a rubber band into a froglike stance—the fetal tuck. The natural position of babies, it is the most calming and the most adaptive: Infants use less oxygen, which conserves energy and wastes less calories, and they digest their food better.

When held flat against our body, we naturally support our baby in the fetal tuck. As we cup one arm under his buttocks, we help him maintain his legs flexed in, while our other arm, usually swept across his back, maintains at least one of his arms flexed in. Similarly, placed on their stomachs, babies curl in more easily, which helps explain why newborns seem to prefer lying prone. (Lying in their cribs does not offer the same flexion as lying against us. When against a flat surface, their bodies are kept neutral; when front to front on the parent's body, their bodies become concave and more flexed in.) But when placed flat on his back in a crib, a baby seat, bathtub, or changing table, the baby loses the fetal tuck. Some wonderfully adept newborns can turn to their side, curl themselves in, find their hand to suck, and self-calm. But many others are unable to gain control of their limbs.

If unable to turn to pull into the fetal tuck, the neonate is also more prone to cold, since curled in is the best position for thermoregulation. This is because the surface area needing warmth is decreased, as is the exposure of the abdomen to the air. The more our stomachs are exposed, the colder we feel because the temperature regulation cells of all primates, including man, are more efficient on the back. And so the kitten sleeps rolled into a ball, and we curl up when we hit the covers at night, our body temperature becoming cooler than during the day. Moreover, when belly to belly, the abdomen, which houses all the receptor and vital organs, is protected. Hence, a dog or cat rolling on its back and exposing its underbelly is a submissive stance that says it trusts you.

So predictable is a newborn's distress to lack of warmth and containment that on the Brazelton Neonatal Behavioral Assessment Scale, the newborn is placed undressed on her back as a maneuver to assess coping capacities. Exposed to both the cool air and uncontained movement, the newborn is *expected* to become distressed. Says Brazelton:

> So disturbing is it to [the newborn] to be undressed and at the mercy of temperature changes, and the freedom of unrestrained movement, that

we have found it wise to hold one arm tightly in flexion up against the newborn infant's body. This keeps him from flying off into random, excited startling behavior that upsets him, makes him cry, and sets off more cyclical Moro startling.

One mother, reclining her newborn on his back for his first bath, plugged in a heater and then touched her infant with a wet washcloth. "His legs stiffened out, his arms stiffened out, and he screamed. I thought I had electrocuted him," she said, not recognizing his innate response to distress.

Frequently separated from our infants, we can forget the importance of the fetal tuck for thermoregulation. This is why, when it's cold, parents often layer their babies with clothing, throw a warm woolen blanket over them, and then put them in their crib or buggy on their backs, often with arms overhead—a position we assume to *lose* body heat and cool off. If too young, or too tightly wrapped to wiggle onto their side, the baby's brain may *register* tuck, but the body says *stuck*.

Some inexperienced parents may not recognize a temperature problem. "One night," a father of a newborn told me, "our baby wouldn't stop crying. Since we just fed, burped, and diapered him, we couldn't figure out what was wrong and so we just kept rocking the cradle. The housekeeper came into the room, said, 'He's cold,' wrapped him in a blanket, and pulled him close to her. Boom. He stopped crying."

Positioning and Sucking

In the fetal tuck, babies' hands are conveniently close to mouth, allowing them to easily find their hands and suck. The intense oral-motor stimulation of sucking—its rhythmicity and its incompatibility with crying—makes it ideal for self-soothing. This is another reason why babies calm best when curled in.

In fact, though lacking hand coordination, the newborn is primed by nature to put her hand in her mouth. Stroke the side of the newborn's mouth and, as if a button were pressed, the hand on that side moves up to the lips. If the hand lands in the mouth, the baby stops crying and sucks. "Handy!" says the baby, unlike the fickle pacifier that disappears when most needed. Press the palm of the newborn's hand and she turns her head and mouth to the side touched, hand-to-mouth programmed as a unit to enable sucking. When we put mittens on newborns, we meddle with the efficiency of this fine-tuned system. Even the fetus sucks for self-soothing.

When babies cannot easily retrieve their hands, as when they are tucked in or overhead, we essentially rob them of this immensely effective self-calming technique.

Many mothers give their baby a pacifier to discourage thumb-sucking, worried it will become a habit difficult to break. This bias is left from the harsh parenting recommended by the early behaviorist John Watson, who encouraged parents to "cure" it at the outset. Wrote Watson:

> Keep the hands away from the mouth as often as you are near the baby in its waking moments. And always, when you put it into its crib for sleep, see that the hands are tucked inside the covers.

In truth, most children give up thumb-sucking before or during early childhood. Those who don't may express an inordinate need for self-calming or may not have had sufficient oral stimulation during infancy.

The Embrace

❧ Henry Moore, famous for his many mother and baby sculptures, felt obsessed with the mother-child relationship and came to appreciate the baby's need for containment. When sculpting *Draped Reclining Mother and Baby*, he experimented with the position of the baby. First, he placed it on and then against the mother's thigh. But it seemed vulnerable and unprotected. A few days later Moore moved the baby, settling it into the space between its mother's breast and forearm. Nestled in the crook of her elbow, the baby now seemed secure against the world.

Of all calming techniques, the embrace is the ultimate baby pacifier. A combination of continuous contact with a steady flow of warmth and pressure, it creates an omnipresent background of pleasurable slow firing vibes that keeps us in that "just right" place. Kept on the parent's body, where infants feel contact both front and back, babies are *kept* in the comfort zone *and* experience a steady flow of sensations. Kept in a crib, where warmth and pressure are diminished and support is felt against only one side of their bodies, babies' comfort zone is narrowed and their sensory input reduced.

When mothers provide a "holding environment" for the baby, as British psychoanalyst D. W. Winnicott put it, the baby feels both physically and psychologically held together. But only if holding *holds* the baby together. To do this, the mother must bring as much of her baby's body surface into contact with hers as possible. The mother must try to re-create the total envelopment of the lost womb.

Fortunately, most experienced and relaxed parents naturally pull their babies into the protective folds of their bodies and quickly calm them. But inexperienced, nervous parents, concerned about harming their "fragile" child, may fear holding a tiny squirming infant. Consequently, they hold their baby loosely and with minimal contact, as do parents who fear intimacy with their infants (discussed at length in chapter 4). As a result, the distressed infant flails ever more ferociously, increasing tension for the baby, insecurity for the parent, and eventual exhaustion for both.

Lisa was such a mother. Waiting for a parenting class to begin, the other mothers had long ago rescued their babies from their containers and were holding them. Only Lisa's three-month-old daughter, Sally, remained in her buggy. Lying uncontained on her back, Sally's arms and legs moved a bit stiffly, and occasionally she tremored and startled.

At the start of class, the mothers held their babies in their arms and danced with them to the music—swaying them, bouncing them, twirling them around. Lisa held Sally facing out, as did another mother with a three-month-old. But while the other mother held her baby pulled close into her body—she had one arm across her baby's chest and the other pulled through her baby's legs—Lisa held Sally with one arm across Sally's chest, and the other arm like a bench under Sally's buttocks. This is okay for the older baby with good trunk support, but not for young infants. Insufficiently supported, Sally continued her random tremors and startles.

Next, the mothers sat down cross-legged and, with their babies lying on their backs on mats, exercised their babies' arms and legs. Between the exercises, some mothers kept a hand quietly resting on their babies' legs, arms, or chest, and occasionally stroked them. Lisa, with a pace a bit more frenetic than the others, touched Sally with tickles and pokes. The tremors and startles continued, and Sally, with a tense face, appeared overexcited.

Asked to pick their babies up, the other mothers pulled their infants close to their body. But Lisa put Sally on her left leg (she still sat cross-legged) and Sally hunched forward. Intermittent tremors and startles continued. Next, Lisa lay on her back with her knees bent up and sat Sally on her abdomen, with Sally's back against Lisa's thighs. To support her, Lisa put her hand on Sally's abdomen, which left Sally's arms, legs, and head unsupported. As Lisa did head curls, Sally kept flopping forward and, twice, completely backward and soon started to cry.

We don't know why Lisa handled Sally so awkwardly, whether it was inexperience or an avoidance of close physical contact. Whatever the reason, young babies left to flop forward or backward or to experience random uncontrolled movements and startles experience insecurity.

Ups and Downs

❧ In some respects, all Western babies are prone to physical insecurity. For one, every time we put a baby down, we change him from vertical to horizontal, or vice versa. This leaves an alarming moment when one kind of support is removed before the other is established, placing babies in the first six months of life at risk for the Moro startle response.

Logically, the less they are put down, the less opportunity for instability. But *think* of the ups and downs in the life of the American baby! Thirteen times a day on average for diapering, nine times or so for feeding, numerous others times for bathing, dressing, playing, sleeping, transporting. Each transition, unless handled with the utmost care, holds the possibility of momentary panic.

Carried infants not fetched to eat, bedded for sleep, wheeled for transport, or entertained in playpen, infant seat, or crib are picked up and put down relatively little and thus experience less panic. "Its bath is practically the only occasion when a child under five or six months is out of arms when it is awake," wrote Margaret Mead of the Balinese infant. And if in their parent's arms when beginning to feel themselves fall, infants can easily grasp onto something—the mother's clothing or hair, for instance. Therefore, they're spared the terrorizing first part of the Moro (the spasmodic throwing out of arms and legs) and only experience the urgent grasping onto something—the mother.

The Art of Swaddling

❧ This kind of physical security has long-term consequences. Consider the Navajo Indian infant. Traditionally carried on her mother's back, tightly wrapped to a cradleboard, she is removed from the papoose only when breastfed, cleaned, and bathed, which amounts to a mere two hours or so a day at two months of age, and six hours at nine months. Yet, so comforting is the experience that the infant is restless when off the cradleboard and will actually demand to be on it. The snugness of the cradleboard reminds the Navajo baby of the snugness of the womb, making her feel more secure than sleeping in the wide open space of the crib. So secure, in fact, that, as Ashley Montagu discovered, these infants grow up without vertigo and a complete lack of fear of great heights. Imagine, they used to work on constructing high-rise buildings in *bare feet without harnesses!*

In carrying cultures, in general, where infants grow up to trust their bodies in space, vertigo appears not to be a problem. Witness Jean Liedloff's interesting experience with the Yequana, a Stone Age South American Indian tribe:

> The women left their firesides several times a day, carrying two or three small gourds at a time, walked part of the way down a precipitous slope that was extremely slippery when wet, filled the gourds in a streamlet, and climbed back to the village above. . . . Many of them carried their babies as well. . . . The Yequana have a superior sense of balance and, like the North American Indian, no vertigo.

Can you see yourself weaving in and out of vines, up and down ledges, around and through riverbanks in search of daily food? Or shopping in the mall while effortlessly balancing an enormous bundle on your head and a baby on your side or back, as do the poised barefooted African women as they amble through the marketplace? Or fetching a coconut for breakfast, as did a Tahitian native for me, by nimbly climbing a coconut tree with bare feet and the speed and vigor of a squirrel?

If all this seems a bit daunting, you were probably not swaddled as an infant. Nor would this be surprising. Though swaddling of some kind by firmly wrapping infants in a blanket or cloths is used routinely around the world in countries such as Russia, Iraq, China, Japan, Yugoslavia, and Mexico, we are one of the few countries with a cold climate not to have embraced swaddling.

We don't swaddle our infants in part because we accept crying as normal baby behavior and in part because we are largely unaware of the baby's need for containment to feel physically secure. We fear also that restricting movement prevents the infant's muscles from developing and delays motor milestones. But this concern hasn't been borne out. Navajo babies, firmly swaddled and bound to the cradleboard most of the first year of life, begin to walk at about the same age as other American babies. What's more, babies in Russia, China, and Iraq, swaddled throughout their first year of life, will, within hours after release from their apparent bondage, demonstrate motor skills equal to same-age counterparts not swaddled during infancy.

The Wild West part of our psyche, limbs flying free, also may indicate not disorganization as much as the zestful protest of a vigorous, assertive baby. To many of us, the sight of a Navajo baby wrapped to a papoose seems highly encumbering. Even worse is the sight of a Chinese infant encased in a blanket like a mummy. It engenders instant claustrophobia; we imagine ourselves buried in the sand, only our head sticking up.

This is unfortunate. Swaddling is hugging. Not just the light hug that does not inhibit movement, but the bear hug: "Hold me!" we beseech when lightly hugged. Acting as a protective womblike cocoon, swaddling relaxes babies by preventing Moros and other startles and reduces crying, which lowers the infant's heart rate and respiration.

While doing my dissertation research in a neonatal intensive care unit in Chicago, I could not calm one little preemie. In desperation, I called Rose, an old-time "grandmotherly" nurse. She took a blanket, wrapped the baby tightly, picked her up, and put her to her shoulder. Instantly, the screaming baby turned into a placid little doll.

Resistance to Swaddling

Not all babies like to be swaddled—especially if the practice is not begun early. This is not surprising. Some babies melt into your arms and easily accept restraint; others scream to be let loose.

Into this latter category fall those active, high-wired babies, who, starting life in the fast lane, defy any restriction. When held, these "noncuddlers" prefer to face out—the "go" position—rather than be tummy to tummy. They don't necessarily object to touch per se, but to restriction: They welcome nonrestrictive forms of touching, such as kissing, stroking, or other "skin games."

There are also, discovered psychologist Daniel Freedman, Professor Emeritus of the University of Chicago, cross-cultural differences in infant behavior right from birth. Due in part to genetic variation and in part to intrauterine environment (nutrition and experiences during pregnancy), as well as to differences in labor and delivery practices, a newborn Asian infant behaves in many respects differently from a Caucasian or black infant.

Navajo babies, who are of Asian extraction, are less active as a rule and smoother in their movements than a black or Caucasian infant. They cry less and are more easily consoled. For instance, if you place a cloth over the newborn's eyes (the defensive maneuver on the Brazelton Neonatal Behavioral Assessment Scale), Caucasian babies get furious, vigorously swiping, kicking, and howling, and Aboriginal babies react even more strongly, and with jerkier movements. Black infants also get irritated, but less intensely so. But the Navajo infants take on a laissez-faire attitude and simply cope: They may take a few swipes and let out a few whimpers, but they soon settle down. If their nose is at all occluded by the cloth, they relax and breathe through their mouths. The popularity of swaddling in Eastern countries such as China, and the cradleboard or papoose with Indians of American descent, may reflect this inborn propensity for smoother, better modulated movement and less overall emotional excitability—behavior more conducive to restriction. Hence, the Navajo baby is comforted easily on the cradleboard, while some Caucasian infants fuss to be released.

The mother's lifestyle also affects the developing fetus. T. Berry Brazelton has been studying mothers in Japan on the Goto Islands who live an active but slow-paced life. He compared them to those in Tokyo, who live a hectic life, and to Japanese mothers in San Francisco whose lives are even more frantic. The newborns of the Tokyo mothers were more jumpy than those of the more relaxed country mothers and had shorter attention spans. This greater activity and shortened attention was even more accentuated in the San Francisco newborns.

Proprioception

❧   Swaddling's calming effect comes in part from proprioceptive input, the sensation of our body in space that allows us to coordinate our movements. Proprioception allows us to zip up our jacket without looking at it, for example.

In the womb, proprioceptive input is ongoing. The tight, impenetrable space and uterine wall causes continual flexion of the limbs, creating steady pressure in the fetus's joints, as does the varying pressure created by the mother's breathing. When an infant is held or swaddled, the pressure of arms and legs pulling and pushing into the body furnishes similar intense proprioceptive input, which reinstates the boundaries of the womb and comforts him. At the same time, pressure against the skin provides tactile input. But in open space where boundaries are undefined—as in the crib, where only one side of the baby presses against a surface—tactile and proprioceptive input are limited. This disconcerts young babies, helping explain why they frequently fret when put to bed.

How do they adapt? They *create* boundaries. Plop them in the middle of their crib and they push an arm, a hand, a cheek up against a "cuddler" or stuffed animal, brace a hand or foot against the bumper pad, or wedge themselves into a corner—head, shoulders, hands, and arms brushed up against the surface of the crib's bumpers.

Some mothers, when their babies resist going to bed, discover boundaries accidentally, through trial and error. One mother, who bought a baby pillow "for fun," contoured to fit her infant's head, found that her infant made a smoother transition into sleep. Another mother, whose baby was restless and "lost and lonely" when put into the crib, hit upon using the narrow bumper pads from the baby's bassinet to create a protective little cocoon.

One can't overestimate the importance of proprioception. Without it, our babies would never learn the coordination needed to bring their hand to their mouth to feed themselves, walk down stairs, or prevent themselves from falling out of bed in the dark. In fact, the security of boundaries may be a more fundamental need than thermoregulation, without which babies will perish. Piglets, who can die of hypothermia if cold, will prefer to lie against a wall or the side of a sow instead of the middle open area of the pen where the heat lamp is located. Human newborns, placed in an open area under a radiant lamp, wail like banshees. Likewise, baby monkeys, deprived of their natural mother, opt to cling to an unheated cloth surrogate rather than sit on a warm heating pad.

Boundaries and the Preterm Infant

So powerful is the baby's need for boundaries that we can even see it in the behavior of the relatively helpless and fragile premature infant. Though unable to do little more than jerk and flail their limbs purposelessly, preemies will miraculously plant a little foot up against the side of the incubator or inch themselves into a corner. Worried the babies could smother themselves, the nurses frequently return them to the middle of the mattress, only to find the infant soon again wriggled up against the wall of their glass booth.

To compensate for the lost containment of the womb and to minimize the frantic, random movements that easily disorganize preemies, psychologist Heidelise Als of Harvard University has devised a protocol of "nesting" techniques. Clothed in bunting suits or tightly swaddled with blankets, the tiny babies are laid down on their sides or tummies—never on their backs—and then surrounded by blanket rolls to help them maintain the fetal tuck position. Before babies can be held outside the incubator, a caregiver may also simulate holding by containing their limbs against their body in the fetal tuck.

Even the very tiny preemies, hooked up to machines, get contained. More relaxed as a result, they don't have to breathe so hard to fight against the ventilator, says Als, and by expending less energy, their lungs heal faster. They also don't waste precious calories on jerky, uncontrolled movements, and the intervention helps them better tolerate painful procedures such as drawing blood. These nested infants show better mental, physical, and psychological development. Ultimately, these techniques may even help them develop a better self-image.

Proprioception and Identity

The ego is "first and foremost a body ego," said Freud. The infant's sense of self begins with body awareness—how her body feels, what it does, and that it belongs to her. In other words, it begins with proprioception.

The baby becomes aware of her body's boundaries by the felt presense of another body: Her fingers feel differently in her mouth than in her father's mouth. This enables her to differentiate "me" from "not me" and to establish clear self boundaries—to know where she begins and ends in space. Our later psychological sense of self originates from body awareness, body functions, and body activities.

The greater the duration of contact and the more extensive the area of the body touched, the more accurate one's body perception and the more we feel at home in our bodies, which leads to higher self-regard. When a parent minimizes holding, and particularly when she fails to pull her baby close to her body and therefore makes contact with less of her baby's body, she may interfere with the infant's appraisal of body boundaries. This sets the tone for the negative sense of bodily and psychological self experienced by insecure, anxious people. It is likely the culprit behind anorexia nervosa and bulimia as well, both on the increase in our society.

But what about the average American baby who, though adored, cuddled, and fondled, still experiences the felt presence of another for at most 25 percent of his day? Given that the infant was designed for continual contact, this reduction could relate to the relative estrangement from our bodies that many of us in modern society are prey to. Stuffing them, starving them, imbibing them, implanting them, and tucking them, we neglect them, abuse them, and transform them. The one thing many seem unable to do is to love them.

One thing's certain, though. The more our mothers loved us, the more we love ourselves.

4

The First Connection

I wither and you break from me;
yet though me dance in living light
I am the earth, I am the root,
I am the stem from fed the fruit,
the link that joins you to the night.
—Judith Wright, "Woman to Child"

Attachment: The Mother

Profound is the tie between mother and baby. So tenacious, separation can't break it. So enduring, time can't erase it. These feelings are a legacy handed down from our own mother, her own mother's mother, and on down the line. At the very heart of the baby's survival, biological evolution spared nothing to assure their occurrence.

First are those "babyish" features that delight us, and that endearing toothless smile that beckons. Then there's the cry that tugs at our gut, making us want to pull our baby to the protection of our body. As we do and our baby stops crying, we enter a state of bliss. Tension seeps out of our pores and time lingers, enveloping us in the warming omnipresence of our baby; until our baby stirs, we sometimes forget she's there altogether, yet we never feel alone. When we put our baby down, these wonderful feelings all but disappear—nature's assurance that mothers (and even fathers) would feel a loss when separated from their infants.

If separation engenders loss for the mother, imagine the infant. Safety means closeness to mother—the source of food, warmth, and protection. Danger means separation from her, since the farther from mother's arms, the closer to harm's way. This is why babies often loudly protest when put down and settle quickly when picked up.

That most babies are no longer in danger of instant death from predators matters little; a strong mother-baby bond, properly called attachment, will always be needed to keep babies safe, physically and psychologically, and will remain a part of our evolutionary heritage destined never to change. Sure, not all mothers feel instant love for their newborns. But generally, within a week or so, most get hooked. When a mother does not develop this bond, her feelings fly in the face of our biology and leave her baby's psychological (and sometimes physical) survival in peril. Love is protection—nature's insurance policy for the survival of the species—and vital touch is its core.

Attached. Connected. Bonded. Even the words used to describe intimacy imply touch. But as obvious as this connection seems, we haven't always made it. Influenced by Freud's identification of the first year of life as the oral stage, we believed for decades that our babies (and our pets) attach to us because we feed them. It wasn't until Harry Harlow came along in the late 1950s that we better understood touch's central role in mother-baby attachment.

Harlow separated infant rhesus monkeys from their mothers at birth. Noticing how the infants clung to their gauze diapers and screamed when the keepers tried to remove them, he decided to offer the infants a surrogate terrycloth mother lit with a bulb for warmth. For feeding, he built a separate wire mother with a bottle attached to it.

What happened then was a turning point that fundamentally changed how we view the mother-baby relationship. The infants spent only the time needed for feeding with the wire mother and clung for up to twenty-two hours a day to the mother who provided contact comfort—a mother, said Harlow, that was "soft, warm and tender, a mother with infinite patience, a mother available twenty-four hours a day, a mother that never scolded her infant and never struck or bit her baby in anger." Left alone in a room with the wire mother, the monkeys felt insecure and cowered in a corner. Left alone with the terrycloth mother, they gave her a few hugs and then felt secure enough to explore a strange object on their own.

Harlow's discovery made two important statements about development: First, touch, not food, binds infant to caregiver. After almost half a century of being dissuaded from fondling their infants, mothers now could feel freer to love their babies without fear of spoiling. It was great news for the father as well. Even if he didn't feed his baby, cuddling secured him VIP status.

This was the good news. The bad news was the second finding: Though the surrogate mother was warm, round, soft, and clingable, the sacred ground of the mother's body knows no substitute. The monkeys survived the experience, but as adults they were neurotic, asocial, displaying abnormal behaviors such as self-clasping and self-rocking, and were sexually inept. Babies don't make emotional attachments to things in the same way they do to a mother who nurtures. Her influence is profound and lifelong.

Building Trust

"Unique, without parallel," said Freud of the mother-baby bond—the mother "established unalterably for a whole lifetime as our first and strongest love object . . . the prototype for all later love relations."

More than twenty years of research in attachment theory has supported Freud's observation. As thematic musical phrases recur throughout a symphony, the strength and character of our first relationship reverberates in our later relationships. When things go well, we've a better chance for development to run smoothly: to learn to love ourselves and other people, to elicit good feelings from others, and to weather setbacks. When things go awry, we're more at risk for bumpy development: for unkindness toward ourselves, impaired relationships, elicitation of anger, annoyance or indifference from others, and poor coping skills.

That course, at the most basic level, is determined by the richness of the body contact between mother and baby. It is the evolution of love. Scientists have been studying this evolution for half a century.

In Touch / Out of Touch?

❧ Following World War II, John Bowlby established a special research unit at the Tavistock Clinic in London to examine young children's responses to separation. He advertised in a London paper for a psychologist to assist him. Mary Ainsworth answered that ad, and the field of child development changed forever.

John Bowlby asked himself how attachment served to promote the survival of the species. To answer this question, he came up with the foundation of attachment theory in three books called *Attachment, Separation, and Loss*—the first scientific study of human love. Mary Ainsworth asked herself how parenting style affects the quality of the infant's attachment to the mother. To answer this question, she came up with the Strange Situation, an assessment that identifies how infants view their mother's emotional availability: I can count on my mother to hug my tears away; I maybe can count on her; I'm unlikely to be able to count on her.

In the Strange Situation, mother and infant (between 12 and 18 months of age) walk into a strange, drab room, which contains two chairs and a blanket with some toys for the baby. Being in a strange place is a bit stressful for the infant. But mom is there, so the infant sits comfortably on the blanket and plays with the toys while mom sits in the chair. A female stranger enters the room and sits in the other chair, which adds a bit of stress. After a minute or so, she sits on the blanket with the infant— more stress but, with mother protectively close, still tolerable. But then mother leaves and stranger and baby are alone for three minutes until the mother returns: stress rises. If the baby starts to cry, as many do, mother does not wait out the three minutes but returns quickly to comfort. The stress drops. Then, at the experimenter's signal, the mother leaves her baby alone. For most infants, the stress level rises to a pitch and they cry pitifully.

Infants who trust their mothers to return are securely attached. When their mother walks in the door, they are terribly relieved, looking, gesturing, and crawling or running to her as she swoops her baby into her arms. A little tenderness, and within seconds her infant is back to play. Sixteen-month-old Richard was like this. When his mother returned, he yelled, "Mommy!" with a big smile, got up, and sauntered over to her. After a quick hug, he sat joyfully on the floor, showing his mother the toy he played with as he jabbered happily to her.

Infants who are unsure their mothers will return are insecurely attached. Though they experience only a brief separation from their mothers, when she returns they behave like children who have been traumatized by long separations, who first show strong protest, then despair, and then emotional detachment.

Insecure, ambivalent infants panic when their mother leaves, as if they feel abandoned. Upon her return, they show confusion. They may run to their mother and then angrily resist her efforts to comfort them. For instance, they may demand to be picked up and then to be quickly put down, arching away from her body. Frequently inconsolable, they cry angrily, petulantly, sometimes hitting and kicking in frustration and throwing away toys offered to them. Unable to derive comfort from mother, they cry for long periods and often do not resume playing.

Seventeen-month-old Diana was like this. When left with the stranger, she held her breath for a second, emitted a piercing howl, threw herself on the floor, and pounded her fists and feet. When her mother returned, a wailing Diana ran up to her. Her mother picked her up, but Diana struggled, arching her back and sobbing. Her mother put her down and sat in a chair. Diana went up to her mother, let out a few sobs, and butted her head into her mother's lap, begging for a pickup. Her mother, speaking softly, gently patted the side of Diana's head and shoulder but did not pick her up. Diana, still crying furiously, held up her arms. Ignored, she threw back her head in frustration, let out several sobs, and then vacillated from trying to climb up mother, to clawing at mother's lap, to circling mother. Her mother never picked her up and put her in her lap; Diana never calmed and never returned to play. In the second reunion episode, however, after Diana was left alone, her mother picked her up, sat down in the chair with her, and warmly attempted to calm her.

Insecure, avoidant infants may also get quite distressed when their mothers depart. Many, though, seem unconcerned—detached—as if they don't expect her to return. They frequently play comfortably with the stranger and busily with the toys, as if they barely notice the change of guard. When mother returns, some scarcely acknowledge her, hiding their need for closeness, as if to say: "I'll reject you before you get the chance to reject me." Mother on her part often makes little attempt to embrace her infant. It's as if baby is confronted with another stranger.

Seventeen-month-old Anna was a good example of an avoidant infant. When her mother left, she looked up: her face blank; her body still. She looked down at the toys on the blanket, fingered a Slinky, and started twirling it around. When the stranger asked her if she liked playing with the Slinky, she babbled to the stranger but with reserve. When her mother walked in the room, Anna looked up briefly, her face expressionless. She looked down and continued to finger the Slinky. Her mother stood at the door with her arms half open. "Come, Anna, come," she said. Anna toddled over to her mother. But when at her mother's feet, she did not hold out her arms to her mother but looked to her right, where a bright red ball had rolled. Her mother, whose body was somewhat stiff, bent down and picked Anna up and sat down in a chair, placing Anna on her lap, facing out. Anna, who made no attempt to fold into her mother's body, sat there for about ten seconds and then got down and toddled back to the blanket to play with the toys.

What distinguished Richard, Diana, and Anna? The degree to which each could feel ownership of their mothers' bodies and therefore assurance of protection. Richard, securely attached, flew into his mother's arms. Diana, ambivalently attached, ran to her mother but failed to feel comfort. Anna, avoidantly attached, dared not extend her arms at all.

The Right Touch

❧ The arms of the sensitive mother invite. When the world looms too large, too loud, too bright, too cold, the infant knows that she will be enveloped in a warm protective embrace. This gives the baby a clear message: "You are safe. You are loved. You are loveable." And so the infant relaxes, secure against the world.

Recalls Kabongo, a Kikuyu chief of East Africa, at the age of eighty:

> My early years are connected in my mind with my mother. At first she was always there; I can remember the comforting feel of her body as she carried me on her back and the smell of her skin in the hot sun.

Assured of comfort, infants come to believe that they can depend on people to come through when needed, that the world is benign and that they are worthy of support and comfort. Filled with basic trust—the basis of all secure relationships—children later form healthy human connections. And hugs are hand-me-downs—if given to children, they will have hugs to give to their own children.

Deeply confident that mother will be there to wipe their tears, to protect them from harm and to reassure them when the world feels too heavy, secure children feel comfortable with both closeness and separation, confident that no separation is as strong as the ties that bind. Thus, as the infant grows from lap baby to floor baby, he seeks less and less to embrace mom and more and more to embrace the world.

During play, he returns occasionally to the secure base of his mother's arms for an affectionate pat or two—"emotional refueling." Then he is off again. Psychologist Alice Honig likens this experience to the Greek myth of Antaeus. If Antaeus, son of Gaea, who was goddess of the Earth, could touch Mother Earth now and again during a battle, his strength would increase and he could fight on unbeatably. Hercules finally conquered Antaeus—by holding him so he could not touch Mother Earth and never attain secure grounding.

But baby in his roaming goes only so far. To ensure ongoing protection, explained John Bowlby, biological evolution tethered mother and baby to a psychic rope. As long as both stay within safe range, mother and baby can do their own thing—mother cooks, her ten-month-old scampers after the kitten in the living room. But when either reaches the end—mother doesn't hear her baby; baby, stuck in a corner, can't see or hear mother—a tug of anxiety signals "too far for comfort," and mother and baby seek each other out.

During times of low stress, the sight or sound of the mother will reassure the infant. For instance, if baby is sitting in a highchair and starts to pucker his mouth, mother softly calling his name might be sufficient to console. As stress intensifies, infants need touch for reassurance—they lean against you, cling to your leg. "When he's lying on the floor and beginning to fuss, if I just go over and give him my hand to hold, he calms," reports one mother. But during times of high stress, nothing comforts but the embrace, and preferably mother's. As we mature, words become better able to hug misery away. But under extreme duress, the savage need for the embrace rules, the hug forever the best antidote for sorrow. When the attachment relationship remains strong, the mother's power to console endures.

Father's Role

What about the other parent in the family equation? Do infants also become attached to fathers? Absolutely. If a father is warmly involved with his infant's care, infants show strong attachments to fathers. They use them for secure bases from which to explore and seek out father when frightened or uncertain. Typically, though, if both parents are present, distressed infants turn to mother as the universal wailing wall. Father is looked to more for fun. If mother is unavailable, however, infants can be calmed as easily by a sensitive father as by a sensitive mother.

These differences can be noted from the beginning—in the way mothers and fathers handle their infants. Mother's touch is mostly about comfort—she smooths her baby down, touches more often, and touches more parts of the body. Father's touch is generally less intimate. He tickles, he pokes, he jabs, jazzing up the baby for play. And a father's impulse is to excite, *even* if he is the primary caregiver. By six weeks of age, babies know the difference. When they see mother, they coo. When they see father, they squeal. As the Zinacanteco Indians of Mexico say, "Mothers hold their children in close, fathers hold them up toward the sky and show them the world." Both styles offer something to the developing child.

A father has another gift to offer his infant. He can make a difference in how well mother can mother. Wrote English psychoanalyst D. W. Winnicott:

> He can help provide a space in which the mother has elbow room;
> properly protected by her man, the mother is safe from having to turn

outwards, from having to deal with her surroundings at a time when she is wanting so much to turn inwards, when she is longing to be concerned with the inside of the circle which she can make with her arms in the center of which is the baby.

When fathers participate in child care and support the mother's efforts, mothers are more responsive to their infants and less likely to have infants insecurely attached at twelve months. And the better mother and father get along, the happier their baby and the better they feel about parenting.

Know Thyself

When the baby is well loved, the baby learns to love himself. When a baby is well understood, he learns *about* himself as well.

Sensitive mothers and fathers not only soothe their infants, they also *listen* to them. They tend to not play with or feed a baby who is tired or put to bed one who is hungry or in the mood for frolic. Nor do they intrusively lunge at and tickle a baby who is fingering a toy or pick up an infant giggling under a mobile. While feeding their infants, they stop, slow down, or speed up on cue. This sensitive responding gives infants accurate information about the effects of their behavior and teaches them that, when they signal a need, they can *expect* a prompt, predictable, and soothing response. The result is a feeling of control over their lives, the importance of which cannot be overemphasized. In control, we feel we can better assure our psychological survival. We need less *to* control, and thus form closer relationships and are happier. We are unlikely to commit acts of violence and have less physical problems and hence live longer.

Control, in fact, affects the functioning of our entire body. Robert Sapolsky of Stanford University, who has been studying baboon behavior in East Africa, found that cholesterol level, stress hormones, and the functioning of the immune and reproductive system all vary according to social rank—the higher the rank, the better the body's functioning. The dominant baboons, in greater control and more able to predict the future, were able to relax; the submissive ones, vigilant of the powers to be, were stressed. Moreover, among those of high rank, those most social had the best physiological functioning; affiliation, not isolation, keeps us healthy.

Other positive things happen when parents respond accurately to their infant's cues. Babies who are fed when hungry and put to sleep when tired grow up learning to eat when hungry and to go to sleep when tired. Babies who are comforted when sad, appeased when angry, and protected when fearful learn to recognize when they *feel* angry, sad, or fearful and comfortably communicate these feelings. Confident that "I hate you" will not incur a slap, an insult, an icy stare, or a guilt inducing, "How could you say that to your mommy?" they grow up to experience the full range of feelings as an integrated part of their sense of self. In fact, sensitive parents encourage expression of their child's negative feelings. For instance, in the Strange Situation, attachment researcher Robert Marvin found that mothers of secure children were more likely to ask their child, upon returning, about their anger at her for leaving. Furthermore, aware of their own feelings, the children respond more empathically to other people.

Quickly and accurately responded to, the baby spends less time in a state of want. This makes the baby happier, which makes the parents happier and feeling more effective in their caregiving efforts. Motivated to continue to quickly meet their baby's needs and keep the smiles coming, the parents shape the baby, while the baby shapes the parents. And the circle goes on.

This does not mean mother always must be available for her infant. All mothers are part loving and part withholding, part goddess and part witch. The question is how the percentages fall. Mothers of secure babies appear mostly goddesses. Sure they have moments and days when they are irritable, tense, or just tired, when their normal nurturant response gets stunted and both mother and baby have a bad day. But if these empathic breaks do not typify the mother-baby interaction, they have little if any long-term consequences. Ultimately, the story recorded is not one of occasional off moments and days—inevitable and easily repaired—but the consistent things we do with our babies day in and day out. If we respond quickly and compassionately most of the time, our baby will be forgiving when our dark side takes over.

But if a mother switches from goddess to witch without warning, or if she is a fake goddess, or worse, if she seems mostly a witch, babies are not so forgiving. From inconsistency, ambivalent attachment results; from rejection—subtle or overt—avoidant attachment results. Neither bode well for the infant's long-term development.

Inconsistent Touch

❧ Mothers who change personas unpredictably tend to be moody and self-involved. Often seeking love never received from their own parents, though the mothers are often well-meaning and loving, they tend to behave more in response to their own needs than their infant's. Consequently, when their infant signals distress, sometimes they offer comfort, sometimes they ignore her. In the Strange Situation, Diana's mother picked her up briefly at the first reunion but then quickly put her down and ignored Diana's bids for comfort. After Diana was left alone, upon return the mother put Diana in her lap and warmly attempted to calm her. Which mom will walk in the door? Diana can't foresee.

Unable to predict her mother's behavior and therefore unsure of protection and comfort when it's needed, the childhood tale of the ambivalent child can get spun in a convoluted web of confusion, mistrust, and uncertainty. Left with both desiring closeness with the good, loving mother—the goddess—and angry at the bad, ignoring mother—the witch—the child neither forgives nor forgets easily. "My mother's perfect; my mother's a monster," said a friend who, at middle age, still remains a prisoner to her deeply ambivalent feelings for her mother.

This pervasive uncertainty of mother's next move creates a chaotic rollercoaster of emotional ups and downs that makes children irritable and difficult to console. This, in turn, makes them harder to parent, intensifying and perpetuating the conflict with the mother. Life often becomes a constant battle for control, bringing out the worst behavior in both parent and child.

Take Brenda and her eleven-month-old infant, Jason. As Jason sat in a highchair facing his mother, Brenda started to play patty-cake with him. Jason squealed and clapped his hands heartily, and Brenda laughed as well. Jason then looked away. Brenda tickled his tummy. Jason shrieked and wiggled around. Brenda tickled his foot, and Jason shrieked louder but then started to squirm and fret. Brenda said, "Oh, you little crab," and poked his nose. Jason started to cry. Brenda grinned. Jason cried louder and began kicking the chair and pounding the table. Brenda sat back expressionless. Jason continued to howl and kick. Brenda's expression now softened and she said softly, "All right, little man," removed Jason from the highchair, and pulled him to her body, as she soothed him with soft words and gentle strokes across his face and head. Jason finally got the soothing he needed, but he had to shout loudly to do so.

There are different kinds of inconsistent mothers, explains Patricia Crittenden, a leading attachment theorist. Some, like Jason's mother, are unpredictable and *under*responsive. When their infants cry, they may not respond or may delay for a long time: "I'll pick you up . . . when I get around to it." When they do come, they are too involved with their own needs to read what their baby wants. When Jason looked away, signaling time out to download stimulation, Brenda, in need of Jason's attention, ignored this signal. These mothers may ignore their infant's holding out their arms to be picked up, but intrude upon their play with a pick-up because they, the mothers, need to be held.

Needless to say, feeling misunderstood makes a baby angry, as it did Jason, and often aggressive. It means as well that the infant does not learn to identify his internal states, so that anger, fear, and desire for comfort blend together as one package of need.

Even two-month-olds get distressed when their mother's behavior doesn't match their signals—even when her behavior is warm and loving. Infant researchers Lynne Murray and Colwyn Trevarthen of the University of Cambridge videotaped mothers and their two- to four-month-old babies playing. The infants then viewed their mother on the videotape. They saw the same mother and all the smiling, oohing and aahing, eye brightening, and exaggerated facial expressions that mothers do. But because their mother's behavior was out of sync with their current actions, the infants frowned, grimaced, and restlessly squirmed. In short, they withdrew from the interaction.

Other mothers are unpredictable and *overresponsive*. When their infant cries, the classic smothering mother rushes to them to "overinterpret any little sound they utter as a signal of distress," says Crittenden. Frantic, they shake, pat, rock their infant in "a rhythmic reflection of their babies' distress." As a result, they increase misery rather than attenuate it. Overprotected, misunderstood, and feeling constantly vulnerable, their infants become angry, too. But they express it less by a tirade than by becoming passive, helpless, and dependent.

To cope with a mother who slips in and out of their reach, which often leaves children feeling in danger to some extent, the child shortens the psychic rope that tethers them and tugs at it frequently. In this way, they keep the mother continually close and unable to disappear, literally or figuratively. Fiercely possessive, a sign that mother might tune out and the infant clings to mother's skirt; in effect, saying, "If you want to leave, you'll have to pry me away." When mother does push her child away physically, verbally, or by tuning out, the child cries, often inconsolably, and then attempts to cling even more: "Nobody's leaving without me." Even with infant monkeys, the more mother pushes them away, the more they cling.

If the crying doesn't prompt the needed nurturance, the child turns to the ultimate weapon: the temper tantrum. Who can ignore screaming, kicking, flapping, and stomping? In this way, explains Crittenden, the infant both punishes the mother for her indifference and threatens her to not let it recur: "If you dare leave me again, this is the price you pay."

During play, the occasional emotional refueling of the secure infant becomes emotional guzzling, as the infant fears running on empty. Worried that mom might vanish if the child absorbs himself in play, the child takes off, less to pursue the wonders of the world than to pursue mom. Games that involve her dominate their play. The toddler will pile her lap up with toys, fuss if she leaves the room, and then shadow after her. Or the child runs from her, forcing mother to chase them and thereby giving them control over her whereabouts: "Mother's running after me." Later, in school, the child is so preoccupied with mother or teacher, he may get easily distracted from learning.

By the second year, children begin to mix threatening behavior with coyness, which disarms their parents and elicits nurturance. By preschool, they become quite adept at using both behaviors to get their way. And though all children use these coercive strategies, ambivalent children use them to the hilt—mixing and matching both threatening and disarming behaviors as "two faces of one coercive coin," explains Crittenden, and alternating strategies with a magician's ease until they get what they want from their parent or teacher. For instance, if after telling the child she cannot have a cookie, the mother loses patience with her shouting, pouting, or tantrums and becomes angry, which threatens withdrawal, the child switches to disarming behavior. With emotional agility, a frown quickly becomes a shy sweet smile, mixed with brief glances, an engaging giggle, kisses, sweet talk ("I love you, Mommy"). Angry children (boys more than girls) turn threats to punishment; they hit, shame, or embarrass the parent. Resentful children (girls more than boys) turn coy enticement to helplessness: "Pick me up or we just don't go anywhere."

Because coercive children behave as if others are primarily responsible for creating *and* for changing their behavior, unless parents become more consistently emotionally available, the children are at risk for growing up wearing their neediness on their sleeves and they remain attention-seeking and childish. The more anxious the attachment relationship, the more extreme these behaviors.

A Rejecting Touch

All mothers love the fruit of their womb. But infants are tiny parcels of need. Some mothers, out of touch with their own need for nurturance, or anxious about this need, cannot tolerate seeing their own unmet needs expressed by their infant's neediness: They want their infants independent of nurturance as early as possible.

When their infants cry, it triggers anxiety, a sense of helplessness, apathy, or irritation—in severe cases, to the point of anger. Sylvia was a good example. Sitting at the table, she sat holding sixteen-month-old Raul on her lap, who passively fingered some blocks in front of him. He looked up with a blank look, grimaced, put his arm across his eyes, and whimpered softly. Sylvia smiled. Raul continued to whimper, and Sylvia continued to smile, making no attempt to comfort him. Then, peeved, Sylvia shouted, "Hey! Stop fussing and pile the blocks."

While Sylvia virtually ignored Raul's distress, other mothers respond to the cry but with delay. Or they pick up their baby but only seem to go through the motions. Or they frantically flood their baby with their own anxiety. Mothers uncomfortable with their infant's neediness range from the garden variety self-absorbed neurotic, who may just be emotionally distant, to the seriously depressed or overtly hostile, for whom too little support or their own internal duress hauls such weight that caring for their infants becomes too much. But arms that are rigid, indifferent, or limp don't comfort—nor do jumpy or listless movements; terse, strained, or monotone voices; or mismatched facial expressions like Sylvia's and Raul's.

Consequently, the mother often fails to quiet her infant, which makes her feel inept. The more inept she feels, the more she resents her infant, which builds up greater hostility. Or the more she may chastise herself, which increases her anxiety with her infant. Or the more she may withdraw, which widens the gap between herself and her infant.

But what about her infant? How does he feel when his cry elicits not comfort but intensified discomfort? Like Alice in Wonderland swimming in her pool of tears, he feels helpless in the face of unrelieved tension—in effect, punished for asking for help. With each prolonged cry, overarousal becomes more intolerable. The more unrelieved his tension, the more he grows up feeling unworthy of help and comfort, and the more his core experience becomes one primarily of depression, unmanageable anxiety, frustration, and anger.

At first, avoidant infants cry often and angrily—similar to the ambivalent infant. But over the first year, they blatantly express anger or anxiety less and less: Since their mothers didn't help them resolve these feelings in the past, they've learned that showing the full range of these emotions only increases the likelihood of maternal rejection. Loud protest is particularly undesirable if mother is openly hostile, since it could intensify her anger and make her dangerous. Take eighteen-month-old Roger. When his mother JoEllen, who was off to the beauty shop, tried to leave him with a babysitter, he started to wail and grab JoEllen's leg. She took him by the shoulders, shook him, and screamed "You'd better stop this crying this minute!"

Not able to fight his mother, which would escalate hostilities or intrusions, and not able to flee her because there's nowhere to run, he looked at his mother and froze, subduing his emotions as his best defense from further rejection. In other words, he shut off his attachment needs and assumed responsibility for his own comfort. Furthermore, if mother's angry, she may not want to take care of you—something no infant can risk. In other words, infants learn that expressing distress could lead to danger. Though adaptive in the short term, this mind-set is maladaptive in the long run, since it distorts perception of reality as always dangerous and threatening. Moreover, anger has survival value: It mobilizes us to help ourselves by warding off something unpleasant or potentially dangerous. If repressed, we may be unable to rid ourselves of unwanted threats from the environment. And, though infants learn how to prevent unwanted rejection, they fail, explains Crittenden, to learn how to elicit desired caregiving.

This emotional dampening starts surprisingly early in infancy and gradually deepens as protests become more and more connected with maternal anger, interference, or apathy. By the second year, babies display muted distress and anger, except under extreme circumstances: They look not sad but just serious much of the time. Anxiety, however, seeps through in other ways: eating problems, sleeping problems, illnesses, thumb-sucking, excessive rocking, and masturbation, and, later, nail biting, nightmares, headaches, stomach aches, eye blinking, stuttering, or the like.

Since wounds fester easily, avoidant infants learn to tune people out and to focus instead on play, which is far less risky. In the Strange Situation, while the secure infants often show their mother a toy and smile at her, avoidant infants never do both together. What's more, while piling blocks and rolling balls the child can shut out a rejecting or interfering mother in a socially acceptable way. But because he never feels quite safe, he remains wary, his play lacks joy, and he becomes increasingly vigilant, particularly if there's been abuse.

This cool demeanor and involvement in play make him appear independent and may later become self-importance, as in: "I'm so great, I can do everything myself." But his independence is pseudo-maturity, compulsive self-reliance, as John Bowlby called it, fueled by inability to use mother as a secure base from which to explore and by the need to shut her out. "It's not that you won't relieve my discomfort, it's that I don't need anyone," is how Crittenden interprets his unconscious thoughts. However, his heart rate accelerates in a flurry of protective activity, indicating suppressed anger when mother comes and goes during the Strange Situation.

In the Strange Situation, if the stranger is warm and friendly, she may lessen some of his stress. In fact, he may feel safer with her than with his mother, whose presence always carries some degree of threat. Rarely, however, does he feel truly safe; rarely does he feel truly relaxed. Gnawing inside him lies an omnipresent craving for love, caring, and nurturance which, feeling unable to reveal his vulnerabilities, he neither expresses nor understands. It's just a diffuse state of unease.

While the ambivalent infant's primary task in life is to keep mother close, the avoidant infant's primary task is to keep mother from getting too close—which would make intrusions more likely and anger more dangerous—but not leave him altogether unprotected. To solve this problem, he juggles a balancing act of advance/retreat: Advance when the caregiver withdraws, physically or psychologically, and retreat when the attachment figure approaches—avert his eyes, turn his body away, stiffen up.

Fear of Intimacy

Touch is the ultimate positive communication. The sensitive mother's hands, fingers, and arms are warm, calm, and receptive, her whole body conveying that her infant is endearing, desirable, adorable, precious. With loving, tender touch more or less a constant, her infant feels loved, lovable, and accepted.

The inconsistent mother gives loving, tender touch also, but when *she*, not necessarily her infant, is ready. Thus, her infant needs constant reassurance that he is loved and lovable—and forever asks for it.

But a rejecting mother is often uncomfortable with physical closeness. For her, the bond can become bondage. Less often tender, her touch tends toward neutral, awkward, or indifferent. In extreme cases, it becomes the ultimate negative communication: harsh, stiff, hurried, hurtful.

It's not that mothers of avoidant children don't protect them. Almost all mothers protect their children. It's that the infant feels at once protected and threatened.

The mother, of course, picks up her infant. But, explains attachment researcher and theorist Mary Main, many indirectly position themselves to avoid physical intimacy. She may stiffen up and hold her baby away from her body, or she may bring her baby into her body with her baby facing out, rather than in close, belly to belly. When her baby's arms fly open for a pick-up, she may leave her arms at her side, or when her baby crawls to her, she may cross her arms and legs to make her body a barricade. When her baby crawls up mother's legs, begging to be picked up, the mother may merely pat him on the head or back. During play, she may be a little rough and poke and jab her baby, rather than use touch primarily to soothe her child. She's unlikely to breastfeed or, if she does, fails at it or gives it up quickly.

When you pick up these infants, they don't cuddle but go limp in your arms. Or their little bodies stiffen, especially if they've been abused. It's as if they fear that, should they relax into you, they won't be prepared when you push them away. In other words, they learn to perceive danger even when it's not there, says Crittenden. Feeling the unwillingness of the parent to be emotionally close, they experience lifelong skin hunger, coupled with a powerful need to protect themselves from these feelings and hide their neediness.

In abusive mother-baby relationships, rejection can be overt: Mother blatantly ignores her infant or angrily yells or taunts her, sometimes even hitting her. But often irritation and anger are suppressed; in their place is a subtle disengagement from the infant. Note for instance the "dance of the hands" of twenty-one-month-old Jane and her mother, elegantly captured on tape in slow-motion analysis by Mary Main:

> Each time Jane's hand approached the mother's, the mother's hand moved slowly out of reach—always too slowly to be perceived in real time, and always just enough to escape what must have seemed to Jane, microseconds earlier, a certain meeting. When Jane did finally succeed in grasping the mother's hand, the mother's hand slid back so that Jane held only the mother's fingers. Her finger then slid gently out of Jane's grasp. As Jane turned toward her mother in renewed panic, the mother smiled with her hand still extended, and the eerie dance of hands began once more. When Jane attempted to seat herself on the mother's lap, the mother stiffened, making her body a flat rather than a comfortable and conforming surface. As Jane lay against her, the mother very slowly began leaning backward.

Painfully out of touch with their infants' need for comfort, mothers fail to recognize and respond to it. When frightened and in need of a reassuring hug, the child might get a pat; when lonely, the child may get put to sleep alone in his crib; when hungering for affection, the child may get a bottle to feed himself; when overexcited, the child may get frenetically shaken, rocked, and patted.

This nonempathy, or what psychoanalyst Daniel Stern calls nonattunement, creates mixed messages that confuse infants. The irony, explains Main, is that the more a mother rejects her infant's efforts to climb into her arms or onto her lap, the more she increases the baby's anxiety, which intensifies the baby's *need* to be held, thus increasing the infant's bids for contact.

This places the infant in a conflict situation similar to a double-bind: to flee from danger (the rejecting mother) or to come toward the haven of safety—the attachment figure (the same mother). Since, when in danger, it is only close physical contact with the attachment figure that will alleviate the anxiety, the infant continues to seek out mother for protection, even though the mother is the predator. "By repelling her infant . . . a mother simultaneously attracts him," says Main.

At one time or another most parents lose their patience, which can create this double-bind. The late author Erma Bombeck wrote of one day at the supermarket with her three-year-old son, who had tipped over and broken a bubble-gum machine and sent the bubble gum rolling all over the store.

> I was furious. I told him he would never see another cookie as long as he lived. Meanwhile, a crowd had gathered. Tears flowed from his eyes, and he grabbed me around my knees, and that was when the realization hit me: I was all he had to turn to, even though I had berated him and embarrassed him in public.

The need for parental protection is so powerful, it is hard to kick ourselves free of the familial gravitational pull, even when it threatens to throw our psychological balance out of orbit. This is why abused children often deny the abuse. But the bad feelings remain.

Bad Touch

As early affection gets etched in our heart, enabling us to later reach out and touch others, cold, lifeless, tense, overstimulating, hostile, violent, or inappropriately sexual touch, particularly in the formative years, gets stored in the dark crevices of our mind and forces us to turn inward and seek forms of self-stroking, or to strike out, to keep people at arm's length.

Wounded, many wound back. And although most abused children do not abuse their own children, those that do have in almost all cases been abused: Violence begets violence.

The United States has the world's highest incidence of child beatings and murders by parents. What's more, 93 percent of American parents use physical punishment on their children. More than twenty years ago, a classic study of American childrearing methods showed harsh and punitive touch to outweigh warmth and affection. Violence, said Stokely Carmichael, is as American as apple pie.

Parents who physically abuse their children use touch to convey power and aggression, rather than nurturance and caring. This teaches children not to trust touch as communication. In other words, violent behavior and body pleasure cannot coexist—the presence of one inhibits the presence of the other.

James Prescott, a neuropsychologist formerly with the National Institute of Child Health and Human Development of the U.S. Department of Health, Education, and Welfare, found a relationship between amount of touch in a given culture and violence. After reviewing forty-nine societies, Prescott discovered that cultures high in infant physical affection—much touching, holding, and carrying—rate low in adult physical violence, with the converse true as well. The principal cause of human violence, concluded Prescott, is "a lack of bodily pleasure derived from touching and stroking during the formative periods of life."

Touch used as violence is touch used as power to subjugate others to our will and to mask our own feelings of helplessness. These low-touch societies thus also rated highest in characteristics representing dominance rather than equality in human relations: slavery, polygyny, and inferior female status. And they worshiped aggressive supernatural gods—a likely carryover of a perception of their first gods—their parents—as belligerent and dangerous if not obeyed.

A striking example of how good touch creates peaceful children and bad touch warlike children is Margaret Mead's comparison of the two New Guinea tribes, the Arapesh and the Mundugumor. With the loving and peaceful Arapesh, infants were always held by someone, and crying was avoided. The breast was given immediately for comfort, and suckling was prolonged and made into an affectionate game for mother and baby. Babies slept either in a net bag against the mother's back, in her lap, or crooked in her other arm as she worked.

With the aggressive and hostile Mundugumor (whose culture has apparently changed since these observations were made in the 1930s), infants, deprived of warm, nurturant touch, lived an "unloved" life. They spent their day hung suspended from a strap around the mother's forehead in a harsh, stiff basket, where little light seeped through. When the infant cried, the mother scratched the outside of the basket, making a harsh grating sound. If the crying did not stop, the infant was suckled but with the mother standing up. When suckling stopped, the child was immediately returned to the basket.

Devoting their time to quarreling and headhunting, the Mundugumor had developed a form of social organization "in which every man's hand is against every other man." The women, as "assertive and vigorous as the men," detested bearing and rearing children.

Defended Children

Avoidant infants, of course, don't necessarily turn into warring children. In fact, long having learned not to make waves and irk their parents, which intensifies the child's anxiety, by preschool some get needed attention by becoming the perfect child—polite, well-behaved, a little helper, involved in their activities, a smiling pleasant kid. So good are some of these children at hiding their distress that preschool teachers are astounded when interpretation of family drawings indicates the child is not a happy camper.

Eager to please in the hope that the parent might like them and therefore take an interest in them and want to care for them, they do what makes parents happy, even when not wanting to do something. In other words, they sacrifice self-development for parental protection. The result is the establishment of a "false self"—a persona in the service of pleasing others. Quick-change artists, when one behavior doesn't please, they immediately try a new one.

Well rehearsed at masking sadness, anger, distress, or hurt feelings, in time the children lose touch with their true feelings altogether, as it all jumbles together in a general state of inner rumblings. Asked if sad, some don't answer or, when older, respond "I don't know" or "I guess so" or "I'm not sure." Fearful that no one will comfort them should they start to cry, many put on a happy face and pretend nothing's wrong. In extreme cases, this denial of self can lead to a sense of depersonalization, as if one is detached from one's body and, in the worst cases of child and sexual abuse, multiple personality disorder.

When intimacy is not a threat, defended children may let down their guard and allow genuine feelings to leak through. Attachment researcher Alan Sroufe found that in preschool, some avoidant children allowed their dependency needs to show—but they sought attention in negative ways, trying to climb onto their teacher's lap and so on. He was able to distinguish them from the ambivalent children—when hurt or disappointed, they retreated into themselves.

If the parent has been only mildly rejecting, the children just tend to avoid them and can do fine often as competent, introverted, mature children who are busy with their activities and just not affectionate. But if the parent has been seriously rejecting—openly hostile and perhaps even dangerous—the child tempers his anger by becoming compliant and quickly meeting the slightest demand. To protect themselves against the feared inevitable blow of rejection, the bruise of hostility, the sting of criticism, they approach with fists up: They side-step toward the parent, make little eye contact, and keep an arm's length between them. If they begin to feel safe, as when in school, the bottled-up rage may explode like a champagne cork: The doll gets yelled at and furiously slapped; the children chased after and, if the teacher's not looking, even hit. Some of them become bullies, as if to elicit from others that which is most familiar from home—rejection.

Rejection comes not only from hostility, whether subtle or overt, but also from withdrawal—from not being noticed, as when the infant is faced with a depressed mother. To cope, children adopt a strategy different from those faced with hostility or intrusion. They seek to keep mother at least minimally involved by behaving to make mother happy, concerned that if mother's not there, no one will take care of them. They act cheerful, though their laughter is often high-strung and empty. To get close to their withdrawn parent, they may use role reversal and become compulsive caregivers, as in, "Here, Mommy, I'll do it." They readily take care of their sisters and brothers and sometimes seem mature beyond their years. In extreme cases of maltreatment infants as young as twelve months of age already show false cheerfulness.

Can a depressed parent fool children and pretend warmth? Not easily. Since accurate appraisal of social cues has survival value, children are wired to pick up subtle signs of hostility or withdrawal. Even babies, who can distinguish between that smile unlike any other that parents use when looking at their infant and a fake smile that becomes a nervous social smile—lips pulled back and teeth clenched.

When parents do not satisfy their children's need for closeness and comfort, these needs do not go away. Rather, they get staked out through the back door. When starved for love, the defended child asks for food. When hurt from rejection, she says her head or belly hurts—a precursor for later psychosomatic illnesses. When lonely, she cries because she wants her doll, not her mother's arms. When frightened following her mother's departure, she greets her return with a request to go to the bathroom—as mother takes her hand, she gets safe touch without revealing a desire for closeness, or that she cares that mother has returned.

Some children become sloppy; getting filthy encourages parents to wash dirty faces and change dirty clothes. Some touch themselves and, when under extreme duress, masturbate excessively. Others become sick, since illness is especially effective in summoning touch. Parents feel their child's forehead with the palm of their hand to test for fever, or put their cheek against their child's cheek. They carry a feverish child to bed, tuck her under the covers, and may lie cuddling with her until she falls asleep. Parents come in periodically during the night to feel the child's forehead, or sometimes even allow the child to sleep with them.

Some children become careless and easily hurt themselves, since sores get washed and kissed. Or they may display excessive fears—"I'm scared" might warrant a pat or two. Others use rough-and-tumble play to gain physical access to the parent: The loving hug becomes a mock-aggressive bear hug, the embrace a wrestling match.

All children, of course, use these strategies to elicit parental attention. But while secure children employ them along with open communication of their needs and feelings and insecure ambivalent children use them in exaggerated form, defended children use them in place of open communication. The more anxious the child, the more extreme the measures used to secure parental protection. In fact, during extreme deprivation, children may behave to invite physical abuse, if that's the only way in which they can feel body contact. Or they may pick fights with other children—a fist in the face is still touching and being touched.

In the poem "Ironing Their Clothes" by Julia Alvarez, a child lingers when pressing her mother's bedjacket:

> If I clung to her skirt as she sorted the wash
> or put out a line, my mother frowned,
> a crease down each side of her mouth.
> This is no time for love! But here
> I could linger over her wrinkled bedjacket,
> kiss at the damp puckers of her wrists
> with the hot tip. Here I caressed complications
> of darts, scallops, ties, pleats which made
> her outfits test of the patience of my passion.
> Here I could lay my dreaming iron on her lap.

By adolescence, when many avoidant families live together in the same household with nary a touch, sexual promiscuity becomes a means for intimacy for some. Or teens may use drugs, which create a steady flow of pleasurable sensations similar to what we experience when we've made intimate contact with a loved one.

Can one mix and match, be sometimes coercive and sometimes defended? Yes. Since some parents switch from rejection to responsiveness, children will select strategies dependent on the parent's behavior. Or, children may behave primarily defended with one parent and primarily coercive with the other: "How come he only misbehaves with me?" mothers often ask. Or he may behave defensively at home but coercively in school: "He doesn't act up like this at home," parents commonly say to teachers. Usually, though, one pattern dominates. In especially disorganized environments, even infants will vary their behavior as stress mounts.

By adulthood, insecure people commonly vacillate between coercive and defended strategies, depending on degree of threat. When mild, one acts coercively; when severe, one acts defensively. Secure people also utilize defensive and coercive strategies. But *they* have the choice to abandon them when no longer adaptive.

Influences on Attachment

Parental Attachment History

Freud proclaimed the mother the prototype for all later relationships. If so, then early patterns of attachment should transmit, like seeds in the wind, from one generation to the next. Indeed, studies on intergenerational transmission of attachment support this. If securely attached to our mothers, we hold within us a blueprint of a warm and loving mother and, in turn, respond warmly and sensitively to our own infant's need for comfort. If insecurely avoidantly attached to our mother and therefore uncomfortable with physical intimacy, we will likely convey this discomfort to our own infant who, in turn, will become avoidantly attached to us.

Our infant's cry, which unconsciously jiggles ancient feelings of what happened when *we* cried, serves as a litmus test. If we were enveloped in warm, receptive arms, our immediate reaction is to offer comfort to our infant. But if no one came when we cried, we may fear opening ourselves up to unresolved loss, and so may ignore his cry: "If I hear my baby's cry, that might put me dangerously in touch with my own unanswered cries."

Or we may pick up our infant but stiffen when we hold him, fearing intimacy might elicit our own frustrated need for closeness. Or, remembering how no one came to comfort us, we may immediately rush anxiously to our infant's side and overwhelm him with our own needs. If our baby does not quickly stop crying, we may feel rejected, and thus distance ourselves from him.

From Cradle to Grave?

Some people doubt the pervasiveness of patterns of attachment across the lifespan, maintaining that we can shed old business like a snake sheds its skin. But research into infant memory supports the profound influence of early experiences on development.

When do your first memories begin? Most people will answer around age four or five. In what Freud called infantile amnesia, we remember nothing of our first two to three years of life—not when we started to walk or talk, or our "birth trauma."

Yet, a part of us *does* remember. Actually, memory functions from birth, perhaps even before. Not memory as we think of it—being able to tell a story about an event in our life—but rather, feelings, sensations, and movements that become associated with people, places, and things. Etched in the limbic system, the primitive emotional brain that we share with other mammals and that functions from birth, these archaic memories remain indelible and influence us all our lives.

In one study, six-month-old infants were asked to reach in the dark for a rattle with a puppet attached. Though given this task to do only once, at one-and-a-half and at two-and-a-half years of age, these infants more correctly completed the task than the control group.

Of course, a puppet is not a mother; her influence penetrates far deeper into the psyche, as this fascinating anecdote from Ashley Montagu's book *Touching* recounts. A two-and-a-half-year-old child had been referred to psychiatrist Philip Seitz for pathological hair-pulling that appeared with the onset of a punitive toilet-training program. While drinking from her bottle, she would pull out some hairs from her head and roll them up against her lip and nose.

Dr. Seitz had a hunch. If the child had once been nursed *and* the mother's nipple was surrounded by hair, this behavior might then be an attempt to recreate this early experience.

His hunch proved correct. But the child was nursed only the first two weeks of her life! How could she have "remembered" the experience two and a half years later? What was remembered was not the actual episode—as early memories are not stored in a verbal filing system, they cannot be verbally retrieved. Rather, we remember sensory impressions: the taste, the feel, the shape, the contour of the breast and the nipple, the tactile sensation of the mother's coarse hair against the baby's face (perhaps a tickling feeling). Later, to re-create the comfort, the child tried to re-create these sensations. When she grew up, she may have found herself attracted to men with beards and hairy chests. Why, she couldn't have said. "How interesting," comments one of my students. "My fiancé's five-year-old daughter always draws him with a mustache. He hasn't had a mustache since she was four months old."

We live in the twilight of our past, bumping into walls of the present, shaped by memories we can't name. Touched by Satie's "Gymnopédies," intoxicated by the scent of jasmine, possessing a penchant for purple—perhaps these were the sounds, scents, and colors surrounding us when nursed at our mother's breast. Those people who feel we should be better able to control our feelings underestimate the importance of the effect of these early experiences on later behavior. Parental warmth, more than economics or whether or not our parents were divorced or alcoholics, determines how fulfilling our lives are in adulthood.

Developmental psychologist Edward Tronick of Harvard University discovered that a stable emotional blueprint of mother guides our behavior as early as six months of age. Tronick asked mothers to sit facing their six-month-old babies and to play normally with them for three minutes and then change their expression to a flat, impassive look—a "still face" like that of a depressed mother. Baby smiles, mother doesn't. How would a baby cope with this mismatch of emotional communication? The answer lies in the baby's relationship with her mother. If accustomed to a consistently warm maternal response, the infant coos and babbles, flashing that impish smile that says, "Oh, come on, Mom. You know you're always happy to see me." If that doesn't get mom to come alive, she may frown, smile again, frown, but, ultimately, persist and smile, or mix smiles and coos with fussing and protesting.

Other infants immediately start to fuss, cry, and thrash about to get mother's attention, the pattern later typical of ambivalent infants, while those whose mothers have been consistently unresponsive to their needs make no attempt to engage mother at all. Neither smiling nor protesting, they may stare at her for a bit and then look away and suck their fingers, clasp their hands, rock, tug at their ear, or pull into the fetal tuck. Or they immediately turn away from mother and not look back at her at all. Tronick describes one such infant:

> He . . . soon looked up at her [mother] and sobered, staring at her for almost fifteen seconds. While looking, his breathing became labored and his hands clenched and unclenched repeatedly until he finally looked off for several seconds but again looked back towards her with his chin tucked, his face tensed, and his eyes narrowed. At no time did he vocalize or even brighten; nor did he cry or fuss. He appeared overwhelmed and stressed as he repeated the tense looking towards and away cycle.

If the infant's environment remains constant, by the second year these behavioral patterns seem set. For instance, in her observations of abused and neglected infants, Patricia Crittenden found that in the first year of life, a sensitive, warm caregiver, in sync with infants' cues, can open up their defensive window a bit and allow a sliver of trust to seep through; with persistence, they'll relax into you, conforming their body to your contours. But, by the second year, that window seems shut: Their bodies remain stiff; their eyes look away.

Recent studies of the brain's functioning back this. The ages between ten and eighteen months appear a critical period for learning how to handle stress, as the orbitofrontal area of the prefrontal cortex is swiftly forming the connections with the limbic brain that will make it a key gatekeeper for distress. After countless occasions of maternal comfort, the infant learns to self-calm and, presumably, builds more little branches in this pathway for handling distress. But when stress overtakes the infant, cortisol streams through the bloodstream and destroys these connections. An infusion of cortisol also increases the area in the brain involved in vigilance and arousal, which is why these children are on continual alert: The slightest stress triggers an outpouring of stress hormones. This tells us the psychoanalysts may have been correct all long: To some extent, we all carry our early baggage with us.

On the other hand, the infant's limbic system continues to mature well into adolescence. If the child's environment changes favorably, formerly insecure attachments can become secure and rewrite the child's tale of woe to include a happier ending. It is not unusual, for instance, for an insecure attachment to mother during infancy to blossom to security during preschool, as mother feels less hassled by the demands of the toddler. Unfortunately, the opposite can occur as well: as stress builds, secure attachments can reverse themselves. If it does, as these recent studies into brain functioning would predict, these children still have an edge. When attachment theorist Alan Sroufe looked at children's coping skills, he found that children securely attached as infants but currently insecurely attached are more likely to bounce back from setbacks—while those currently secure but insecurely attached as infants tended to have lower self-esteem and to regress under stress. In other words, if the road turns in their favor, wounds can be sutured. But the minute the ride gets bumpy, they smart all over again.

Security of attachment also varies. An infant can be securely attached to both parents, to only one parent, or to neither. Predictably, the children with secure attachments to both parents do better in every way—in love, in friendship, in school, in work—and those with insecure attachments to both do the worst. When Mary Main and Donna Weston watched how babies would react to a friendly clown, those infants who were securely attached to both parents were more playful with the clown than those securely attached to only one parent, with those insecurely attached to both parents being the least friendly.

And children don't just make attachments to parents. They will attach to anyone who cares for them—grandparents, aunts, sisters, babysitters, and teachers. This is nature's safety guard against loss of the parents. If secure, these other attachments can help buffer some of the pain of the child's early experience; later, it can make a difference in their own parenting. For instance, though most secure infants have parents who are secure in their own early attachments and likewise for insecure attachments, there are some secure infants of parents with insecure attachment histories. In people who have been abused, the presence of a nonparental caring person in one's past can help break the cycle of abuse from one generation to the next. Therapeutic intervention can also help change the tide. In the new field of infant mental health, psychologists are often successful in helping parents to overcome their obstacles to bonding with their infant, and often in ten sessions or less. (For more information, see the Resource Guide.)

Insecurity also has a broad range, depending on the degree of anxiety experienced in our first relationships, our current circumstances, and our coping skills. Some insecurely attached people are not necessarily unhappy adults, who, though not especially intimate, function well in the world.

Moreover, while our early environment plays a profound part in writing our life story, it's important to consider that the infant also comes with a unique sense of self.

Temperament's Role

Babies emerge from the womb with distinctive personalities that mix and match with their parents'. Sometimes there's a good blend, sometimes there isn't.

Some babies are born good-natured. Mostly content, they quiet easily when upset. They love to snuggle and mold their body into yours but don't fret when put down. Easy to love and easy to care for, they bring out the best in even a stressed parent and increase the likelihood of a secure attachment.

Others emerge edgy. Easily emotionally aroused, we call these babies reactive or emotionally labile. It takes little to set them off and much to calm them down. More unhappy than calmer babies, they tend to remain so and grow up more prone to emotional upheaval, moodiness, and nervousness.

Most of these newborns become shy and cautious infants. Typically happy only when in your arms, they cry easily when put down. If a mother is too busy to fill her infant's need to be held, she may feel guilty and, thus, inadequate. Moreover, an active outgoing mother may lose patience with a slow-to-warm baby.

Other babies are more outgoing but are difficult. They quickly set off and easily exasperate parents. If under stress, lacking sufficient supports, or inexperienced, a parent who may be sensitive under ordinary circumstances may be unable to cope with an irritable infant. Consequently, mothers might withdraw from their infants, holding them less and with less warmth and affection. This can create a negative feedback cycle. The infant perceives the mother as rejecting and begins to withdraw, further increasing mother's feeling of rejection and ineptness, which further distances mother from baby, increasing the likelihood of insecure attachment.

The situation may be worse when babies are both difficult and "noncuddlers," infants who are restless when embraced. Turning their face away, they begin to struggle and push you away, wriggling and arching their backs and only stopping when you put them down. Some are reacting to subtle or overt maternal rejection, while others seem born touchy (see chapter 8). Often highly active and alert, they seem too busy and interested in the world to sit still and cuddle and often demonstrate advanced motor milestones and high intelligence. They make their mothers feel rejected, which can cause mothers to draw back.

Temperament affects also how easily children cope. Some fall apart in the best of circumstances, others weather the worst of circumstances. Take my neighbor's child. Though her mother is volatile, Tonya, who is easygoing, lets her mother's rages roll off her back. Most of the time, she's friendly and in a good mood. Four-year-old Nadia, on the other hand, is shy. Though adored by her warm and affectionate mother, she smiles rarely, cries easily, and hides herself behind her mother's back when I come to visit.

Some theorists, such as noted Harvard psychologist Jerome Kagan, feel that temperament slots an infant into a particular attachment category: easy into secure; difficult into ambivalent; and slow-to-warm into avoidant. But the relationship between attachment and temperament is not linear. Secure babies run the gamut from easy to difficult, as do those insecurely attached. Nor do difficult babies become necessarily difficult children and vice-versa. Indeed, most studies find little prediction between temperament ratings and security of attachment at twelve months. In other words, though temperament can put a baby at higher risk for insecure attachment, sensitive parents tone their baby's arousal and bring out the best in their babies, while insensitive parents bring out the worst in their babies, making even easy babies fussy.

Insensitive parenting and infant irritability is especially lethal when it includes few social supports, a combination that often leads to maltreatment. "Why did you burn him?" asked a reporter of a mother who "accidentally" scorched her baby. "I couldn't stop his crying. It made me so nervous, the pot of boiling water just went flying out of my hands."

And, whether it's water, hate, or indifference that burns babies, all abused, neglected, or ill-cared-for infants are at risk for becoming psychological casualties. In a high-risk American sample, only around half the infants are securely attached. Even rhesus monkey mothers, when isolated, avoid their infants more.

Fortunately, most babies are not fussy and, fortunately, the majority of middle-class American mothers are sensitive. In a typical middle-class U.S. sample, 65 percent of infants are secure, 13 percent ambivalent, and 20 percent avoidant. Yet, when our children turn two years of age, the percentage plummets to around 40 percent secure, with the largest increase in ambivalent coercive children. And though some are just testing out their newfound ability to push around their parents and will return to more reasonable behavior and secure attachment, for others their formerly supportive environment has become threatening, causing a shift in strategy to seek parental protection.

This shift is understandable. While it's relatively easy to care for an infant, it becomes inconvenient for a busy mother, lacking help, to run after a two-year-old or to hug a crabby baby when she's feeling crabby herself. As for the children, when holding out arms no longer elicits the needed pick-up, they turn to whining to force the needed closeness. Consequently, the American child has gained the reputation as whiny and petulant. Cross-cultural comparisons lend support.

Attachment Across Cultures

❧ Picture yourself on a lounge chair at a beach in Honolulu. All around you are mothers and their young children. Some are Hawaiian American, some Japanese American, and some Caucasian American. If you are developmental psychologist Mary Martini, you are not basking in the sun but carefully noting the differences between the three groups.

The Hawaiians are gathered together in large extended families with lots of children but few fathers. The adults chat with one another, rarely playing with their children, who, playing with each other, don't seem to care. When parents speak to their children, it's mostly bantering, commanding, and scolding. Children, self-reliant, do mostly for themselves and get much help from older brothers and sisters, seeking their parents out infrequently. There's little sibling rivalry. They explore widely.

The Japanese form mostly little enclaves of nuclear family units— mother, father, and one or two children. At their children's beck and call, the parents do everything for their children's happiness, rarely engaging in solitary activities and spending little time talking to each other. They stay close to their children, play with them, follow them, comment on their activities, monitor them, protect them, structure their environment, minimize frustrations, and demand that they be polite and stay clean. When the children are hungry, the mother pulls out carefully prepared "snacks." Confrontations are rare. Rather, the parent tries to distract the children from undesired activities. Talking little, communication is mostly through touch and gesturing.

The Caucasians are about half nuclear families, half single mothers with children. The mothers are sunbathing, reading, talking to one another, doing crossword puzzles, even swimming and jogging alone, encouraging their children to entertain and care for themselves. At requests from their children to play, mothers say things like: "It's your father's turn to play with you"; "Please stop bothering me, I'm trying to read"; "I'll play with you when I finish this chapter"; and "This is my time to relax." When their children are hungry, they pull out peanut butter and jelly sandwiches or

run to McDonald's. To get their parents' attention, children do much talking, gesturing, even yelling, looking like insecure coercive children. Mothers seem harried and unable to relax. Confrontations, power struggles, and
sibling rivalry are common. Touch is minimal.

In another observation of American mothers and infants at the beach,
this one done in 1966 by Vidal Clay at three different beaches—a public
one, a country club, and a private one—there was little affectionate touching between mothers and infants. Rather, touch occurred mostly when
babies needed to be controlled. The mothers also seemed more interested
in socializing with their friends than interacting with their children.

Other anthropological data are in accord with mainstream U.S. mothers
as more self-involved and less affectionate toward their children and the
children, in turn, acting out more negative behavior. Tiffany Field, who
recently watched mothers and preschoolers on a playground in Miami and
in Paris, found the French mothers watched over their children more,
while the Miami mothers were more self-absorbed. More important, the
French mothers and teachers stroked, held, kissed, or petted their children
more than their U.S. counterparts. Transferring this affection to each
other, the French children hugged, held, and stroked each other more and
grabbed toys and hit each other less. All total, aggression occurred 29
percent of the time among U.S. children and only 1 percent of the time
among the French children. Harvard developmental psychologist Jerome
Kagan watched Japanese mothers and their young children on a playground
with their mothers. He noted a gentleness in the children's play: The
children did not seize property or strike another child. Anthropologists
Beatrice Whiting and John Whiting, who compared our culture to Japan,
India, Kenya, Mexico, and the Philippines, found almost three times as
much attention-seeking behavior in American three- to eleven-year-olds,
while toddlers here were more active, more demanding, and more sensitive
to emotional changes in their mother. In China, American researchers
were astonished to not find terrible twos, which we consider a two-year-old
rite of passage. Neither are the tantrums or sibling rivalry commonly reported here generally found in young children in indigenous cultures.

Cultural Norms and Quality of Attachment

What accounts for such differences in parenting style and children's behavior? Cultural roles for one.

The parenting role is crucial for the self-definition of Hawaiian parents,
and they seek to nurture their children. But they also see their child as

belonging not just to them, but to the whole family, who share in the caregiving, and they prepare their children for integration into the whole social milieu of the extended family. At the same time, they encourage self-reliance. The adult role is less to focus on caring for children than to meet the needs of the whole household.

In Japan, by contrast, motherhood has traditionally defined the Japanese woman. Her whole life centers on caring for her baby, whom she never leaves; there are almost no babysitters in Japan. The mother-infant bond is so intensely intimate, the Japanese call it *skinship*. The mother carries her baby for long periods on her back, prolongs breastfeeding, co-bathes, and sleeps with her infant until he reaches age five. She attempts to soothe her infant into a continual state of calm, lying down next to her baby and patting him, singing to him, and comforting him until the baby falls asleep. Totally involved with her infant, the mother's relationship with her husband comes secondary, and the father may sleep separately.

In the United States, we too place great importance on mothering but, encouraged to seek self-fulfillment, define ourselves through other roles as well—career, leisure activities, other children, and our spousal relationship. To preserve the marital bed, we sleep with our partner rather than with our infant. Forced to juggle many roles and worried that everyone gets the short end of the stick, our do-all, be-all lifestyle drains us.

Does the Japanese mother's continual protection of her infant carry bigger emotional dividends than our more distant parenting? In some respects, it does. In Japan, 77 percent of infants are securely attached to their mothers, and 23 percent are ambivalently attached. Where are the avoidant infants? Because of the Japanese mother's quick attention to her infant's needs, most studies have found few avoidant attachments.

Skinship

When mother and baby are rarely separated, as in Japan, a mother becomes acutely sensitive to her infant's signals. Able to perpetually anticipate her infant's distress, she can respond *before* rumblings become a tempest.

The more skinship, the greater maternal sensitivity, as mother and baby literally communicate through their skins. The !Kung mother, who carries her baby skin-to-skin, senses tension in her infant's limbs, changes in breathing or heart rate, and movements in the abdomen that enable her to anticipate waking and hunger. Knowing when her baby is ready to do his business, she holds the baby away from her body. The Eskimo Netselik mother does the same. When asked precisely how she knows it's time for her baby to do his business, she was amazed that any mother would not know. A mother can't get much more hooked into her baby than that!

Psychologist Elizabeth Anisfeld of Columbia University found herself in an ideal situation to conduct a skinship experiment. Left with a bunch of donated Snuglies (soft baby carriers), she distributed them to some poor mothers, whose infants are at high risk for insecure attachment. What happened next was beyond her expectations: At one year of age, 83 percent of the babies carried in the Snuglies were securely attached to their mothers, compared to 38 percent of babies carried in plastic infant seats (the control group)!

Differences emerged early. As one would expect, at two months, few carried infants had regular periods of crying, compared to half the control infants. At three months, experimental mothers enjoyed their babies more than the control mothers did. In appreciation, their babies looked more at their mothers.

Anisfeld repeated the study with premature infants, another population at increased risk for insecure attachment. She got even better results. Ninety-three percent of the carried babies were securely attached, compared to 57 percent of the control group babies. That figure far exceeds the normal middle-class American population, which reports 65 percent secure. At seven months of age, carried infants and mothers were better cued into each other and spent more time joyfully playing together.

In both studies, increased carrying led to increased maternal sensitivity, which resulted in less crying (which made the infants easier to parent) and in quicker bonding (which created greater investment in parenting). With their babies less fussy, mothers felt more competent and thus more desirous of nurturing their baby, circuiting mother and baby into a nice positive feedback loop.

But separation of mother and baby sacrifices this fine-grained moment-to-moment awareness and increases the likelihood of misinterpreting the infant's signals. This is the case even with the most sensitive mothers, who get intensely frustrated when unable to know what their babies want. With insensitive mothers, the problem is intensified. When Brenda played patty-cake with Jason and he turned away, she interpreted this as disinterest and continued to overload him until he started to fuss. But if Jason had been in her lap, Brenda would likely have felt his limbs tense up and his body squirm. This would have increased the odds that she would accurately interpret his eye averting as related to stress, rather than disinterest, and she would either draw back or soothe him.

Marten deVries and Arnold Sameroff looked at temperamental differences between three African tribes: the Kikuyu, the Digo, and the Masai. All three tribes indulged their infants with extensive carrying, co-sleeping, prolonged breastfeeding, and a quick response to the cry. Modernization, however, brought changes for some infants—namely, sleeping alone in a cot, scheduled feeding (breast or bottle), outside child-care helpers that drastically decreased mother-infant contact, infant seats versus carrying babies on the back, and Western-style clothing, which limits skin-to-skin contact. Of the three, the Kikuyu were most rapid in transition to modern living, and of the three, Kikuyu mothers also rated their babies as having the most difficult temperament. In other words, with increased separation came greater fussiness.

Attachment Does Not Equal Dependency

Childrearing methods in any given culture reflect what kind of child the parents want. For the Japanese, who champion interdependence, mother-baby closeness furthers this goal. But for us, who champion independence, mother-baby closeness suggests dependency—in other words, helplessness, powerlessness, and lack of control.

But *does* it? A close look at cultures who indulge their infants' need for closeness throws doubt. The continuously carried !Kung San infant, for instance, initiates separation before his mothers does, who rarely leaves his side until well into the second year. As toddlers, !Kung infants ventured farther from their mothers and played more with peers than did their middle-class counterparts in England. Nor do they become excessively attached to their mothers but transition easily to attachment to a peer group. As for concerns about autonomy in adulthood, leave them aside, says Melvin Konner, reminding us how the !Kung woman gives birth *alone* in the forest. Can you imagine us being so self-reliant?

By the age of four, children of the Yequana, a Stone Age tribe in the Venezuelan rainforest, contribute to the workforce in their family and are described as extraordinarily self-reliant. In Kenya, the Nyansongo tribe entrusts their two-month-old infants to five- to eight-year-old siblings as child nurses, who feed, bathe, and care for the infants while their mothers work in nearby gardens or go to market. Our five-year-old picking up our two-month-old would send us into panic.

All this suggests that our children are *less* self-reliant than those of more "indulged" cultures and that indulgence of the baby's need for close bodily contact does not result in unhealthy dependency, but rather both in closeness *and* ease of exploration. In other words, indulgence creates autonomy and intimacy—healthy *interdependency* that allows us to define ourselves in relation to others and to feel comfortable in giving and receiving support without loss of personal identity.

Early Self-Reliance

The largest percentage of insecure infants are found in cultures that require the earliest self-reliance—the Israeli kibbutz and in northern Germany.

The Israeli kibbutz is a communal farm where infants live in infant houses, separate from their parents. Cared for by a metapelet (nurse), the mothers come and go during the day to feed and bathe their infants. By six months of age, however, mothers go back to work full-time and, other than a half-hour visit during the day—the "love hour"—visits occur primarily in the evening. Hence, infants go back and forth from the mother to a caregiver, who may or may not give sensitive care. At night, the infants sleep alone in the infant house, separated from both metapelet and mother. If they cry, a night watchwoman is summoned by an intercom—a process that, as imagined, takes time. Half of the kibbutz infants were ambivalently attached to mother and to metapelet.

The largest number of avoidant middle-class infants found in any cross-cultural sample is in northern Germany—49 percent, and similar to the American high-risk sample. These mothers push their infants into early self-soothing. Writes psychologist Karin Grossman of the University of Regensburg:

> As soon as infants become mobile, most mothers feel that they should now be weaned from close bodily contact. To carry a baby who can move on its own or to respond to its every cry by picking it up would be considered as spoiling. The ideal is an independent, nonclinging infant who does not make demands on the parents but rather unquestionly obeys their commands.

Fewer than half the mothers in the northern Germany sample showed any tenderness while holding their infants. When the child was twelve months, the majority of the mothers offered their crying infants a toy or a pacifier, rather than picking them up, though the infants would not calm without close body contact. When the parents did try to pick them up, their infants rejected the closeness.

Although the secure infants cried less than the insecure, eleven of the infants in the sample never cried longer than five seconds at ten months, which supports Patricia Crittenden's observation of the early inhibition of distress in infants whose bids for contact were rebuffed. Further, the wish that their infants "unquestionably obey their commands," suggesting the mothers may get annoyed or even angry if the infant does not, risks later compulsive compliance.

At first, psychologists viewed these findings as less anxious attachment than cultural adaptation. The avoidant attachments of the German children were not extreme. These children lived in middle-class families with parents who were interested in and concerned about their children but just didn't want them clinging. But by age ten, these avoidant children had less confidence, self-reliance, and resiliency. They did not have close friends and often felt excluded, taken advantage of, or ridiculed. As John Bowlby concluded, "No matter where the rejection comes from, it is bound to have the same outcome." The Grossmans, who conducted the study, agree and are encouraging more nurturing parenting in northern Germany.

Support Systems

If emphasis on early self-reliance is a risk factor for insecure attachment, lack of supports, which greatly increases maternal stress, is as well. Child abuse, for instance, occurs most often in societies where mothers are seldom relieved of their child-care responsibilities. Here in the United States, child abuse and neglect is most common among poor mothers in unstable homes with few supports, in which a large percentage of infants are insecurely attached.

We also see a larger than usual number of insecure attachment among twin boys, half of whom one study found insecurely attached to their mothers. Why boys and not girls? Boys get sick more often and are more active than females. Without help, mothers literally have their hands full.

Like urban mothers in the United States, young urban mothers in Japan suffer from isolation and lack of psychological support from husbands, close friends, and neighbors. At the same time, skinship is decreasing and baby carriages are popping up, as are cribs.

With some Japanese mothers, lack of supports has spawned a syndrome called "childrearing neurosis." Lacking confidence, they don't enjoy mothering as much as they see it as serious business to be done to perfection. A tiny percentage commit double-suicide with their infants, which seems to be a uniquely Japanese phenomenon. With this onset of depression as a syndrome among Japanese urban mothers, it's likely we'll begin to see avoidant attachment increase in Japan.

Unlike the United States and Japan, Sweden, which is a stable social democracy with a low rate of unemployment, provides parents with extensive social supports: health and welfare services and full-time parenting leave (available for mother *or* father) with 90 percent pay for the infant's first nine months, as well as another nine months at a reduced salary rate with job position guaranteed for three years, and sixty days sick leave annually for the child. When their babies are born, Swedish mothers are able to stay in the hospital until they've successfully established breastfeeding. All this may give an edge to some mother-infant relationships. In Sweden, 76 percent of infants are classified as secure.

In the Anisfeld study, 38 percent of the control infants in the high-risk population were securely attached to their mothers. What made the difference, Anisfeld wondered. As it turned out, these mothers lived in extended families: More social supports and helping hands aided in overriding some of the burden of poverty and the stress frequently found in the mother-infant relationship.

On the other hand, the kibbutz has probably the most extensive social support system of any society. Mothers have guaranteed work, housing, food, baby-sitting, medical care, and education for their children. They don't have to cook (there is a communal dining room), do laundry, pick up and drive their infants to day care or to the dentist—it's all on the kibbutz. Why would extensive supports not make mother more relaxed and reduce the insecure attachment of Israeli kibbutz infants?

Actually they do. In those kibbutzim that have abolished the infant houses and allow infants to live with their parents, insecurity of attachment has dropped to 30 percent, lower than that of the American middle-class population. Apparently, the overriding factor in insecure attachment was not multiple caregivers and frequent separation from mother during the day, but the insecurity resulting from the traumatic night separation and delayed response to the cry. Furthermore, unlike children in day care here, kibbutz infants and young children have multiple means for attention and affection beyond mother and metapelet. During the day, grandparents, siblings, and children who just want to be with the infants visit periodically. Taken on frequent walks, the infants come into daily contact with familiar adults who pet them and babble to them.

Perhaps there's something to learn from the massive social support system of the kibbutz, sorely lacking here. In the history of mankind, few societies have taxed the coping resources of parents as we do in the West, making close physical intimacy with our infants harder to achieve. Kibbutz-like housing may save the day. Certainly the parents at EcoVillage in Ithaca, New York, feel that way. There, families live in a small cluster of townhouses where, kibbutz style, they share washers, dryers, a large play-room, a group dining room, and a safe, large patch of grass for the children to run on. Doesn't sound like such a bad life.

5

Rock of Love

Rock-a-bye baby, on the treetop,
When the wind blows, the cradle will rock;
When the bough breaks, the cradle will fall;
Down will come baby, cradle and all.

Why the mass appeal of this nursery rhyme? Perhaps the image of the baby tranquilly swaying back and forth—the wind stroking its skin, the sun warming its soul—wipes out the horrific ending.

Or perhaps we ignore the words altogether as the cadence thrusts us into that natural sway that parents spontaneously assume when standing and holding their baby. In fact, it's hard to know who gets more pleasure from this primal tick-tock, our baby or us.

Rock of Ages

Rocking is a natural baby tranquilizer because it reminds the baby of being in the womb—a virtual "floating hammock," as poet Diane Ackerman described it. In fact, were we to use a metronome, we would discover that we spontaneously rock our babies at precisely the walking rhythm in utero during the later stages of pregnancy, around 60 to 70 cycles per minute (our normal walking rhythm exceeds 100 paces per minute). This is also the heart rate of the average resting adult that accompanies babies throughout their nine-month sojourn. Rocked at this rate, the infant stops crying within fifteen seconds. A preventative medicine as well as a cure for baby blues, rocking also delays the onset of crying.

We may not consciously remember when our mothers rocked us, but our bodies never forget. Forever imprinted in our psyche, this primitive rhythm is at our beck and call at a moment's notice: If we start rocking when relaxed, we hypnotically lock in to it. Lovers embrace and rock to fuse their link, adjusting to each other's pace until they sway in perfect sync. Mourners rock for self-comfort with ferocious abandonment, both alone and with another. In the movie *Prince of Tides*, Tom, suffering an emotional crisis, breaks down and begins to weep from the pain of his childhood. Quite spontaneously, his psychiatrist, Dr. Lowenstein, takes him into her arms and rapidly rocks him. Such honesty lends the scene a courageous and realistic feel.

But rocking is more than relaxation and consolation. It stimulates the tactile receptors in the skin, developing muscle tone. It increases cardiac output, helping in circulation. It promotes respiration, discouraging lung congestion. It aids in digestion, assisting the movements of the intestine like a pendulum, making it highly recommended after a feeding, particularly for the fussy or colicky infant. And, not the least important, it creates a mother-baby rhythmic duet that helps forge their bond.

The Vestibular System

The calming effect of rocking comes from its effect on the vestibular apparatus. Located in the inner ear, the main job of the vestibular apparatus is to maintain equilibrium. This makes it possible for our baby to find her place in space.

The vestibular apparatus accomplishes this through three semicircular canals that together form the shape of a pretzel: One oriented for side-to-side balance, one for up-and-down balance, and the third for back-and-forth balance. Every time a person moves, the fluid in these canals moves against tiny hairlike filaments that vibrate and send nerve impulses throughout the muscles of the body. Lean to one side and we are cued to lean back to the other side. Through these cues, babies learn to balance and to keep their head in a neutral position, which is no small feat. Until babies get over their initial wobbliness, they can't begin to develop bodily control.

When in a parent's arms, babies automatically receive movement in all three directions: back and forth from the parent's walking motion, side to side from swaying, and up and down when bounced, repositioned, tossed in the air, and, if they sleep with us, from the rhythmic rise and fall of our chest as we breathe.

But if we don't sleep with them, as few parents do, and if we use a stroller rather than tote them, as most parents do, our babies receive vestibular stimulation largely from the motion of a rocking chair or the popular infant swing. This limits movement experience to primarily one direction: back and forth.

Think also of the variety of movement when we carry our baby. We stop; we bend down; we turn around; we scoot our babies up as they start to slip down onto our hip; we reposition them to our other hip. But when kept in an infant swing for long stretches, babies experience ongoing repetitive and monotonous motion. This can overwhelm some infants and force them into a stress sleep as their only means to shut out unrelenting stimulation.

And parents not only move in varying directions—parents move! For nine months, as the mother stepped, turned, bent, and caressed her belly, the developing fetus buoyantly swirled and somersaulted through the amniotic water and lightly collided against the uterine wall. At birth, then, the vestibular system is programmed to *expect* movement. For the newborn baby, who, with only slight body awareness (proprioception) will move little on her own, the stillness felt lying in the crib is disconcerting. If they're left in a crib twelve hours a day, in these twelve hours the newborn receives virtually no movement stimulation, unless the crib is one that rocks and vibrates.

Some of the newborn's tremors and jumps may be an attempt to generate movement to energize their nervous system. Even the fetus appears to seek out movement. During the day as mother moves around and the fetus gets jostled about, it is relatively quiet. But at night when mother rests, the fetus starts jitterbugging, as if needing to create its own movement. This need to be kept moving also explains why babies in buggies fidget. One three-month-old I know, when placed in an infant seat, would immediately grunt and push his body forward. His mother was convinced he would be an early walker.

Though we take all this squirming and fidgeting for granted, it may be more a casualty of separation than universal infant behavior. Jean Liedloff, who observed the Yequana tribe of the Venezuelan rainforest, was struck by the relative calmness of their babies, who were held in close contact most of the day. Almost never crying, they "did not wave their arms, kick, arch their backs, or flex their hands and feet. Rather, they sat quietly in their slings or slept on someone's hip." As adults, they were at ease with themselves and greatly enjoyed life.

Vestibular Stim Calms and Alerts

Vestibular stimulation not only calms infants, it also makes them alert. Witness, for instance, what happens when six-week-old Latisha, howling away, gets picked up. As her mother puts Latisha's head into the crook of her own neck, like magic Latisha's eyes "pop" open: She stops crying and looks all around her.

What caused Latisha's transformation from cranky to bright-eyed, content, and curious? Moving from horizontal to vertical also stimulates the vestibular apparatus. This, in turn, fires neurons in the reticular formation which, located at the brain stem, controls alertness. The mere effort of holding her head up to maintain balance also stimulates the vestibular apparatus.

The more time babies spend vertical, the more time they are alert and calm. Even newborns, who spend most of their time sleeping, stop crying and perk up when picked up and placed on our shoulder. Interestingly, how alert a newborn is relates to *where* he is. Upright in an infant seat, he is less alert than when upright in arms, even when in a comparable position.

Vertical positioning as optimal for infants makes perfect sense. Once walking, we spend most of our day upright, as do the carried infant and the fetus in the womb. In other words, upright is the natural position for infants. Yet, think of how much time our infants spend horizontal—flat on their back in crib or buggy. Might this affect their alertness? There's a good chance. Researchers found that infants too young to sit independently learn more when placed in a vertical or a semivertical position. Of course, we didn't need research to convince us. Try finishing this chapter lying flat on your bed, or even inclined, and see how long before your eyelids start to droop.

Furthermore, it's not just position that regulates level of arousal; movement does as well, explains occupational therapist Patti Oetter. In fact, she says, to stay alert we must move, even if just turning our head to the side. If our baby is in a buggy or infant seat and his head is stationary and there's nothing interesting for him to look at, he will start to drift off if we don't move him. This is okay if we want our baby to go to sleep, but if we want him alert and scanning and taking in his environment, infant seats fall short. If a parent wants to put his baby down in a protective seat, Oetter suggests he use bouncies so the baby can experience movement.

In fact, says Oetter, not moving a child is almost worse than not touching them. After eight hours of stationary position, people begin to hallucinate. Swaddling pacifies infants precisely because it minimizes movement, lowering arousal level. When we want to do the opposite—to arouse some-one—we jiggle them. When preterms "forget" to breathe, we reinstate respiration by spontaneously shaking them.

Vestibular Deprivation

In traditional cultures, carrying and movement come as one package and babies experience a steady flow of vestibular stimulation. But in modern society, we've cut back drastically both on how much we move and, with our babies in cribs or infant seats a good portion of the day, how much movement they experience. Furthermore, some child development experts discourage rocking babies to sleep, claiming that it interferes with the baby's learning to fall asleep independently.

This leaves the infant to find other means to get needed movement. They do this in two ways: They "request" it by letting us fervently know they will not quiet unless walked, rocked, or taken for a ride in the car. Or they furnish it themselves through repetitive movement, by squirming, body rocking, and, later, whirling like dervishes.

The more movement-deprived, the more babies generate their own motion. In neglected infants and in those in institutions left alone in a crib most of the day, extreme body rocking and head rocking are common.

In Harry Harlow's experiments with monkeys who were removed from their mothers, those monkeys did a lot of self-rocking. But when provided a terrycloth mother who moved, which furnished approximately nine to ten hours a day of vestibular stimulation, none developed self-rocking. Of ten monkeys raised on a stationary mother, all but one did.

Premature infants, confined to an incubator with little time for normal holding and loving, miss out on weeks and sometimes months of womb rocking, as well as the normal movement felt in the mother's arms. But if they are placed on oscillating waterbeds that simulate gentle movement (set at the approximate breathing rate of an adult), they jump about less, sleep better, become more alert, and breathe better.

Even normal infants seem to benefit from increased vestibular stimulation. In one study, one three-month-old twin was given supplemental vestibular stimulation and the other was not. At four months of age, though both had started out with identical pretest scores, the infant given the added stimulation had mastered head control and could sit independently, while the other twin was only just starting to develop head control.

Learning Disabilities

The ability to concentrate, to sit still, and to perceive letters all relate to the integration of the nervous system which, in turn, relates to the integrity of the vestibular apparatus. This makes feeding the vestibular system especially important for learning-disabled children, including those with hyperactivity. In fact, predicting which infants are at risk for later hyperactivity or learning disabilities begins with testing the integrity of their vestibular functioning: Do they lose their balance when held upright? Do they react with alarm when suddenly picked up or hung upside down? Do they startle to fast movement or respond with sheer terror when held out in space? Do they have stiff or flaccid limbs?

Both hyperactivity and learning disabilities are on the rise. The reasons are many: greater use of drugs, more carcinogens in the environment, earlier and higher diagnosing, etc. But there may be another: a mother's inactive lifestyle during pregnancy.

Throughout our history, women were engaged in work during the day that kept their bodies, and their babies, in perpetual movement. As mothers planted rice or ground cornmeal, their body pulsed up and down, which rocked their baby, often lulled to sleep by the perpetual movement. The fetus experienced this constant, regular movement until the end of pregnancy. The !Kung mother, for instance, does her usual gathering routine—walking to find food, bending, climbing, etc.—until going into labor. But women today, many of whom work at a desk job, are more sedentary than ever. If movement is food for the developing vestibular system, what effect might diminished movement have on the developing fetus? We know, for instance, that hyperactive children, as their mothers will tell you, were jumping-beans in the womb. Were these children preprogrammed by genetics to be hyperactive? Or did they need more movement than they received from their mother's movements? We don't know. Either way, the message of the fetus to the mother is clear—lots of movement!

Kinesthetic Stimulation and Movement

When we cache our babies, we cut back on more than just vestibular movement. We remove much calming deep-pressure touch and kinesthetic stimulation—the sense of the movement of our limbs. When we hold our baby, we move him about frequently in response to cues from him, as well as to cues from our own body for a change of position. We nestle him into our neck for resting, place him across our legs for patting, set him on our lap for arm and leg calisthenics, and so on. Every bend of finger or foot, lift of arm or leg, turn of torso or hip provides the infant with some skin pressure and a kinesthetic spurt.

But in a container, young infants move little. If he is too young to change his own position, the position we choose for him in is the position he stays in, greatly diminishing movement and thus kinesthesis and deep-pressure touch. If he slumps, as young infants do frequently in swings and infant seats, he remains that way until rescued.

When the cradle was popular, there was compromise—though alone, the infant was rocked to sleep. But the bassinet and the crib, lacking rocking, touch, warmth, containment, and rhythmic sounds, rob the baby of these natural womb comforts, making baby more fussy than he was designed to be and rendering parenting more taxing and frustrating than *it* was meant to be.

Toting as a Great Baby Workout

❧   The simplest way to ensure that our babies get enough vestibular and kinesthetic stimulation, to say nothing of tactile stimulation, is to carry them more. Why don't we? Well, for one, babies are heavy!

How did our gathering sisters do it? The !Kung woman carried her baby on her hip in a pouch made of antelope skin, until the baby was around two years old. From two to four, she carried him straddled on her shoulder. Foraging around three days a week, she walked an average of two to twelve miles at a time and carried home, in addition to her baby, food weighing fifteen to thirty-three pounds. Wrote Elizabeth Thomas of the !Kung women in *The Harmless People:*

> The women got up and walked off together into the veld [bush] to search for wood. In an hour or so they came back . . . , Tsetchwe with her kaross [leather cape] bulging with melons, perhaps twenty in all, a great load of wood on top of them piled higher than her head, and Nhwakwe [her child] riding on top of it all. Even in the cold air she perspired, and as her load must have weighed almost a hundred pounds, she walked leaning forward.

But unlike our gathering sisters, few modern women spend their day in manual labor for their daily bread, nor can most of us spend hours a day at the gym. Consequently, we do not have the well-developed back and muscular strength of our ancestors. Lugging around a fifteen-pound baby is an effort; add a diaper bag and a bag of groceries, and carrying a baby becomes a job. "I can only hold this baby for so long," bemoans a drained mother at a picnic in Winnetka, Illinois, as she eases her baby into a buggy. Why become a beast of burden?

Well, in addition to the multitude of benefits for the baby, toting our baby builds the back strength *needed* to carry a baby, and it rights our posture. And, as the yogis say, a bad spine is a bad life. Further, carrying babies around need not be as strenuous as we think; we just haven't quite got the hang of it.

Defying the Laws of Physics

Universally, babies are carried on hip or back. In Bali in the South Pacific and in the Kalahari Desert of Africa, mothers straddle babies, skin-to-skin, astride their hip in a sling. In Kenya, mothers carry babies on hip or back in a dashiki, mother and baby wrapped together as one colorful package. In Mexico, mothers backpack babies in a shawl called a rebozo. But in the United States, we tote our infants predominantly front-to-front in a soft baby carrier.

This soft carrier entered the scene in the 1970s with the introduction of the Snugli, invented by two people who, while in the Peace Corps, noticed how calm carried babies were. Back carriers popped up for older infants and, gradually, the sling made its entrance. Stubbornly, though, the common mode of carrying babies, for the relatively few parents who do, remains predominantly front-to-front.

As wonderful as this position is, simple physics and body mechanics discourage its use after more than a few months. If we carry extra weight in front, we throw our back out of alignment—one reason older babies are universally carried on the hip or back. Once, at a health conference in Miami, I met a modern Jamaican mother carrying her two-year-old on her hip, kept there by a colorful dashiki. She told me she carried seven babies this way and never experienced back pain.

Once past the age of wobbly heads, babies, unless they want to nod off, also don't much like front-to-front carrying, which creates sleepiness, restricts their view and movements, and confines them. In some front-to-front carriers we can turn our baby out, broadening his view and increasing his alertness and interest in the world. But this will not help our back. Nor can our baby turn in to nestle into our body. And if the parent's belly protrudes, the baby's legs dangle straight down, which does not support the comforting fetal tuck as does engulfing the baby in a sling-type carrier. As a result, parents who use frontal carriers soon find that aching backs and squirming infants send babies off to the stroller. (See Resource Guide for information on soft baby carriers.)

Baby Calisthenics

Ironically, the more we hold our babies, the sooner they leave our arms. Carried infants, as more than fifty studies from Africa, Asia, and Latin America demonstrate, sit, stand, and walk earlier than Western infants. At first, this make little sense. If carried all day, how do they exercise their muscles? Actually, they must do their lion's share to hold on, and this effort helps develop the muscles later needed for sitting, standing, and walking.

To begin with, explains occupational therapist Sandra Edwards, vertical positioning forces the baby to use his head to maintain his balance, developing the neck muscles needed for sitting. What's more, the baby's balance and vision are in the same plane as when he begins walking, stimulating the antigravity reflex in the vestibular apparatus. His neck and back are extended and his hips are flexed and rotated out, placing him in the same stance needed for sitting, and eventually standing, building necessary muscle strength. And to stay comfortably seated, he must pull his legs into a straddle, forcing him to use leg muscles needed later for walking. Even the turning of the baby's head flat against his parent's body influences holding on, as James De Boer described with the Netselik Eskimo infant:

> The infant assumes a sitting posture with its tiny legs around its mother's waist or slightly above and with its head flexed right or left, which usually elicits the tonic neck reflex that facilitates the straddling placement of the legs as extensor tonus decreases in either of these limbs.

We see this incredible workout even in newborns. Away from the parent's body, they seem to do little more than cry and suck from time to time. But, notes Heinz Prechtl of the University of Graz in Austria, "if you watch a baby on the skin of its mother without clothes but at a warm temperature, it shows a lot of things: rooting, crawling, grasping, and numerous antigravity postural responses."

Contrast this active workout with the baby lying flat in a plastic container. Not needing to use his muscles to fight gravity, upright his head, or straddle onto you, he is relatively passive.

The African Baby

The most physically precocious infant is the well-studied African baby. Ahead of U.S. infants in motor milestones, babies in Uganda and Kenya, who are traditionally carried, also surpass westernized African urban infants, who are kept in cribs most of the time and held and carried much less frequently than their village counterparts.

Could the precocity of African babies relate to innate tendencies? Some, like psychologist Dan Freedman, think so. Freedman found that black newborns, compared to Caucasians and Asians, demonstrate less head lag, stronger neck and shoulder muscles, a more brisk automatic walk, and, in general, more integrated movements. What's more, in skeletal maturation and ossification at birth, native African babies are advanced beyond Western Caucasians. Even the westernized urban infants in Uganda and Kenya average around one month ahead of American Caucasian infants in sitting, standing, and walking. And in the U.S., African-American babies walk a few weeks earlier than Caucasian infants.

But the African village mother has a different explanation for her baby's precocity. She believes that she trains her baby to learn to sit, stand, and walk by the way she positions and plays with him. For instance, in the first month of life, babies in Kokwet, Kenya, are sitting in their mother's lap about 60 percent of the time when awake. Our infants, in contrast, sit about 40 percent of their waking time, and primarily in an infant seat, which requires little exercise of the trunk muscles.

Then there's play time. Starting at around the fifth or sixth month, Kokwet mothers help support their babies' back by sitting them in a special hole dug in the ground, or they nest them with blankets until the child can sit independently. Our babies, in contrast, play mostly lying down on a blanket or in their crib.

As for walking, by around one month of age, mothers bounce their babies upright in their lap, and the infants respond with the standing or stepping reflex that is present from birth: Place a newborn upright, with her legs flat on a surface, and most spontaneously "march." In continuously carried infants, this reflex remains with them, as they use it to push themselves up and latch onto their mother's body. But in our infants, who, lying in a crib, have no need for it, the reflex disappears and reemerges later on in the first year. And it disappears even though the kicking movements our babies make while on their backs seem to reflect these same early stepping movements.

But would it disappear if we, like the African mothers, exercised our babies? And would our babies walk earlier? The answer, researcher Philip Zelazo found, is yes to both questions. If we exercise them, they keep the walking reflex and walk on their own by ten months of age. But if we do the usual things—pump their legs, for instance, which babies also do on their own when on their backs—they walk at around eleven and a half months, the norm for the American infant. Practice with sitting shows similar early advancement. And normal babies spun briefly in a swivel chair twice a week for a period of four weeks, which increased vestibular stimulation, showed earlier head control and independent sitting.

Some parents worry that carrying babies prevents them from learning to crawl. But the African baby, who uses his muscles to ensure he doesn't slip off his mother's body rather than to slither across the floor, often skips crawling altogether and goes straight to walking—as do most of the world's babies. In other words, it is a myth that babies must crawl before they walk.

African tribal infants are not only physically precocious but, in the first six months of life, are smarter than our babies as well. Melvin Konner, the renowned author and anthropologist from Emory University who assiduously studied the !Kung San, found that these infants surpassed ours on items such as "shakes rattle with regard to sound" and "transfers object from hand to hand with visual regard"—tasks typically used to assess early mental development.

Are these mental advances largely a reflection of the !Kung infant's advanced motor development? Perhaps, but Konner is unconvinced. His bet is that they result from environmental enrichment—close and continuous bodily contact and extensive upright positioning. Unlike our infants, says Konner, !Kung infants are either on their mother's hip in a sling, sitting or standing in her lap when awake, or on the ground immediately in front of her; *rarely* are they lying down. This gives them practice in compensatory movements in response to the pull of gravity, which allows them to learn, from early on, to keep their head upright and their body balanced in equilibrium.

Still, we might wonder, if the infants are carried all the time, when do they play? How would they develop hand coordination, as our infants do when we hang various toys from their cribs, above their infant seats, or scattered on a blanket when on the floor? We need not worry. Carried naked in a sling on their mother's bare hip (allowing constant skin-to-skin contact), !Kung babies have easy access to their mother's clothes, jewelry, hair, mouth, nose, ears, fingers, and her naked breast. In fact, with almost continuous tactile contact, extensive vertical positioning that keeps their vestibular apparatus well tuned, and incredible opportunities for reaching and grabbing, the natural environment of the !Kung, said Konner, is one "well-designed infant stimulation program."

Is Speed Important?

How important *is* it for our infants to walk at ten months of age, rather than twelve months? After all, our Olympic records hardly speak of children unable to compete on the world's racetrack. Furthermore, even the Ache infants of Paraguay, who don't start to walk until around eighteen to twenty months of age and show the slowest development of any human group, show normal motor development by the time they're eight or ten years old.

Nevertheless, there are advantages to the fast lane. Motor maturation has a clear effect on both mental and social-emotional development. Take sitting: The sooner infants are able to sit upright without toppling over, the more easily they can reach for, grasp, and shake their rattle, swipe at their rubber duck, or push down their jack-in-the-box; this gives them greater mental advantages. And once infants begin to walk, they can combine movements in quick succession—run to the bed, grab the big red ball, throw it on the floor, run after it, and bend down to pick it up. This both advances their play and frees their dependence on mother and father. In other words, the earlier they maneuver on their own, the greater their independence—the buzzword in our culture.

In addition, the earlier babies crawl and walk on their own, the more sophisticated their understanding of space and the greater their interest in it. This has advantages. For instance, while babies do not initially show a fear of heights when beginning to creep around and are in danger of falling, they will when they become expert crawlers: Fearfulness apparently emerges as infants are better able to calibrate distances more accurately. The sooner that occurs, the less the risk they will topple down a flight of stairs.

Motor development influences depth perception in other ways. Both eyes work together at about five months of age. Babies judge depth from relative size and differences in shading, but to do so they have to know about actual size and other properties of a block, a ball, or a teddy bear. The more objects are handled, the more information they absorb.

Carrying our infants confers further physical advantages. As we saw, carried infants grow up to experience less vertigo and more physical agility. Perhaps it's not coincidental that martial arts such as judo and tai-chi, characterized by superior balance (the vestibular sense), precision of movement (the kinesthetic sense), and an exceptional awareness of one's body in space (proprioception), all emanate from the East, where infants have traditionally stayed in close contact with their mothers.

There are psychological benefits as well. In addition to shortening the dependency period and thereby lessening the burden on the parent to entertain and transport the baby, the infant can seek out mommy or daddy at will or take her own initiative in exploring the forbidden pots in the cabinet. This increases the infant's sense of control, helping her to develop mastery of her world, all of which boosts self-confidence and self-esteem. And, helped in part by depth perception, crawling babies can better learn to differentiate themselves as separate from the rest of the world.

Furthermore, parents universally applaud early motor milestones. Nevertheless, I'm not optimistic that toting babies will replace strolling as the transportation of choice in this culture. As long as we lack helping hands, it's hard to assume this kind of continual burden. In all cultures that show advanced motor development, parents have lots of help. In fact, the more people in the household, the higher the motor scores of the infants. In other words, increasing the number of people who handle baby during the day may inadvertently boost motor development, as well as spicing up baby's sensory menu.

6

❧

Sensory Nourishment

What is it, then, this seamless body-stocking, some two yards
square, this our casing, our facade, that flushes, pales, perspires,
glistens, glows, furrows, tingles, crawls, itches, pleasures, and pains
us all our days, at once keeper of the organs within, and sensitive
probe, adventurer into the world outside?

—Richard Selzer

Joshua is ten minutes old. Is he lying on his mother's belly,
loudly imbibing his first meal and bonding with his mother? No. Joshua is
getting his first test.

Carolyn Goren, a researcher from the University of Chicago, has him on
her lap, looking at four paddle boards with different drawings: a human
face; a scrambled symmetrical face; a scrambled nonsymmetrical face; and a
blank. Moving each in an arc, a protractor measures how much Joshua's
head moves to follow the image. Joshua and thirty-six other newborns
make no bones about their preference—the human face every time—nor
where they prefer to be—propped in Goren's lap. Placed in the same angle
on a comfortable bed, they don't follow the drawing as well.

Newborn Sensory Preferences

❧   Babies are natural sensual adventurists with a highly specific preference from birth: other humans. They will look longer, turn their head more
often toward, and quiet sooner to sounds and sights of people over things.
This tells us that the human brain is designed to seek company, not solitude. And not just any company. Since the newborn's survival depends on

closeness to his mother, a particular fancy for *her* touch, *her* odors, *her* sounds, *her* face evolved to meet that end.

Our Odor

By an infant's sixth day, if we place a gauze breastpad damp with a mother's milk on one side of her newborn's head and another mother's on the other side, the baby will turn to the side with his mother's odor 80 percent of the time. But he will not recognize his father by odor, nor, if bottle fed, will he recognize his mother by odor. Breastfeeding, it seems, acts as a kind of scent marker for bonding. The newborn, guided by the mother's odor, will crawl to the breast. If the right breast is washed with soap and water, the newborn will crawl to the left breast and vice-versa.

By one month of age, an article of our clothing imbued with our natural body odor placed in our baby's crib will help comfort him to sleep. Incredulous, we think, so accustomed are we to think of body odors as anathema. But how many of us have slumbered through the night, wearing our absent lover's unwashed T-shirt?

Our Sounds

Mothers often feel that their newborn knows their voice—and they're right. By three days of age, when the fluid has cleared from their ears, babies recognize their mother's slow, high-pitched, singsong chatter over a stranger's. Part of the myriad maternal behaviors designed to assure the infant's survival, the melodic tone of motherese says, "Look at me," explains psycholinguist Anne Fernald of Stanford University. In this way, infants, who are very responsive to the human voice, hook into social communication from early on, and especially to the person most committed to their survival.

T. Berry Brazelton loves to demonstrate the newborn's maternal preference. He asks mothers to stand on one side of their baby and softly whisper their baby's name, while he does the same into the other ear. Without fail, the baby turns to his mother's voice. The newborn recognizes daddy's voice as well, but since mothers evolved as the primary caregiver—presumably because only she can be assured the baby is hers—the newborn prefers the higher-pitched female voice over any other sound in his environment.

Mother's and father's voices are well known to the newborn. Beginning around 26 to 28 weeks gestation, the cochlea (the center of hearing in the inner ear) is fully formed. From then on, the fetus responds to loud or very close sounds coming from the outside, including his parents' voices, with dancing limbs and pounding heart. This means that for at least the last four months of fetal life, salient sounds from outside the womb are well known to the fetus. Once born, he will calm more quickly to these familiar voices and other habitual sounds as well. Psychologist Peter Hepper of Queen's University in Belfast, Ireland, studied seven women addicted to a particular soap opera, estimating their babies to have listened to the theme music as much as 800 times during pregnancy. As newborns, two of the seven immediately stopped crying when the soap opera was turned on, while six of the seven adopted a quiet alert state, as if they were actually watching the program. In another group of babies whose mothers did not watch the soap opera, only two of eight showed any interest in the music.

"What the mother sings to the cradle goes all the way to the coffin," wrote Henry Ward Beecher in *Proverbs from Plymouth Pulpit*. He was right, both figuratively and literally. Boris Brott, a conductor, had an unusual ability to play certain cello pieces sight unseen. One day he mentioned this to his mother, a professional cellist. She quickly solved the mystery for him: "All the scores I knew sight unseen were ones she had played while she was pregnant with me." In other words, if you wish your infant to grow up a Beethoven aficionado, you might consider playing the *Moonlight Sonata* while practicing Lamaze.

For the fetus to hear such things, the outside sounds must be loud enough to override the clatter (as high as 95 decibels) of the inner sanctum. The *thump* of the mother's heartbeat, the sibilant *swish* of her blood flowing through her veins, the churning of her lunch working its way through her digestive tract, the roar of her nourishing blood passing through the umbilical cord are the fetus's constant companions. Even before the fetus can hear, the vibrations of the mother's heartbeat creates a gentle rhythmic pulsation of movement against the fetus's skin. Once born, the heartbeat, associated with the sounds, comfort, and security of the womb, becomes the neonate's mantra: Played a recording of the sounds of the womb, or a heartbeat, newborns readily calm.

With all those sounds coming from inside and penetrating from outside, the noise level of the womb is anything but quiet. In fact, it has been compared to that of a factory. This explains why newborns calm most easily in an atmosphere of white noise—continuous droning sounds, such as that of the vacuum cleaner or the continuous steady sound of the mother's heartbeat and other bodily sounds. How then might newborns feel about sleeping in a quiet crib, alone in a quiet room? If we eavesdrop on their brain, probably a little disconcerted. Silence and prolonged lack of stimuli do not match the conditions in which we evolved, where trees rustled, branches fell, birds sang, animals growled, winds whispered, waterfalls roared, and the sky thundered.

Our Face

Ever wonder what newborns see as they stare at us? Not much. Legally blind at birth, they see only around eight to twelve inches in front of them. Programmed to fixate on the human face, this is the conveniently approximate distance between the nursing infant and the enraptured mother's face.

Actually there's a simple explanation for this fixation. Newborns have poor visual acuity, and so they zero in on curves and high color contrast, of which our face is replete: our round iris, set against the white of our eyes; our oval-shaped mouth, set off, when we smile, by the white of our teeth; our arched hairline, set against our face.

But not just any face interests the newborn. When a mere two days old, a baby will look longer at mother than at a strange woman. Of course—our mother is our first protector, and we need to know at all times the status of those we protect or those who protect us. Are they okay? Are they tuned into us if we need help? Do they still care? This explains why three-month-old infants in the "still face" experiment become distressed and turn away from mothers who look at them with disinterest. Intense gazing into mother's eyes also excites mother and makes her feel she's important to her baby, which enhances bonding.

Of course, it's not just exclusively mother's eyes that fascinate. All eyes do, as watching them offers important social cues that have survival value: Is this person enemy or foe? Are they looking at something we, too, should be looking at?

There's another reason why the face captivates the baby: It is both familiar and yet keeps changing. We ooh and aah; we giggle; we blow bubbles; we open, close, and pucker our mouths. And this is precisely what babies prefer—stimuli that is familiar and whose safety has been established and yet, to keep interest, continually varies. And so they drink in our faces, like nectar from the gods.

And they drink in the rest of the world as well. This is especially the case when babies are upright, as carried babies generally are, which gives them free rotation of the head and an unobstructed view that keeps varying. In fact, if we increase the amount of time we hold our babies, we also increase their visual attentiveness.

Imagine the view of the baby kept on the mother's back all the day as she works in the fields. As mother moves, the infant's perspective keeps varying, forcing the infant to make sense of the world from assorted angles. Ashley Montagu suggests that this may account for the extraordinary spatial abilities of the Eskimos. Given a picture to look at, they view it at whatever angle it's presented—even if upside down or horizontal—amused that the "white man" has to turn it right side up to make sense of it.

Mothers Know Their Baby

Just as babies come with an inborn sensory menu, so do mothers. Primed for nurturance, mothers within a day or two can distinguish by smell an article of clothing worn by their infant from similar clothing worn by an infant of the same age. If kept with her newborn an hour or more following birth, there's a 70 percent chance that, if blindfolded and marched along a row of babies, the mother will identify her own just by feeling the back of her baby's hands or her cheeks. And fathers have this ability too, although they recognize their newborns only by the feel of their baby's hands.

Pick up your baby and notice on what side you place her or him. If you are like 83 percent of right-handed mothers or 78 percent of left-handed ones, you will place your baby on your left side, where your heartbeat is. Though we are not conscious of it, the primeval part of our psyche programs us to keep our baby close to our heart and to the rhythm imprinted in our baby's brain. Furthermore, our left arm, nearer the heart, is warmer.

But this tendency toward left-sided holding is not only a maternal whim. Newborns show a distinct right-sided lateral preference. Thus, they appear to be programmed with this heartfelt response. And for more reasons than just mother's thumping heart: The right side of the body is better for digestion, making left-sided placement a baby antacid as well as a tranquilizer.

More recent hypotheses for left-sided holding connect it to brain functioning. Because the left side of our body connects to the right side of our brain, our emotional side, the left side of our face, some claim, is more expressive. When gazing at the mother's face, this gives the baby better emotional cues. In addition, the mother's left eye and ear would be more tuned in to emotional changes in her baby. In other words, baby may see the more expressive side of mother, while mother, by showing her good side, may be better prepared to pick up her baby's cues.

Inborn Gender Differences

Every day, science discovers more biological bases for human behavior, and that includes gender differences (though a politically unpopular view). Consider the origin of female intuition. In males, emotional responsiveness is concentrated in the right side of the brain. In females, emotional responses reside in both the left and right sides of the brain. This means women can pick up emotional cues regardless of what side of the brain receives them. Furthermore, in women, the corpus callosum (the bundle of fibers that divides the right and left hemispheres of the brain) is up to 23 percent larger than in men, permitting easier transportation of signals between the two hemispheres. This makes women better able to recognize emotional nuances in voice, gesture, facial expression, touch, and other sensory information and therefore more likely than fathers to pick up their infant's cues: For example, a slight stiffening of their infant's trunk when held on the right side, and mothers unconsciously adjust their baby to the other side.

From an evolutionary standpoint, women as nurturer and man as aggressor gave each distinct survival strengths. Women needed sensitivity to detect nuances in their babies' behavior before children learned to speak, as well as good verbal skills to negotiate sibling rivalry and to keep peace with the other women they were in close contact with during the day. Men needed aggression to hunt food for the family and to fight off enemies, and good spatial ability to discreetly maneuver through the forest, tracking animals.

How do we know that these differences in brain functioning don't come exclusively from early stereotyping? Differences in emotional communication are evident at birth, before social learning takes place. When only a few hours old, the hands and fingers of newborn girls are strikingly more sensitive to touch than those of newborn boys—so much so that the most sensitive male feels less than the least sensitive female. Baby girls are less tolerant to sounds than males, becoming more easily irritated at noise, pain, or discomfort. When they do get distressed, however, they are more easily comforted by soothing words and singing. In other words, even before they can understand language, girls appear better than boys at identifying the emotional content of speech.

Baby girls spend almost twice as long as boys maintaining eye contact, and they gurgle more at the human face, indicating they are more interested in communicating with people than are baby boys. Boys, who show superior spatial reasoning to girls, spend as much time talking but gibber away at toys or geometric designs as much as to their doting parents. Boys are also more active than girls. If you spend enough time with newborns, these differences are readily noticeable. Dr. Benjamin Spock could pick out newborn girls and boys in the nursery with about 80 percent accuracy.

Infant Stim

~❧~ According to Darwinian theory, species-specific behavior evolved to allow individuals to best adapt to their environment and attain the resources necessary for survival. The smarter we are, the better the resources we acquire: desirable mates, supportive friends, rewarding jobs, and lots of toys. As such, all parents want to produce the smartest baby they can. How do our babies become smart? Through a combination of good genes, which we attempt to control by marrying the smartest mate we can find, and "infant stim."

Sensory stimulation is the stuff of which the infant's brain is built. As such, the baby's brain hungers for excitement, rebelling against inertia and boredom. Every caress, stroke, hug, squeeze, and playful game; all the rocking, swaying, swinging, spinning; all the sights, sounds, smells, and tastes in our baby's world—*all* feed our infant's need for sensory input and spark the neurons in her brain to grow and branch out to encompass other neurons. The greater the arborization, the greater the brain growth. In other words, the more we shower our infant's hungry brain with sensory input, the more likely he or she will reach the upper limits of intellectual potential and better his or her chances for competing for limited resources. Since the late 1950s, experimenters have been petting and holding baby mammals and then comparing their brains to those of animals deprived of handling. Studies with rats show that the handled ones have a general increase in gross brain mass, an increase in the synaptic junctions that connect neurons, and a higher ratio of cortical functioning.

How consequential is brain growth during infancy, which covers only 2 percent of our lifespan? Very consequential: 80 percent of our baby's total brain growth takes place in the first two years of life. In the first year alone, the brain more than doubles in size, reaching 70 percent of its adult weight and growing more than it ever will again. In other words, infancy lays the foundation for all later learning. And the more work our baby's brain does, the more it becomes capable of doing, hungering for new knowledge. Not capitalizing on all the sensory experiences in our infant's world is tantamount to educating adults by limiting their access to a library. Unfortunately, we do—at least when it comes to touch. It might make a difference.

Touch is our most sensitive sense. Nerve impulses conduc
impulses are generally larger than those associated with other ?
ing our skin so exquisitely responsive that our brain registers to...
slightest pressure. "Human skin is like a field of grass," describes anthropologist Helen Fisher, "each blade a nerve ending so sensitive that the slightest graze can etch into the human brain a memory of the moment." The
average human body, which has around five million nerve endings or touch
receptors, contains—in a patch of skin $3/4$-inch square on the back of our
hand—nine feet of blood vessels, 600 pain sensors, 30 hairs, 300 sweat
glands, four oil glands, 13 yards of nerves, 9,000 nerve endings, six cold
sensors, 36 heat sensors, and 75 pressure sensors. When held, two-thirds of
our infant's body surface is stimulated; when lying in a crib, only half of his
body is stimulated—to say nothing of the monumental difference in
warmth, pressure, and texture—especially when flesh touches flesh.

From Africa to Bali, from New Guinea to the Brazilian Amazon, tribal
mothers in warm climates carry their unclothed babies nestled against their
bare breast. Where mother goes, baby goes, skin against skin, creating a
sensory feast of motherly touch, warmth, pressure, movement, sound, smell,
sight, and taste. "Primitive!" some say. "Life doesn't get any better than
this," say their babies.

Skin-to-skin is the most meaningful human contact. In some parts of the
world, even when mother is clothed there is mutual nakedness, as her baby
lies inside her clothing and against her skin. In parts of Kenya, mother and
baby wrap together as one unit. In cold Alaska, the Eskimo baby is naked
against the mother's bare back, inside her parka.

But here, removed from our sensual nature, we design our clothing to
separate parent and baby and thus to minimize reciprocal touch. Even in
warm weather, some parents, uncomfortable with a sweaty baby, avoid bare
skin contact. "I wouldn't carry a sweaty baby around in this heat," responds
one mother as to why she prefers the buggy. In cold weather, babies may
feel skin contact only on their hands and faces. Even during nursing,
there's often little more shared flesh between mother and baby than the
mother's nipple and areola and the baby's lips and mouth. And co-bathing,
which further intensifies luxurious skin sensations, is more occasional than
customary.

We even leave clothing on when it can be safely discarded. Take our
habit of putting bathing suits on our baby. Naked, our baby's whole body—
nuzzled by our smooth, supple skin, bathed by the warm rays of the sun,
caressed by the breeze, gently sprayed by the ocean water—*pulses* with
effervescence, as does ours. Add a bathing suit and she loses the play of air,

wind, and sun from parts of her body and the feel of our skin against hers. True, suits help protect our baby's skin from the sun, but even when it is safe to remove them, we often don't. As a result, we unknowingly transform our baby's sensory experience from a feast to a snack. This, in turn, reduces those buzzing neurons in her brain anxiously seeking one another out, and her pleasure as well. No wonder that by age two, when children have the motor coordination to remove their clothes, off they fly at the first opportunity.

In the 1970s, infant stim became a buzzword, and parents made every attempt to shower their infants with smart toys. But the smartest infant toy ever invented is free and accessible to every infant.

Our body is a sensual cornucopia where smiles, aromas, and laughter mingle amid undulating caresses that put the entire sensory world at our baby's fingertips. Our baby gets tactile or cutaneous stimulation from our skin touching hers and proprioception from the pressure of her limbs flexed into our body. She gets tactile, olfactory, and gustatory stimulation from the feel, smell, and taste of our skin and, if we nurse, of our milk, and vestibular stimulation from the gentle rhythmicity of our movements and, when held upright, from her efforts to right her head and maintain balance. She gets visual stimulation when she looks all around her, auditory impulses as we softly whisper endearments, and kinesthetic stimulation as we change her to our other side.

In addition to covering all sensory bases at once, in a parent's arms, sensory input is ongoing and paced to allow for easy digestion. Consider, for example, the mother in the seat next to me on a flight, cradling her three-week-old infant. Save an occasional extended break of a minute or two, during the three-hour flight, the mother did *something* to her infant an average of every ten seconds. The mother looks into her baby's eyes and smiles. She straightens his clothing. She gently rocks him. She slowly strokes his cheek. She pulls his arm into his body. On and on. Add to this the mother's own movements, which stimulate the baby's skin, and you have a brain continually fed. Since all this input was low-key, her baby slept most of the three hours and *never* cried. The mother, equally calm, alternated from doting on her baby to doting on herself—reading, eating, resting, and occasionally conversing.

When we put our babies in a container, and especially if out of sight, most of this sensory nourishment is lost.

PART 2

· ·

Out of Touch

The precursor of the mirror is the mother's face.

—D. W. Winnicott

7

⌖

Container Crazy

I envy the Mexican babies carried within a wide scarf around the mother's body. . . . When I look into Mexican eyes I wish I had been born there, in the warmth and emotional richness of their nature, with feeling at the core.

—Anaïs Nin

$\mathcal{O}$ne Sunday at an outdoor festival in Florida I did a casual count of how infants under one year of age were transported. Babes-in-arms totaled five, one carried by mother, and four carried by father. Babies in buggies numbered thirty, divided equally between mother propelling and father propelling. This indicates that even on a Sunday, when both mother and father can share carrying, babies are primarily wheeled. In other words, not carrying our babies goes beyond our lack of helping hands. If Florida is at all representative, it has become a national habit.

Wheeling Deficits

⌖ If our childrearing practices were put to trial, Exhibit A, responsible for disarming our infants, would be the baby carriage. Invented in 1848, it is something few parents could *imagine* living without: Visit any mall, walk down any city street, and you see a bevy of fashionable buggies stroll by, with only an occasional carried baby. And yet, the buggy is a relative rarity—aside from the few industrialized nations that dot the globe, most babies venture forth piggyback or straddled on their parents' hips.

Does it make a difference how a baby is transported? Judge for yourself. Carried, our infant experiences body warmth, frequent position change, deep-pressure touch, containment, and rocking, to say nothing of the opportunities to balance her head, upright her posture, or use her muscles for clinging. When babies are wheeled, all this is lacking.

Carried, our baby hears our voice and smells our odors. Wheeled, she hears a cacophony of screaming, screeching, scraping, shattering street noise. Garbled language replaces audible human language, and soothing human odors are absent altogether.

And her world view? When carried, the same as ours. When wheeled, much more limited. In an umbrella stroller, she may see little more than feet and knees if she's looking straight ahead; in a buggy, she will see a ceiling if she's lying flat or, if the top is up, whatever pattern the manufacturer chose, which even the youngest baby quickly tunes out. Moreover, the sides of the stroller restrict her visual scope. Does it matter what infants see? Absolutely. Babies are lookers before they are mature enough to become grabbers; in the first four to five months of life, sightseeing is the infant's primary mode of learning about the world, and interesting sights help to maintain alertness. There's another concern: In a stroller, the baby cannot see her mother. If unable also to hear or feel her, the baby may lose sense of her mother altogether and feel alone.

As for all the variety of stimulation during carrying—the frequent kissing and stroking of hair, nose, cheeks, eyebrows, and forehead, the change of positioning, the rearrangment of clothing, the swaying side to side and back and forth—it all but disappears during wheeling.

True, mothers depend on the buggy to save their backs and for its convenience: Often lacking helping hands, it's hard for mother to carry baby, a diaper bag, a purse, and hold the hand of another child all at the same time. But there are disadvantages for mother as well. The buggy is awkward, heavy, hard to store, hard to clean, and hard to transport.

And the buggy encourages distance between mother and baby. If our baby is sitting in a buggy, for instance, it's easier to prop a bottle in her mouth than take her out of the buggy and feed her in our arms. We feel this promotes independent feeding (which it does), but it also removes mother as a source of nurturance. Food and love are inextricably intertwined. Wrote Margaret Mead of the prolonged suckling of the Arapesh infant of New Guinea, "The whole matter of nourishment is made into an occasion of high affectivity and becomes a means by which the child develops and maintains a sensitivity to caresses in every part of the body." In fact, unless a baby has a pleasant time during feeding, the necessary fluids for digestion are not activated. That Harlow's monkeys were left to dine alone with a wire "mother" likely contributed to their poor outcome.

Moreover, when nurturance and the mother's body part ways, so does the social connection to feeding. All the little conversations that take place during feeding time—verbal and nonverbal—teach important social lessons. To begin, baby learns turn taking, the core of human communication: I speak, you wait; you speak, I wait. And this lesson begins on day one, at the mother's breast. Baby sucks and then pauses. When baby sucks, mother is still. When baby pauses, mother gets active—jiggling her nipple, talking soothingly to her baby, smiling. When baby resumes sucking, mother pauses again.

In her 1980 poem "Greedy Baby," Alicia Ostriker portrays this nursing dialogue:

> Greedy baby
> sucking the sweet tit
> your tongue tugging the nipple tickles your mama
> your round eyes open appear to possess understanding
> when you suckle I am slowly moved in my sensitive groove
> you in your mouth are alive, I in my womb
> a book lies in my lap I pretend to read
> I turn some pages, when satiated
> a moment you stop sucking
> to smile up with your toothless milky mouth
> I smile down, and my breast leaks
> it hurts, return
> your lashes close, your mouth again clamps on . . .

When fed with a propped-up bottle, feeding becomes perfunctory and loses this back-and-forth rhythmicity and vital communication, which encourages later detachment.

Wheeling puts us out of touch in other ways. If we can't see our baby's face, as with a stroller, we lose moment-to-moment awareness of our baby's well-being and cannot fine-tune to her signals. Since separation leaves a baby more vulnerable to nuisances like sun and to danger, with any mishap we feel terrifically guilty. Nature, of course, made separation and guilt frequent traveling partners to motivate mother to keep her baby close and thereby reduce potential harm.

Plastic Infant Seats

❧ Young infants are often toted around in plastic containers that double as car seats. Though essential for safety in the car, as infant carriers they have all the disadvantages of the buggy and then some. For mother, they're awkward and heavy, adding rather than saving weight to her back. For babies, the list is considerably longer: For the young infant, they offer too little restriction of movement; for the older infant, too much, especially in the trunk area. Explains Sandra Edwards, an occupational therapist who returned from Kenya a staunch convert to babes-in-arms transport, neurological development progresses best in an environment that encourages opportunities to explore and experiment with movement. "Devices that restrict movement may deny the child important opportunities for sensorimotor development." Little wonder babies get restless when tied down in these seats and grapple to move about and to upright themselves.

Plastic infant seats are also stiff. Babies' soft, flexible bodies are suited to fold into the crook of an arm, nuzzle into a neck, enfold into a breast, not to press against rigid, solid, unyielding surfaces. Infant seats are a particular problem for children at risk for motor delay, explains occupational therapist Patricia Wilbarger, since they position babies "so the back muscles can become abnormally stiff." If misused, infant walkers, swings, and jumpers can cause problems as well in muscle flexibility, unlike infant snugglers, backpacks, and hammock sleeping devices, she says, which "give a rich 'sensory diet' of movement and pressure touch that have proved helpful to infants."

Infant seats are also difficult to maneuver in and out of cars, through doorways, and up and down steps, jolting the baby. And if baby is put down abruptly, causing his head to move backward, he responds with the Moro reflex. At the supermarket recently, I watched a four-week-old lying in an infant seat in the shopping cart. Each time the mother pushed the cart over very thin rugs on the floor, the baby startled.

Baby is also left in a horizontal position. If there is nothing interesting for him to look at and his head position doesn't change, he will become drowsy. Plug him with a pacifier and, if nothing catches his eye, sucking and lying flat create double lethargy. That's okay if you want him to go to sleep, but not if you want him to learn.

Infant seats also do nothing to promote attachment between mother and baby. The mother's body draws the baby into a pulsing circle of warmth, softness, and roundness that contains and cushions his shape in supple, receptive contours; that adjusts and adapts in sync with his turns, squirms, and stretches; that massages him with slow, fluid motions that vary his day and give rhythm to his existence. This cements the connection between mother and child; plastic containers do none of this. As such, they dramatically change the baby's sense of life and of human relationships.

Cache or Carry?: Sensory Differences

❧ Cache or carry? What's the actual difference in sensory input? Occupational therapist Stephanie Day decided to find out. She observed the tactile agenda of a typical all-American infant: a baby between four and six weeks of age, born of middle-class parents, breastfed, and described as a happy, contented child of a caring, loving mother.

For about seven hours a day, or a little over 25 percent of the time, the baby received tactile stimulation when fed, diapered, cleaned, dressed, carried, held, and played with, all primarily from mother. For about an hour and a half a day, or around 5 percent of the time, the baby received vestibular stimulation, primarily during holding or carrying. But for twelve hours a day—half her day—the baby was alone, both asleep and awake. In other words, the greatest chunk of the baby's day constituted the *least* amount of stimulation.

This is because our babies tend to sleep alone in a crib. If we measure alone time by average sleep time, that would equal around sixteen hours a day alone for neonates, and fourteen hours alone for six-month-olds. And even when with mother, babies are often separated—in a buggy, an infant seat, a swing, a playpen, a highchair.

Other researchers in the United States, in Cambridge, England, and in Holland have corroborated Day's results: The average Western infant gets touched 25 percent of the day or less. By nine months of age, touching time goes down to 16 percent of the day. In a model day care center, Tiffany Field and colleagues found touch time to average only around 14 percent of the day for even young infants. As for actual holding time, between the ages of three weeks and three months, the average Western infant is carried a little more than two and a half hours a day.

How do our babies look in comparison to a high carrying culture like the !Kung San? Deprived, says Melvin Konner. In touch with their mother for approximately 70 percent of the day and in someone else's arms most of the rest of the time, !Kung infants receive in the first months of life more than *triple* the touch of a typical American infant, as well as the vestibular-proprioceptive input that accompanies contact. And the contact is skin to skin!

As for time alone? About zero. Not only is the !Kung infant's landscape literally never without people, says Konner, but they are rarely separated from a caregiver.

We would probably worry that this would interfere with our baby's independence. Most child development specialists recommend that our babies spend some time alone during the day to learn how to entertain themselves. This makes sense since few babies live in a household where multiple loving hands are around to provide ongoing entertainment, nor can mothers spend their day amusing their baby.

Yet, it's easy to view the !Kung experience as baby utopia. Day and night on their mother's naked body, the world a sensory rainforest that bathes the baby all the day in a perpetual shower of lush sensations—who would turn down such a start in life?

Touch Deprivation

✤ We don't know how much touch babies need for normal development. But we do know what happens when we seriously touch-starve infants, for instance, those brought up in orphanages and left alone a good part of the day in a crib, like the well-publicized Romanian orphans. Lacking appropriate tactile, vestibular, and proprioceptive input, as well as visual and auditory stimulation, many become mentally retarded; some even look autistic. At the same time, there's less than a 20 percent difference in touch time between typical American infants and institutionally reared infants.

Of course, we can't experiment with babies to find the precise cut-off point as to what is too little touch for normal development. But we have experimented with primates, and the results reveal some surprises. At the University of Illinois, infant monkeys were divided into three groups: a control group behaving naturally with a high degree of physical contact with their mothers; a second group housed with a peer and given normal interaction for only four hours a day and, for the other twenty, separated from their mothers by a glass partition that permitted seeing, hearing, and smelling her but no touching; and a third group totally isolated—each individual could neither touch, see, hear, nor smell the other.

The control group did not develop brain damage; not surprising. The totally isolated group did—in the cerebellum, a part of the brain controlling motor coordination and influencing learning and memory; again, no surprise. But the partially isolated group also experienced some brain damage. *This* was a surprise. Though in contact with the mother for a full four hours a day (around 17 percent of their day), the infants suffered damage in the cerebellum as well. The authors concluded that only a relatively small amount of touch denial, in combination with reduced activity, is sufficient to cause brain damage.

The Primal Beat

🍂 Babies who are touch-denied will self-rock, as will primates. They do this to feed their vestibular system. But there's more to it than that. They do it because primitive rhythms reside in the very depth of our psyche and influence our behavior in ways never fathomed.

For instance, if I told you that frequent use of the infant swing to calm your baby might mean he may later be a rap music fan, you'd probably find the connection strange. But think of the rhythm of rap music—steady and monotonous. Now think of the rhythm of the infant swing—back and forth, back and forth, without variation. When did the infant swing come on the scene? Around thirty years ago, around the time Generation X was being born.

"I've Got Rhythm"

Harvard researcher Barbara Ayres looked at the rhythmicity of the music in fifty-four different societies from across the globe; her findings are intriguing. When mothers carry babies on their bodies, the music of the culture is more rhythmic, modeled on the gentle swaying sensation felt in the regular up-and-down or side-to-side motion of the mother's movements, as well as the regular "on the beat waltzing" rhythm of the heartbeat.

In Bali in the South Pacific, where babies are kept on the mother's body as she works in the fields, the tempo of Balinese music is the same as the movement of the women during rice pounding. The steady, continuous movement of the mother walking and working, as well as the steady rhythm of her breathing and heart rate, remains imprinted in the psyche. Later, the music is used to evoke the feelings of relaxation and pleasure experienced as an infant.

But here in the United States, where babies are cached and therefore experience relatively little movement, Ayres found that irregular rhythms in which accents are unevenly distributed predominate in our music—for example, from $^2/_4$ to $^5/_4$ to $^3/_4$ time. The movement babies do experience, which is in large part from the buggy, reflects this arhythmicity. Wheeled on a flat concrete surface, movement rolls evenly, occasionally punctuated with bumps that momentarily jar the baby; on a rough surface, such as dirt or grass, movement is jagged, with baby and buggy bumping and grinding.

As if a reflection of the muffled, indistinct sounds heard in the buggy, where language was drowned out by street noise, in our culture we dance to songs in which the lyrics are often garbled and barely audible. Our youth's speech, often speeded up, seems also to reflect a discordant rhythm. Statements, often spoken as a question with raised pitch at the end, throw intonation out of sync.

Music may be affected not only by how much babies are carried but also by whom. Music in West and Central Africa tends to be "hot" rhythm, characterized by several simultaneous rhythms of regular beat that may be proceeding at a different tempo. These cross rhythms are typically played by drums or other percussive instruments. Ayres wondered why simultaneous rhythms seem to predominate West African music. Perhaps, she thought, it's because polygyny is high in these areas and infants are typically cared for by several co-wives. As a result, infants become accustomed to being carried by women with different, distinctive tempos and rhythms of movement.

In Africa, not only are babies traditionally carried throughout infancy, but in this hot climate, some are carried naked against the mother's skin. The greater the skin-to-skin contact, the greater the opportunity for directly experiencing the rhythm of the mother's movement, which may explain why rhythmic music dominates African life and culture more so than in other carrying cultures.

Which rhythm do infants prefer—the stroll of the buggy or the stroll of mother or father? No contest. Infants calm and listen longer to rhythmic lullabies than arhythmic music, so that the majority of children's music in the world remains in simple $^2/_4$ time. Nor, at our most primal layer, does this ever change. "If we were to ask the brain how it would like to be treated," wrote Itzhak Bentov in his book *Stalking the Wild Pendulum*, "whether shaken at a random, irregular rate, or in a rhythmic, harmonious fashion, we can be sure that the brain, for that matter the whole body, would prefer the latter." We can't help it. It is ingrained in us through entrainment, the physical law in which one pulsating system causes another one to link with its vibratory rate or rhythm and pulsate in unison. And it starts at the most basic level: with the tom-tom beat of our mother's heartbeat, rhythmic breathing, and rhythmic movements.

What better example than the rush of the ocean surf—repeating the primal surge of the sounds of the womb, it draws us to its bosom like no other sound. Hypnotically, we sleep "like a baby" to its pounding. And then there's the timeless still of the meditative state and the religious trance that, often achieved by repeating a sound, gives us a glimpse of the internal harmony of the womb. That meditation is common practice in Eastern nations but not here may relate to the extensive carrying of their infants and its ongoing rhythm. Later, the use of continuous rhythmic sounds as a vehicle for achieving inner peace seems natural and familiar.

Preterm infants grow better on waterbeds that oscillate to the adult breathing pattern, and breathe better if you place a "breathing bear" set at a normal neonatal rate inside their incubator. And we spontaneously rock our infants to a heartbeat rhythm, which replicates the ambling movements our infant experienced when inside us.

If we pat our baby's back with the palm of our hand, we put him to sleep *if* the strokes are the natural heartbeat rhythm, that is, about two to three times a second. If we stroke five to six times per second, which is the faster heartbeat of a person when excited, our baby awakens ready for play.

In utero, the fetus's sleep states seem to coincide with mother's sleep states. After birth, entrainment of each other's breathing and movements continues to influence coordination of mother-baby sleep states, as we'll see in chapter 11.

If you videotape a parent talking to her newborn infant and then replay it in slow motion, you see the baby's arms and legs move in synchrony with the rhythm of the parent's speech. Similarly, microanalyses of three-month-old infants in play with their mothers show that they move their heads in marked time with one another.

Just as the rules of conversational turn-taking start at the mother's breast, the origins of adult interactional harmony likely emanate from the many ways we employ rhythmic stimulation with our babies. Explains developmental psychologist Barry Lester:

> In soothing an infant, we introduce cadence and patterning in our voices; we use rocking, walking, music, sucking on a pacifier—all forms

of rhythmic stimulation that establish the temporal patterning of social interaction.

Temporal patterning during social interaction gets affected not only by
rhythm but by speed as well. If we're on a fast track, our babies will be also,
and vice versa. Let's now look at what impact this has on babies' ability to
process sensory information.

8

··

❧

Sensory Overkill

She blows on the patch of water around me. It dances with her breezes. I glide upon it, picking up speed, exhilarated. . . . We play leapfrog with the dance between us. . . . Suddenly her wind shifts. . . . It is upon me. It strikes. I try to meet its force, to run with it, but it jolts me through and through. I quake. My body stalls. I hesitate. Then I veer off. I turn my back to the wind. And I coast into quiet water, all alone.

This quiet place quells the turmoil inside me. It dies down and comes to a rest. I am comforted.

—Daniel Stern, *Diary of a Baby*

*I*n a tale of two mothers—one American Navajo and the other Anglo white middle-class from Chicago—both sit facing their five-month-old infants and are told to "get your baby's attention in whatever way you wish." Researchers from the University of Chicago are videotaping the mothers in their own homes and are interested in the different rhythmicity between mother and infant: how much the mother's behavior is in sync with her infant's signals. What emerges from the two mothers are two distinct rhythms: one adagio; one allegro.

The Navajo mother, with a beatific Mona Lisa smile, gazes quietly at her baby in her lap. She doesn't talk to him, doesn't rock him or wiggle him. She just looks at the wide brown eyes that, unflinchingly, remain fixated on hers, mother and baby interlocked in mutual radiance. When her baby looks away at other sights, mother doesn't interfere.

The Anglo mother, her eyes bright and her mouth opened in an O, holds her baby in her arms in front of her and delivers a deluge of nuzzles, jiggles, and kisses, all accompanied by a stream of chirping utterances. Her baby in turn squeals, screams, and flutters her arms and legs in a little choreographed dance of delight. Then, overloaded, arms and legs squirm and head turns for time out. Mother sits back and waits. Her baby turns around, looks at mother and gurgles, and the whole mother-baby dance begins anew.

The Animated Anglo Mother

The Navajo mother, with her adagio tempo, made little attempt to engage her infant in play. Rather, she allowed her infant to come and go at his own rate and didn't overstimulate—when her baby turned away, she waited quietly until he looked again at her. The result was prolonged mutual gazing and long states of calm but little mutual play.

The Anglo mother, with her allegro tempo, offered her baby much ongoing stimulation. This resulted in short bursts of attention from the infant followed by turning away to download stimulation. Excited and easily engaged, the Anglo baby smiles, moves around, and chats much more than his Navajo counterpart. Since American culture favors spirited and spunky people, this parenting style jibes well with what parents wish their babies to become.

But there's a down side as well. All this stimulation builds up. By the end of the day, fussiness is rampant among infants in this culture. Our buzzing style also contributes to the overall greater irritability of our infants and creates a need for ongoing stimulation.

Also, the Anglo mother relative to the Navajo has a tendency to sometimes "demand" that her infant look at her, which increases the likelihood for overstimulation. Of course, no parent *has* overstimulation as a goal. Fussy infants do not attend to the world around them but to their own discomfort. This puts the baby at risk, since the less aware of external signals, the less fit are we to avoid danger. Consequently, parents universally seek to maximize calmness and alertness and minimize fussing.

Does our spirited style create spunky babies, or are our babies born this way? Probably both play off each other.

Ethnic temperamental differences, as Dan Freedman's cross-cultural work with newborns demonstrated, are evident at birth. With the Navajo mother, a quiet approach fits her baby's more easygoing nature, while the lively and talkative approach of the Anglo mother fits the easily excitable and more emotionally shifting nature of the Anglo baby. The greater incidence of eye averting of Anglo babies fits their lower tolerance of stimulation and more irritable nature, while the longer eye contact of Navajo infants reflects their easier soothability and greater adaptability to stimulation.

Nevertheless, these differences are open to cultural influence. In Japan, the mother takes great pains to keep her infant continually calm and placid. But the Japanese-American mother, like her American counterpart, attempts to physically excite her baby, who responds by becoming more animated. This switch in style might be the Japanese-American mother's attempt to fit in with the more animated American nature. But I think it also has much to do with our long periods of separation.

Both Japanese mothers in Japan and Navajo mothers in the United States remain in continual close proximity to their infants until they can walk. "Night and day, wherever the mother goes, whatever she is doing, the baby is either being held by her or is within sight of her eye and almost always within reach of her hand," wrote Clyde Kluckhohn of the Navajos. With continual opportunity to feel, glance at, and smile upon her baby, neither the Japanese nor the Navajo mother feels the frustration of longing for her absent infant, frustration that makes sustaining her infant's attention more of an imperative. Moreover, in touch, she is more sensitive to her infant's signals, and thus her baby does not experience the disorganization and distress of one left to fend for himself.

We, too, when holding our babies for an extended period, remain low key—although, befitting our more active nature, we furnish a more steady stream of sensory dialogue than our Navajo counterparts. But when out of touch with and even out of sight of our baby for a substantial part of the day and night, we experience each separation as a loss and are greedy for the next hug. Often, we can't wait until they awaken. Says former First Lady Betty Ford of an experience with her son:

> The first time I remember truly feeling like a mother was during those first few nights after we brought Michael home. I could hardly sleep for listening to our new baby breathing, fearful that at any moment he might stop. It was a relief when I heard his hunger cry, because I could then hold him and cuddle him.

As excitement builds up, reunions become an outpouring of love. When our infants turn away, we are less able to tolerate this disinterest. Thus, it's not quantity of sensory input that overstimulates as much as intensity. When out of touch, we're also more likely to overstimulate because we miss more of our baby's subtle time-out signals, such as squirming the body or arching the back.

More vulnerable infants have an especially hard time with our endless procession of arrivals and departures and take longer to regroup when put down. For the American infant in general, long stretches of lack of human touch, interspersed at times with exciting touch often accompanied by almost nonstop dialogue, sets up a pattern of expectation of intense stimulation. This likely contributes to the later stimulus frenzy in which we live.

"I'm Bored"

If frequent separations and reunions lend themselves to overstimulation, leaving our young babies alone lends itself to understimulation. Infants, when old enough to reach and grab and crawl (around eight to nine months of age), entertain themselves easily for short periods of time, thereby satisfying their stimulus hunger. But before the world is at their fingertips, life gets quickly monotonous and frustrating, and babies get mad.

Take six-month-old Nina. While her mother is cooking in the kitchen, Nina is lying on her tummy on a blanket on the den floor with her bunny within reaching distance. Excitedly she grasps it, brings it to her mouth, sucks it, and knocks it around a bit. But soon she tires of it.

She then spots her red-and-white-striped rattle and attempts to slither toward it. But, unable to propel herself far enough to reach it, she falls just short. Frustration! Able to see her toy but not to feel it or listen to the funny sounds it makes when squeezed or banged, she is at a loss. Her brain registers "bored," and she begins to fuss. Mother must now stop her cooking and amuse Nina.

Now let's look at Mora, a child from Bali in the South Pacific. Held on mother's body most of the day, Mora hears, feels, smells, tastes, and "talks" to her mother, all the while exploring her mother's face, hair, clothes, or jewelry. Moreover, when off her mother's body, children and other women continually vie for the opportunity to play with her. Stimulation ongoing but modulated, Mora gets neither bored nor overwhelmed. Rather, she experiences moderate excitement and then relaxation. Nina, in contrast, got quickly excited and then crashed—a pattern T. Berry Brazelton described as typical of babies when they play alone.

Of course, some frustration is necessary for development. In fact, it is the driving force for babies to learn and should not be discouraged. But frustration that sends babies fussing and giving up on an activity is not productive. Frustration is useful only within the context of control.

Holding and Contingent Behavior

When in touch, learning is not only more modulated but also more likely to be contingent—that is, as a result of something the baby does.

For instance, six-month-old Rafael, lying in his playpen, reaches toward a ball with a bright butterfly on it, but he can't reach it: He did something, but his butterfly didn't respond. He swipes at his fuzzy duck, but as he touches it, it moves away. Again, his efforts didn't bring him the expected response.

But in your arms, when he grunts you say, "Oh, really!" When he sucks on your clothes, you say, "Are you hungry?" And when he gives you his flirtatious smile, you, like the Cheshire Cat, flash back with a broad one of your own. He emits a behavior and you respond, in more perfect attunement than any toy.

When babies or anyone feel their actions create a response—that *they* make something happen—they connect their actions with the response and learn the association between cause and effect: If I cry, someone comes to pick me up and my discomfort goes away; if I smile, I get a smile in return and I feel happy. This behavior allows them to feel control over their world. If the response is not to their liking—the puppy bites their hand when they bang his nose—they learn to discontinue the behavior. But if the response piques their curiosity—the puppy licks their hand— they repeat the action until they lose interest. "It's not the noise of the rattle that makes babies laugh," says psychologist Martin Seligman, "it's the fact that *she's* rattling the rattle."

And the *more* they feel in the driver's seat, the *more* excited they get. For instance, developmental psychologist Michael Lewis of Rutgers University took two groups of babies and showed them a color slide of another child's happy face, accompanied by children singing the *Sesame Street* theme song. One group of babies had strings tied to their wrists, which activated the show; the other did not. Both groups of infants saw the same slides, but the ones who caused it to occur by movement of their arm viewed the show longer, fussed less, and smiled more. Were we to peek into their brains, we would see more neural connections.

Of course, infants feel the most control when playing with those animated toys that laugh when you laugh and squeal when you squeal. To a three-month-old, explains Melvin Konner, "the mother and father resemble gigantic controllable mobiles that thrill and delight the infant precisely because she *is* able to control them . . . with her eyes, smiles, coos, and cries." And this is why they never cease to find us interesting objects.

Touch by nature is always contingent: We can avoid looking at someone looking at us, block out what another says, close our nose to another's smells, but it's impossible not to touch someone touching you. Little children learn this very quickly: If screaming doesn't get mother's attention, poking her will every time!

And, sometimes, with the dishwasher swishing, the microwave humming, the TV blasting, and the phone ringing, poking her may be the child's only recourse.

Noise, Lights, Action

↯ Modern life in all its flashing, thumping glory has become a three-ring sensory circus that trounces on our nervous system. Hyped up, we unconsciously hype up our children. How did we get to be such stimulus junkies?

Our brain, wired for survival, must evaluate if a stimulus is dangerous or safe, or if we care. As such, we quickly tune out the familiar, whose status is known, and zero in on anything new or different. If we shine a light in a sleeping infant's closed eyes, her heart rate and respiration speed up, and she moves about a bit. After repeating the light shining several times, she habituates to it and stops responding.

But detection of changes, according to Weber's law, depends on the size of the stimulus: the louder the noise, the brighter the lights, the stronger the perfume, the greater the change needed to detect a difference. Hence we seek out music with louder amplification or flashing lights with brighter whirling neon colors or perfumes with greater pungency. In one experiment, three-month-old babies were given an overhead mobile with ten objects to view. When shifted to a mobile with two objects, babies lost interest, becoming sad or angry; some began to cry.

Accustomed to ever more intense stimulation, our homes throb with noise and lights. I taught in a Head Start program for five years and made, during that time, more than four hundred visits to my preschoolers' homes. With few exceptions, I had to politely request that the mother turn off her soap operas so we could hear each other talk. So embedded was the TV in their environment, they didn't think to do so on their own.

This continual sensory onslaught causes our nervous system to work hard to either process the information or to tune it out. Often draining us, this effort contributes to our high levels of stress. Nor does all this buzzing go unnoticed by our infants.

In the last trimester of pregnancy, if we shine a bright light on the mother's abdomen in the fetus's line of vision, or if we make a loud noise, the fetus will startle. If we shine a softer light or make a soft noise, the fetus actively and smoothly turns toward the stimulus, seeking it out. If, toward the end of pregnancy, we play a Bach concert, the fetus reacts with smooth rhythmic kicks. If we play a rock concert, the fetus reacts with sharp, jerky movements. A mother whose infant reacted strongly to noise once told me that, when pregnant with her son, he would stop moving during rock concerts. In other words, the noise so overloaded his system that it shut him down.

Bombarded with sensory input all day, babies in this culture are no-torious for end-of-the-day fussiness. Inescapable noise, such as that of a loud droning TV, can also disrupt normal sleep cycles and cause a "stress" sleep, meaning that babies bypass light REM sleep and go directly into deep sleep.

A neonatal intensive care unit is a real sensory nightmare, as tiny fragile infants get bombarded with a constant hum of throbbing and buzzing machines, alarms going off, and people chatting. Add bright overhead lights and periodic aversive touch, combined with the infant's neurological immaturity, and you have babies so stressed they spend much of their day in a spasmodic dance. Observing preemies as part of my dissertation research, I assumed this behavior to be normal. I was pleasantly surprised to see that, when held on their mother's body in a quiet corner, the babies slept quietly and this jerky activity all but disappeared. If you place earmuffs on the ears of these fragile infants, as one clever researcher did, the babies breathe in more oxygen, breathe more slowly, sleep longer and in a more quiet state, and appear more relaxed.

Ironically, the things we use to quiet our babies—the nightlight next to their beds; the swings we swing them in; the cradles we rock them in; the white noise, sounds of the womb, or heartbeat recordings we place in their crib—*add* noise with their humming motors, as does the baby monitor next to their crib and the mobile over it.

If you question how much your baby really notices this humming, consider this. In the United States and Canada, where electricity operates on an alternating current of 60 cycles per second, the resonant frequency relates to the B-natural tone on a musical scale. In Europe, the alternating electrical current is 50 cycles per second, which relates musically to G-sharp. Music professor R. Murray Schafer asked American, Canadian, and German students practicing meditation to sing spontaneously whatever tone came naturally. For Americans and Canadians, B-natural was the most frequent tone hummed; for German students, it was G-sharp. In other words, whether we consciously hear the humming or not, electrical current permeates our cells, causing us to entrain to it.

Not all people are bothered by this sensory madness. Some people are thrill seekers and actively seek intense stimulation. It takes a whole blast of air to ruffle their feathers. Such people are extroverts and easily bored—the ones you see working out at the health club while watching TV, listening to music on a headset, and reading all at the same time. For them the louder, the brighter, the higher, the faster, the more dangerous the world around them, the better.

Such sensation-seeking likely evolved because fearless people were needed to lead the pack, to stake out dangerous territory, which explains why males typically outnumber females. Following them on the other end are people whose feathers get ruffled by only a slight puff of air: They don't need to seek out danger, they experience it easily—some on an ongoing basis. Many, if not all, are sensory defensive.

Sensory Defensiveness

❧ Meet twelve-month-old baby Dustin. He cries for twenty hours out of twenty-four and refuses anything in his mouth but his mother's breast. He screams if you try to pick him up, change his clothes or diaper, or give him a bath. He cannot walk, crawl, stand up, sit well, or roll in either direction, nor does he finger objects. He's never slept more than two hours at a time. And he won't look at you.

Dustin was referred to the pediatric unit of Walter Reed Army Hospital, where he was hospitalized for seven weeks because of failure-to-thrive and severe developmental delay. Evaluated by multiple specialists, he was given a CAT scan, an MRI, and every other imaginable test. Total hospital cost: $80,000.

Still, no one could diagnose Dustin, and therefore no one knew how to help him. But they did know that if he didn't eat, he wouldn't survive. On Monday, Dustin was scheduled to have a feeding tube put in. He never did. On the Friday before, occupational therapist and counseling psychologist Patricia Wilbarger was called in to evaluate him and immediately identified his problem: severe tactile defensiveness.

To prevent the insertion of the feeding tube on Monday, she had Dustin's mother start an immediate intervention, a brief but specific protocol utilizing deep pressure touch (DPT)—in between light touch, which annoys, and heavy touch, which can be painful—and joint compressions to furnish proprioceptive input. She instructed the mother to repeat the protocol no fewer than twelve times a day.

Why twelve times a day? Deep-pressure touch sparks volts of electricity that send our neurons aflutter and releases endorphins, our brain's natural morphine, which revitalizes our nervous system and calms us. The effect lasts an hour and a half to two hours. If done frequently, millions of tactile receptors could be quickly stimulated, and Dustin's system wouldn't have a chance to regress.

Dustin also had to be treated for oral defensiveness: Since the mouth is heavily imbued with tactile receptors, tactile sensitivity commonly extends there as well.

By Saturday, Dustin had started to take naps and slept for six hours straight. By Sunday, he had his first meal—three full jars of baby food—and slept eight hours straight. By Monday, the day the feeding tube was to be inserted, he took a full bottle along with his baby food, cried less, rolled over, played with toys, made eye contact, and started to laugh. Within thirteen days, he started to crawl, and two months later, started to walk and talk normally. At the time of this writing, he is ten years old and functioning normally.

On the Defensive

Tactile defensiveness is part of a larger general syndrome called sensory defensiveness, which is a tendency to react negatively and intensely to sensory stimuli that most people consider nonirritating and tune out. And, while few people experience sensory defensiveness to the severity that Dustin did, it is common in milder forms and extends from infancy through adulthood. It's called sensory defensiveness because people *feel* a need to defend themselves against a perceived danger, typically something quite harmless.

We are born prepared to evaluate sensations as dangerous or safe. If we feel a bug crawl down our leg, smell smoke, feel ourselves falling, or hear a snake's hiss, our body goes on alert, ready to take protective action. If confronted with harmless stimuli—the ticking of a clock, a tap on the shoulder, the headlights of the car a half mile away—the senses abandon their defenses.

But when sensory defensive, harmful and harmless lose their distinction: The senses invade the psyche unmercifully, explains Wilbarger. Leaving the person on continual alert, what should be perceived as benign gets misperceived as dangerous or alarming or, in the very least, irritating—no matter how many mattresses, you still collide with the pea. And when you do, your sympathetic nervous system goes into action: Your heart pounds, your breathing accelerates, your palms sweat, your legs stiffen, your hands clench, the blood rushes from the gut to the extremities, readying your large skeletal muscles for action (explaining why sensory defensive babies have frequent feeding problems), and your whole system gets flooded with stress chemistry, a response that, in the normal nondefensive person, wouldn't occur except in a true emergency.

Unable to tune out the aversive stimulation, the sensory-defensive person may not recover to a comfortable level of arousal but may remain in an alarm mode, ready for fight, flight, and the extreme—freeze, when all one's energy turns inward. Often perceiving the world as an emergency or crisis, hypervigilance and overarousal can become a steady state, and stress hammers away at their well being.

Babies can be sensory defensive to only touch. Or sensory defensiveness can scramble the whole nervous system and cause babies to react defensively to a multitude of sensations: Turn on an overhead light, drop a can on the floor, laugh too loudly in their face, approach too quickly, pick them up suddenly, take them from the warm outside air into cold air conditioning, and they can go into a tailspin.

Some especially compromised infants need stimulation toned down to near zero. In the developmental follow-up clinic at Prentice Hospital in Chicago, a nurse was trying to weigh a screaming cocaine-addicted baby who would not calm. "Turn the overhead lights out," the director told the nurse. The director then took the baby, swaddled her tightly, pulled her close to her body, and sat holding her still in the dark. Slowly, the baby quieted.

Infants don't outgrow defensiveness. Rather, they adapt by avoidance and by training everyone around them to offer special handling. Tactile-defensive children teach parents to refrain from touching them with light, tickling touch, with pokes, jabs, or shaking, or with sudden touch; to hold them away from their bodies—remember the non-cuddlers—or to constantly hold them firmly and close. Parents learn not to wash their child's hair or to cut it often, to buy clothes of a particular texture (often cotton, rather than denim, since it's softer) and to cut out labels, to turn their child's socks inside out because seams are irritating, to allow them to walk around without shoes and hats, and to avoid taking them to the dentist.

Because sensory defensiveness is not commonly recognized as a syndrome, some people walk around their whole lives tactile defensive to some degree and not realize it. Instead, they feel different, weird, or even crazy. When possible, they eliminate socks, slips, bras or undershirts, shoes, belts, ties, and hats, and the clothing they do wear tends to be soft and loose. All labels are, of course, removed. At night, those who can afford it sleep with silk nightgowns on silk sheets—no muslin linens please! Often cold from poor circulation, they gravitate toward warm climates. Many shun touch. Drawing or even jumping back from light touch, the tactile defensive person may repel a gentle sweep across her brow from her infant's hands, placing the infant at risk for avoidant attachment.

Because the tactile receptors in their mouths may be insufficiently developed for their tongue to taste everything, tactile-defensive children often have strong food fetishes but without a set pattern: They may prefer only soft food or chewy food; avoid very spicy foods or seek them out. These children frequently don't like rubber bottles or pacifiers and, when mouthing an object, may immediately reject it.

Since infants learn through their senses, avoiding touching, mouthing, tasting, looking at, listening to, or smelling the things in their environment can cause developmental gaps. As such, tactile defensiveness puts "a lid on development," says Wilbarger.

Take oral tactile defensiveness. Infancy, as Freud first said, is one long oral adventure, oral-motor stimulation as a way of meticulously evaluating a shape, a texture, a form. Infants who don't freely mouth everything lose one of the most important ways infants gather information about the world. In fact, touching an object helps the infant to recognize it later by sight. Infant researcher Andrew Meltzoff gave month-old infants either a regular nipple to suck or a nobbed one. When shown the two nipples, the infants looked longer at the one just sucked, telling us they can identify what something looks like by what it felt like in their mouth.

Lack of Sensory Integration

We used to think we had just five senses: vision, hearing, taste, touch, and smell. But as the work on cross-modal integration indicates, the senses are far more intimately connected than previously thought. In fact, with the exception of our aloof sense of smell, which operates independently, our senses are massively connected in our nervous system. Touch alone has at least four senses: pressure, pain, warmth, and cold. This makes it difficult to look at the senses in isolation. There are sensory cells for hearing or vision that will not fire off unless preceded by touch or movement. Thus, when we want to tune the world out, as during meditation, we lie alone and still.

Without vision, we don't plan movement well—close your eyes, and you'll have a problem balancing and walking down stairs. The same with our sense of touch. The vestibular and the tactile are close partners in our family of senses: When out of touch, we are often out of balance, literally. In fact, said Jean Ayres, the founder of sensory integration theory, if you were to cut off the sensory nerves to your hand, in five minutes you would lose coordination.

As such, tactile-defensive children often have problems with movement—with their place in space—ranging from minor clumsiness and fear of fast motions or unstable positions (like being turned upside down) to the stiff or flaccid muscle tone frequently seen in children with learning disorders and hyperactivity. Since anxiety is mediated through the vestibular apparatus, a shaky vestibular system creates jitters throughout their system, adding to their level of anxiety.

To balance out their system, some children seek constant movement. They rock and spin themselves, and they "train" their caregivers to keep them in perpetual motion—to rock them, walk them, spin them, jump with them, toss them in the air, swing them around. To keep Dustin calm, his parents had to jump him up and down, jerk him around, and take him for extended car rides (made doubly difficult by his intolerance for car seats). Needing continual motion, these children can look or be hyperactive.

Sensory-defensive infants are also prone to a strong Moro reflex so that the slightest jiggle may register in their brain as falling. Dustin was so alarmed by any change of movement from the horizontal to the vertical that he had to be maintained at a horizontal angle. These infants especially require smooth movement and great care when being lowered backwards into the crib, tub, or changing table. If the parent's movements are tentative or jerky, the infant will associate being carried with a feeling of dread.

Early Detection

Because the integrity of the vestibular apparatus relates to the integrity of our nervous system, clumsiness combined with tactile defensiveness is often a sign of later potential learning problems. And though learning problems are estimated at around 15 percent of the school-aged population, they're more common than thought. When Patricia Wilbarger screened 2,100 kindergarten children in California, she found an astonishing 30 percent were at risk for later learning problems, though some differences were subtle. Following these children for twelve years, she found many of her predictions to come true.

It's unfortunate. Later potential problems can be prevented, says Wilbarger, if children are given an adequate "sensory diet." Dustin is the proof: Had Dustin's mother not met up with Wilbarger, he would have continued on a path of severe motoric delay, mental delay, and later hyperactivity and attention problems—a huge trial for both Dustin and his parents.

Tactile defensiveness can be recognized by two weeks of age, and the intervention protocol begun at two months of age. As with Dustin, within two to three weeks of treatment, Wilbarger finds that sensory defensiveness has gone from decreased to eliminated, even in severe cases. This change is permanent and occurs regardless of age. (For information on the intervention protocol, see the Resource Guide.)

The deep pressure touch experienced during the intervention protocol is not the same as infant massage. In fact, occupational therapists caution that infant massage may not be an effective intervention with sensory-defensive infants, since one needs to intervene quickly and fire off tactile receptors and then quickly stop stimulation—the opposite of what baby massage does. Further, unlike infant massage therapists, occupational therapists do not believe in stimulating the head or the stomach, where all the visceral organs lie.

Causes

Sensory defensiveness can be inherited, or it can come from prenatal trauma, such as substance abuse, birth complications such as asphyxia, or postbirth trauma. There was some evidence Dustin was asphyxiated at birth. And, though born full term, he was small for his gestational age (five and a half pounds), indicating he stopped growing in utero and this affected the development of his nervous system.

Since their nervous systems are immature, hospitalized preterm infants or those medically compromised are especially prone to overreact to noise, light, even touch and smell. For instance, if you walk to the incubator of a preterm infant and slam the door shut—something the medical staff often unknowingly does—the infant goes off the deep end: His face turns red, his heart beats wildly, he throws out a spasmodic Moro reflex, followed by cycles of startles, tremors, kicks, and airplanes (both legs stiffly extended out).

The more intense the stimulation in their environment, the harder the preemies have to work to shut it out. This effort creates stress, which can cause hypoxemia (decreased oxygen intake to their brain) and, in some cases, lead to cerebral hemorrhaging and damage to the nervous system. In fact, postnatal trauma may help explain why a large percentage of premature infants, though born healthy, end up later with learning problems and hyperactivity. Moreover, subjected to painful medical procedures like heel sticks and insertion of feeding tubes, touch for many premature infants becomes associated with negative feelings, which can, in and of itself, create tactile defensiveness.

On the mild to moderate end of sensory defensiveness are normal infants of difficult temperament. Easily irritated and often colicky, their intense cry is a way of balancing out their overloaded system and shutting down from overwhelming sensory input. In fact, colic is believed to be a major symptom of sensory defensiveness. This would surprise no parent of a colicky infant, who find themselves tiptoeing around the house. And, though the crying stops at around three months, the symptoms often shift over into other systems—feeding, sleeping, and separation anxiety.

Shy or cautious children, whom psychologist Jerome Kagan of Harvard University has identified as constituting from birth about 15 to 20 percent of the population, show all the symptoms of sensory defensiveness. More fearful than the average child, they perceive new people and new situations as a threat and respond defensively. For instance, while uninhibited children will barge into the room with a smile, inhibited children hover near their mother, their eyes peering warily at others.

If you look at them, they may look underaroused. But when physiological measures are taken, their hearts are beating faster and their level of cortisol is higher than that of uninhibited children. In fact, Kagan believes that cautiousness during the Strange Situation explains the seemingly nonchalant reaction of avoidant infants, who are inwardly anxious, not primarily deficits in the mother-infant relationship.

One of the ways Kagan tested for inhibition was to assess children's response to noxious odors. Predictably, after exposure to harsh smells, the heart rate of shy children stays elevated longer than that of their more outgoing peers. Kagan also found that, while more uninhibited children had brown eyes, more inhibited children had blue eyes, which are more light sensitive than brown eyes. Kagan even discovered that when inhibited adolescents went from sitting to standing, they have larger rises in blood pressure—a clear involvement of the vestibular apparatus.

The sensory defensiveness and extreme caution of shy infants is a direct result of a lowered threshold for reactivity in the limbic system and specifically in the amygdala, the part of the brain that mediates fear and defense. When we smell, hear, see, touch, or taste something, the amygdala scans the sensation for trouble. If the verdict is danger, the amygdala acts instantly and triggers the body's fight-or-flight response, stirring the sympathetic nervous system into action. The hormone norepinephrine is released, heightening our senses and putting us on edge. Kagan, in measuring indices of sympathetic arousal in shy children, found higher resting blood pressure, greater dilation of the pupils, higher levels of norepinephrine in the urine, and cortisol in their saliva. Even when asleep, inhibited children show higher heart rates with less variability. Kagan postulates that their low threshold for excitement may relate to an inherited chronically high level of norepinephrine or other brain chemicals that activate the amygdala.

In utero, the hearts of shy children consistently beat faster than 140 times a minute, which is faster than the heartbeats of other babies. And in the newborn period, one can see biochemical distinctions that predict later sensitivity. Newborns with high plasma levels of dopamine-beta-hydroxylase (DBH), an enzyme that catalyzes the conversion of dopamine to norepinephrine, are unusually sensitive to light, sound, and new food at five months of age; at one year, they intensely dislike unfamiliar foods. At age one and two years, about half of four-month-old infants who showed intense movements and frequent crying to visual, auditory, and olfactory stimulation were highly fearful. In other words, as they develop, many inhibited infants continue to live in a chronic state of stress.

Since sensory-defensive children show extreme responses to normal events, Patricia Wilbarger postulates sensory defensiveness at the heart of extreme reactions in general—anxiety, phobias, hyperirritability, hyperactivity, anorexia and bulimia, explosive behavior, all indicate a nervous system out of balance. For instance, some aggressive children lash out because any little touch makes them feel attacked. With the onset of puberty, normal events like a first crush or taking an exam can trigger a panic attack in timid children.

Sensory defensiveness itself does not cause psychological disturbance. Rather, it sets up the potential for an extreme response to life's events. How symptoms specifically manifest themselves depend on the collision of sensory defensiveness with other constitutional factors, individual coping skills, and with the emotional climate of one's current and past life. In unprotected environments, both emotionally and sensorily, one's reactions become more intense. In low-key protective environments, sensory-defensive people may look normally agitated; in fact, Kagan found that a third to half of severely inhibited children look uninhibited by age seven.

Much has to do with how well parents cope with their child's sensory defensiveness—which is not easy. When mild, sensory defensiveness is a nuisance; in the attempt to ward off or to avoid noxious stimuli, these children are more picky, more easily irritated, more difficult to console, and harder to please. When severe, it is crippling—clothes can feel like "spiders on their skin, and stairs seem like cliffs," says Wilbarger—and it disrupts every aspect of the child's life, as it did with Dustin.

Parents, often held hostage to their children's whims, can spend their day putting out fires and going to extreme measures to reduce threats in their child's environment. To curb the intensity of their infant's reactions, they must create a predictable atmosphere. Since parents may not always have the patience to do so, these children are at risk for insecure ambivalent attachment and at risk as well for avoidant attachment, since their extreme demands and irritability make them easy to reject—especially since *they* make parents feel as if they're rejecting them. Writes a parent in a letter to *Parents* magazine:

> I hate to admit this, but I don't think our one-month-old son likes me. I try to cuddle with him, but he acts as if he wants to push me away— his face gets red, he arches his back, and sometimes he gets so upset that he spits up. . . . What am I doing wrong?

If both sensory defensive and insecurely attached, the child must cope with two major threats: an inclination for perceiving the world as unrealistically alarming, and an attachment relationship that intensifies the perception of the world as threatening rather than buffers the threats. The two together make a lethal combination that create a litany of woes.

Emotional trauma—both touch deprivation and negative touch experiences—can also *create* tactile defensiveness. In Harlow's isolation-rearing studies, monkeys deprived of maternal contact were hyperreactive to touch, hyperactive, and depressed. Avoidantly attached infants deprived of soothing nurturant touch, as well as those physically or sexually abused, often stiffen up when you try to cuddle them, their whole body locked into a defensive posture. And though the nervous system appears fixable—Dustin is proof—emotional withdrawal from touch, which bruises the soul as much if not more than the skin, is more stubborn to remove.

Infants suffering from nonorganic failure-to-thrive, a syndrome believed to derive from extreme lack of appropriate physical affection, are so severely tactile defensive that they withdraw from human contact as if painful. In a constant state of sympathetic nervous system arousal, blood leaves their organs and, to help the muscles, goes instead to the extremities. As a result, the food they eat may pass through their intestines without being digested. This, along with lack of sufficient tactile stimulation to stimulate growth hormone, helps to explain their failure to gain weight.

Is Sensory Defensiveness a Modern Phenomenon?

Is sensory defensiveness a modern phenomenon? Possibly, at least when severe. Anthropologists who have studied carrying cultures do not report babies who are inconsolable, babies who reject food, babies who withdraw from their mother's touch, or babies who move about in an agitated manner.

Perhaps sensory defensiveness got factored out of the gene pool. In the environment of evolutionary adaptedness, only the hardy survived. Those most at risk for tactile defensiveness—preterm infants, full-terms born with neurological and medical problems, and autistic children—would have died. If they did survive, their mothers would have abandoned infants with severe defensiveness, since to carry a baby who cried unconsolably or who pulled back from your touch would have presented too much of a struggle. Furthermore, neurologically compromised infants have a more grating cry than normal infants, which creates greater rejection. Even mildly tactile-defensive full-term babies may have presented too much of a challenge in a harsh environment. In today's culture, irritable infants are at high risk for child abuse.

And in an environment where swiftness and agility of movement can mean life or death, children delayed in their motor development or awkward and slow in their movements—as some sensory defensive infants are—could imperil the lives of others. And in an environment dependent on manual dexterity, children with delayed or awkward hand skills may not acquire the necessary tools for independent living and survival.

If sensory defensiveness did get left by the evolutionary wayside, why does as much as a fourth of the population in the United States suffer it to some degree? One possible reason is the greater stress experienced during pregnancy by women in more complex cultures. Maternal stress hormones pass through the placenta, reducing oxygen and nutrient flow to the fetus; this can provoke a fetal stress response. Persistent maternal stress could influence infant temperament. For instance, it's been suggested that the more placid nature of the Navajo baby may relate, in part, to varying blood pressure during pregnancy among Navajo and Anglo women. And there is a difference in the activity level of Japanese newborns born in Tokyo and those born in rural areas of Japan.

It's also possible that sensory defensiveness always existed as the extreme end of the temperament scale but that it was not evident in our ancestral environment, which was nonthreatening. Though sensory-defensive people may complain about bright neon lights and noisy motors, they don't complain that the stars in the sky are too bright or that the surf is too loud. In fact, the more acute one's senses, the more adaptive one would have been in an environment where danger could lurk at any moment.

Shyness also may have gone unnoticed in a hunter-gatherer environment. In a village of fifty to one hundred people, it was unusual to encounter many strangers, new situations, or even new foods as we do in modern society. Furthermore, while shyness is nonadaptive in a culture in which people must make social contacts and take chances, this kind of behavior among people living in a small clan could lead to a long-term commitment between a dominant male and a submissive female and add to the survival of the tribe. Consequently, in a less competitive environment, this temperamental style could have been adaptive. In other words, sensory defensiveness may be an anomaly of modern life—a casualty of our sensory circus, supreme self-reliance, maternal stress, and frequent separation of our infants.

9

．．

The Body Forbidden

> I was the son of a beautiful, word-struck mother and I longed for
> her touch many years after she felt no obligation to touch me.
>   —Pat Conroy, *The Prince of Tides*

In José Orozco's bold and vivid painting *Mother and Child*, a
Mexican mother is bent over and kneading bread; her breasts are exposed
and her naked baby is strapped to her back. Thinking the painting might
be interesting to show in my child development class for a cross-cultural
comparison of parenting, I took it to be copied onto a transparency. When
I handed it to the copy machine operator, he looked at me and uttered—
"Oh, pornography! Can I see your ID?" That comment is telling.

Uncomfortable with the biological basis of the mother-baby relationship, touch taboos pervade every aspect of parenting in the United States
and give us the message that intense mother-baby intimacy is unhealthy.
Touch as the language of love—intimacy—distorts into touch as the language of sex—erotica. This has profound implications for how we define
intimacy and how, where, and how often we touch our children.

Human sexuality begins at birth at the mother's breast. As a mother
caresses her baby's arms, sucks on her baby's fingers and toes, strokes her
baby's forehead and cheeks, and, in some tribal cultures, fondles her baby's
genitals, her infant learns the language of sensual pleasure. The more often
flesh meets flesh, the more pleasurable life is for the infant. This sets the
stage for human intimacy, both emotionally and sexually.

Ideally a mother should have carte blanche for touching her baby, an
entitlement that attenuates slowly throughout childhood and does not end
until puberty, when the need for privacy dominates, and boys especially
become body shy. (Desmond Morris describes the cycles of infancy, child-

hood, and adolescence as "hold me tight / put me down / leave me alone.") But here, as we give a mother her newborn to hold for the first time— swaddled in a blanket rather than naked—cultural attitudes against intimacy creep into the nursery and wedge themselves between mother and baby. Being caressed in mutual nakedness becomes a rarity and the most innocent touch can come with a wagging finger.

Noelle Oxenhandler, in an article in *The New Yorker*, describes how the "eros of parenthood" haunts her relationship with her young daughter. It's as if, says Oxenhandler,

> a stern and frowning face were hovering over my shoulder. I feel this hint of censure when my daughter climbs into my bed in the morning to wake me, wrapping her muscley little arms around me. I feel it as I stand, at her command, outside the glass shower door and wait for the pink blur of her silhouette to turn into her perfect, dripping body. This unease makes it difficult to speak of the sheer pleasure that parents and children take in each other's bodies.

Michel Odent, the obstetrician who runs the natural birthing clinic in Pithiviers, France, blames the technological takeover of birthing for the destruction of human sensuality. "It is no exaggeration to speak of total erotic neutralization of the body from birth onward," he says.

We can thank as well the influence of the early behaviorist John Watson. According to Watson, the natural close physical contact between mother and child fell into the camp of our base sexual impulses. He warned that, though on the surface mothers wish to coddle their children because they want their babies to be happy and because they want to express their love, at the bottom of this coddling is "a sex-seeking response in her, else she would never kiss the child on the lips."

And his influence on mothers was powerful. Dr. Benjamin Spock, born in 1903, recalls his own mother's puritanical view of sex. "She suspected 'naughtiness' everywhere, and subjected her cowed sons and daughters to regular interrogations about their deeds, thoughts, and friends. The mildest lapse from purity registered on their guilty faces . . . with a vestigial cringe."

Certainly, there is an eros to parenthood, but not as we define it. It is a sensual love, not a sexual love; a protective love, not a seductive love. It gets playful and titillating but seeks primarily to pacify and relax. The !Kung San mothers of the Kalahari Desert and Yanomami tribe mothers of the Amazon know this intuitively. Lacking inhibitions about the naked body and about sexuality, mothers regularly caress, lick, and otherwise mouth their baby's genitalia, regardless of sex. For them the act is not sexual, as we perceive it to be and thus blatantly forbid it, but to express affection, for hygiene, and to relax their infants. This practice, according to German ethologist Irenaüs Eibl-Eibesfeldt, is the natural progression of sexuality. "Patterns of caressing primarily evolved in the service of parental care and secondarily became incorporated in the repertory of courtship behavior."

By preschool, the incest taboo is firmly in place and parental fondling of a child's genitalia becomes universally forbidden. Nudity, however, remains lax in many cultures. But in our sexual climate, where innocent touching gets easily misread as eroticism, sex now rears its ugly head and we try to avoid any behavior that might imply impropriety: letting our children see us in the nude, sleeping with or embracing a naked child past infancy, showering with our children.

Nudity

🥕 When the Puritans settled in the United States, so did repression of our sensual nature. The pleasures of the flesh were thought to be evil, an attitude that continued through the stiff-laced Victorian era. Today, though more comfortable with our bodies than one hundred years ago, we remain prudish: Nudity continues to equate with sexuality. Consequently, unless intending to seduce, our "private parts" need to be hidden.

To some extent this is worldwide. All adults cover up the genitals. Even the natives running through the thicketed Amazon jungle wear a "modesty leaf," a loincloth, or a string. But in the United States we've extended the definition of private parts to include something as innocent as the nursing mother's breast, which we view primarily as an erogenous zone.

We accept a bare-breasted woman on magazine covers, in the cinema, and at some progressive beaches. But a woman suckling a baby in public with even *no* breast showing is viewed as immodest, animalistic, uncivilized, and peasantlike—a cause for public outcry, to some, as former *Today* show host Deborah Norville discovered. In 1991 a photo of Norville feeding her infant son appeared on the cover of *People* magazine, which caused a media stir. "There's no breast. There's no nipple. There's nothing," said Norville. "My strapless gowns show a heck of a lot more. I was dumbfounded—and amused."

Barely warranting a glance in most of the world's cultures, breastfeeding in public was considered "indecent exposure" only a decade ago in New York City, and punishable by law. In 1993 Florida became the first state to enact a statute to allow a mother to perform her body's natural function in public. Nature has continued to gain respect. Today, twelve states have enacted this statute, and thanks to a mother named Dina Tantimonaco, Connecticut will likely soon become the thirteenth. On August 30, 1996, Dina sat in her truck, nursing her baby. A police officer pulled up alongside and told her to stop. She complained to the police department, her state representative, and the La Leche League. If the law is passed in Connecticut, Dina won't have to worry about getting arrested for nursing her baby. But that won't stop her from getting booted out of restaurants, like one mother last year at a restaurant in Fort Lauderdale, Florida. Fifty breastfeeding moms ganged up and came back the next day to protest.

This prudishness affects the ease with which mothers can nurse. During breastfeeding a mother is defenseless—she cannot easily flee with her baby. If someone glares, walks past and snickers or whispers, or threatens expulsion, the brain would perceive this signal as potential danger and milk flow would naturally suppress, readying the mother for flight. In other words, a mother faced with a hostile environment not only feels uncomfortable nursing but produces less milk. "I wouldn't nurse in public," says one mother. "Instead I pumped before I went out. I refused to sit in a bathroom to feed my daughter."

This prudishness about the naked breast is only the tip of the iceberg. From infancy on, small children wear colorful bathing suits that cover their genitals and for little girls, their unformed nipples as well. In a study done in 1966 by Vidal Clay, who observed and recorded touch behavior between mothers and their children at the beach, Clay reported seeing only one naked baby—a thirteen-month-old little girl—after a whole summer's observation. Not only were negative comments heard from other mothers about the nudity, but the curiosity of two little boys made the mothers uncomfortable.

Things haven't changed much in the last thirty years. While sitting at a beach in San Diego, I watched a three-year-old undress herself and run around nude. "That's disgusting, Kathy," shouted her grandmother. "Put some clothes on." A whole beach of bare-bottomed children would get a parade of gawks. What a difference if we cross to the other side of the ocean. In Europe, unclothed children in public is a more natural sight, especially in Scandinavia. "I didn't get my first bathing suit until around age ten," a Swedish student tells me. "When my mother visited, she found it ludicrous that we put bathing suits on our babies." In Israel in the 1970s,

I was struck by all the children freely romping nude at the beach. In India, children regularly run around naked until age six or seven.

Throughout the history of our species, people lived together in close quarters, and privacy was a foreign concept. Children witnessed nudity as a natural part of life. But seeing parents naked has been and still is uncommon in the United States. Robert Crooks and Karla Baur, professors of sexuality, have asked thousands of students over the years this question: Did you feel comfortable with nudity around the home while you were growing up? "In a class of 75, the number of hands raised often can be counted on the fingers of one hand," they report. Consider one account:

> I can remember accidentally walking in on my father when he was shaving, naked as a jaybird. His response was off the wall. I got the message loud and clear that there was something wrong about a little girl seeing her father naked. My mother was quite prudish, too, as I think back on it. I didn't see another adult male naked, I mean close up so I could really look him over, until I was involved in my first heavy sex experience.

Part of our squeamishness stems from the classical psychoanalytic perspective that allowing children to view the parent in the nude could be sexually stimulating and possibly traumatic, leading to potential later difficulties in adult sexual functioning. In the marketplace of ideas, this has become a staple that has placed loads of restrictions on the American child. Along with keeping our children's and our own private parts covered, in our climate of sexual abuse, we commonly forbid children in day care to view one another's naked bodies. Nor are books containing natural pictures of nudity readily available. *Where's Waldo?*, a popular children's book, has been banned in some places because one of its puzzles contains a minuscule profile of a female breast. In fact, says sexologist John Money of Johns Hopkins University, allowing a child to see a nude adult or allowing a nude picture of anyone under the age of eighteen to be seen by someone else falls under the definition of child sexual abuse, as defined by some professional victimologists.

With scant opportunity to observe nakedness naturally in adults or each other, a child holds in his mind a cultural script that says certain parts of the body—and thus, oneself—are unacceptable, even dirty. At the least, we become uncomfortable being nude with a sexual partner; at the most, this inhibition can lead to sexual dysfunction.

Growing up accustomed to nudity, in contrast, does the opposite: It gives children accurate information about their body, providing a healthy framework in which to place themselves on a continuum of development. The tribal little girl, wrote Margaret Mead, views herself "as one of a series of girls, up through the nubile girl with budding breasts to the mature young woman, and finally to the just pregnant, the fully pregnant, and the post-parturient and suckling mother."

In cultures such as Japan's, where families traditionally bathed together until the children were prepubescent (although this happens less so today), nudity is treated as neither forbidden nor erotic but as a normal part of life; children grow up to view the naked adult body as natural. Recently, as I undressed in the locker room of my athletic club, a four-year-old boy, accompanying his French nanny, stood nearby. "Uh oh," I thought, prepared for the usual giggling or gaping. But nothing happened. The child looked at me briefly without reaction, turned around and sat next to his nanny. I asked the woman, who had been with him since age one, if he were accustomed to adult nudity. "I don't prance around naked in front of him," she said. "But if he walks in on me, I don't make anything of it or attempt to cover up." Hiding our bodies, in contrast, piques the child's curiosity, drawing the child to the forbidden parts; like little detectives, they will seek to uncover the naked truth.

In the United States, children do, of course, see nudity in the media. But, as concerns John Money, rather than getting an "honest portrayal of naked human bodies, they see the body in exaggerated, eroticized form." Later, when their own bodies begin to develop, they compare themselves to an unrealistic image of the human body. Thus in the United States we see excessive dieting of even prepubescent girls.

The Primal Scene

⚜ Children growing up in a primitive society see not only their parents nude but occasionally catch them "in the act." Classical psychoanalysts cautioned that, like nudity, viewing parental coitus could overstimulate, traumatize, and potentially damage the child. Thus, parents take great pains to avoid uninvited guests in the bedroom.

But this concern, in light of a simple fact, appears to be psychological nonsense. Since 75 percent of the children in this world sleep with their parents and always have, it's likely most if not all of them *would* have witnessed "the primal scene," as Freud called it, at one point or another. If this were psychologically damaging, that would constitute considerable pathology. In fact, there is no evidence that the sights or sounds of parental lovemaking have any damaging effects on infants or children. The openness, for instance, of the Aboriginal camp permits many opportunities for children to observe intercourse among adults. Rather than become neurotic adults, the Aborigines are described as "extremely mild-mannered, easygoing, and relaxed," with none of the "armored defensiveness of the Western personality structure."

Furthermore, before technology eliminated animals for work, food, and transportation, children who did not observe parental coitus likely observed it, along with genital differences, in animals. It is only in recent history that, with our animals frequently neutered and the overwhelming majority of children sleeping separately from their parents, we grow up less educated about both anatomical differences in animals and about the birds and the bees.

Something else is brand-new to our hominid history—television. If children do see a frank depiction of copulation, it's usually from the media and depicted often as lewd or violent, which leaves them in the dark about sexuality as a natural act. This distortion easily leads to a view of the act as not only wrong but obscene, and could contribute to later guilt, anxiety, and conflict regarding sex.

In truth, peeking in on mommy and daddy doing their "work," as !Kung children call it, is not only not psychologically damaging for children but may be essential for developing a healthy gender image. Observation is a principal mode of learning. As with witnessing parental nudity, it gives children a script of how growing up gets played out. Psychologists Robin Lewis and Louis Janda of Old Dominion University, in Norfolk, Virginia, queried 210 college students about their early exposure to nudity and sexuality: How often did you see your parents naked? Did you sleep in the same bed with your parents? Did you ever witness your parents having sex? Could you discuss sex with your parents?

What they found was encouraging. Exposing children to nudity, sleeping in the parental bed, and witnessing the primal scene creates adults who are more relaxed about touch, about their body, about nudity, and about sexuality. Boys who slept with their parents later enjoyed increased self-esteem, less guilt and anxiety, and greater sexual freedom. Girls who slept with their parents were more comfortable with physical contact and affection and with their own sexuality.

The common thread running through both groups was the casual attitude with which their parents viewed nudity, sleeping together, and witnessing parental intercourse. In other words, it's not the nature of the sexual act itself, but the parent's response to getting caught that determines the child's feelings. If there is good family communication and if the parents do not overreact, children will treat it with normal interest and little harm will be done. But if parental anger, anxiety, guilt, or punishment highlights the act, children will imbue it with immense importance and see it as forbidden and dirty.

This does not mean parents should leave their bedroom door open. The psychoanalysts were right on one account: Under certain circumstances, witnessing adult intercourse can be overstimulating and damaging. Repeated exposure to coitus (either from witnessing parents or by seeing it from the media), disturbed family relationships, parental brutality (which makes children misconstrue sex as aggression), and seductiveness or sexual abuse toward the child all sully normal sexual attitudes. That there is so much of this today likely accounts for much of our sexual pathology and explains some of the obsessive and disturbing sexual acting out that child-care workers report, and that we read about in the newspapers.

Childhood Sexuality

⚡ Parental discomfort about sexual matters has further ramifications than bolting the bedroom door and discouraging children from romping in the raw. Parents are likely also to react with dismay when seeing their infants and children touch "forbidden" parts.

Take one mother of a two-year-old son. Walking into his bedroom to get him up from his nap, what she saw "shocked" her. Her son was undressed and had an erection. "He was touching it with this spaced out look on his face. 'Oh, God,' I thought," she says. Her response was quite typical, part of our legacy that our body contains evil sexual impulses. In 1906, Margaret Morley warned parents to watch their children carefully, almost from the hour of birth; children may sin against themselves and lose their sexual purity. In 1914, *Infant Care*, a publication of the U.S. Department of Labor, cautioned that the infant has "strong and dangerous impulses" which easily "grow beyond control." The mother must fight her child's sinful nature by taking forceful measures to prevent masturbation, or children could sometimes be "wrecked for life." To eradicate masturbation, the mother should tie the baby's feet to opposite ends of the crib so that he cannot rub his thighs together; his nightgown sleeves should be pinned to the bed so that he cannot touch himself. The baby may achieve the dangerous pleasures to which his nature disposes him also by his own movements or may be seduced into them by being given pacifiers to suck or having his genitals stroked by the nurse. The need to stifle the infant's sensual nature is also what led to severe restriction of thumb-sucking.

By the 1940s, we emerged from the Dark Ages and touching of the genitals lost its notoriety as an evil deed. An updated edition of *Infant Care* described the genitals as a normal object of exploration—the same as the toes, the ears, or a toy. The solution was not tying down but diversion—if the baby has a toy to play with, he will not play with his genitals.

This change was undoubtedly due to the influence of Freud's landmark discovery that deriving pleasure from playing with the genitals is normal infantile behavior. In fact, René Spitz, an early psychoanalyst, discovered that infantile genital play is not only normal exploration, it is an indicator that a baby is receiving adequate affection. When mothering was optimal, Spitz found virtually all infants engaged in genital play. When mother-infant encounters were problematic, genital play was more rare. And infants reared in families exhibited genital play almost two months earlier than those cared for in nurseries.

Today, we are more lax about infantile genital play and encourage parents not to interfere with it. But old attitudes die hard. Our gut reaction can still be negative as we tend to "adultomorphize" the infant. But genital play for infants is a source of security, not a source of eroticism.

Newborn males often get erections—some during nursing, which is often followed by relaxation. And female babies show a capacity for lubrication in the first months of life. At around four months of age, when babies have the motor coordination to do so, they discover they too can create sensual pleasure. At first, they may randomly finger their genitals. After six months of age, they may do so with greater frequency. Some infants, through rocking, discover the pleasure of rhythmic genital stimulation. Resembling coital movements, this pelvic thrusting occurs in infants eight to ten months of age, usually as part of affectionate play, when the infant will clasp the parent and rapidly thrust and rotate the pelvis. Primate infants exhibit pelvic thrusting as well, suggesting that infantile sexual behavior may be the rule in all mammals.

For most children through age two and a half, genital play is pleasurable but not emotionally exciting or stimulating. But in some children genital manipulation apparently gives rise to orgasm—at least according to Kinsey, who noted in 1948 to have observed orgasm in boys of every age from five months to adolescence and for a female baby of four months. After the experience, most relax and go to sleep.

It is impossible to tell what these experiences mean to infants, but one thing seems clear. If, because of our own discomfort, we spontaneously pull their hands away, say no, or frown, babies will begin to hesitate and then inhibit their behavior. As early as nine to twelve months of age, infants rely on their parents' facial expression to make decisions about what to touch, body parts included. If the message is "don't touch," this could inhibit a progression of very normal—and healthy—interest in their bodies.

By age two, strong sexual curiosity makes children want to see, to touch, to pull at, to talk about, and to play with their genitals and those of other children. First of all, toilet training increases awareness of genital sensations. Second, children start to notice gender differences. Curious, they explore one another's bodies and in this way learn what it means to be a little boy and a little girl. It is innocent; it's our reaction that gets distorted. Take that of a father watching his two-year-old in play with her two-and-a-half-year-old cousin one afternoon. "They had been playing with their dolls on the bedroom floor," he says. "When I came back into the room, they had all their clothes off and were patting baby powder all over each other and their dolls, giggling and poking away at each other's bodies. I froze. I was *not* prepared for sex play at their age." His response was not unusual. Many parents, ill-informed about childhood sexual play, react with discomfort when suddenly confronted with a two-year-old's sexual curiosity.

In some extreme cases, gross misunderstanding of the normal behavior of the child, coupled with adult pathology, leads to severe abuse. For seven-year-old Christina Holt, it meant death. On September 16, 1994, Christina Holt was killed by her stepfather, John Zile. The case caused a media frenzy because Christina's mother, Pauline, had reported Christina missing, abducted from Sunrise, Florida. For one month, lies and cover-ups kept the nation looking for the child, until the stepfather finally confessed the murder. Christina had angered him. Her crime? Playing doctor. Terrified by his rageful reaction to finding out, and knowing a severe beating was imminent, Christina soiled her pants. At that, he began to beat her. Attempting to stifle her cries so the neighbors wouldn't hear, he put his hand over her mouth. She went into convulsions, choked, and died.

Certainly the stepfather's fury over innocent sexual childplay is a rare example. But parents becoming hysterical over children acting out sexual play is not. Recently, a director at a day care center in Miramar, Florida, told me that a parent, irate that a three-year-old child "touched" her three-year-old, reported the incident, and the next day Child Protective Services came out to investigate. Stories like this abound in the newspapers. It was just last year that a six-year-old first grader was suspended for kissing a girl on the cheek.

Nor is the media always especially enlightening. Recommends the April 1995 issue of *Parents* magazine:

> It's not necessary or even desirable to permit sexual play, especially when other children are involved. . . . Preschoolers who are playing "doctor" should be separated with a matter-of-fact statement such as, "I know you're curious, but I don't want you taking off your clothes when you play together."

To avoid parental wrath, child-care workers discourage children from seeing one another nude, touching one another's private parts, or acting out the sexual act. Monitoring children's behavior to ensure that two children are not alone together, they set up rooms so the children are in sight at all times, demand that children go to the bathroom individually, and allow only one child at a time in hiding places. When they get "caught," children are reprimanded and the parents informed. This not only smacks of the early sexual repression of the Victorian Age but may be psychologically damaging for the young child.

Normal Sexual Development

❧ Normal sexual exploration is, within the context of normal development, a natural and necessary step on the path of sexual identity. "The child is, above all, shameless, and during its early years it evinces definite pleasure in displaying its body and especially the sexual organs," wrote Freud.

As children learn how to walk by going through progressive stages of sitting, standing, and taking practice steps, so must they go through sexual rehearsal play to reach healthy sexual maturity, explains John Money. Holding hands, kissing, hugging, flirting, exploring each other's naked body, and simulating the sex act are all rehearsals for later sexual roles. If our children pick up that something is shameful about certain areas of the human body, sexual feelings and interests become a source of conflict, which lowers self-esteem and affects sexual behavior. As an adult, points out Margaret Mead, one is then faced with having to unlearn the "wickedness or dangerousness of sex, a lesson which was impressed upon him strongly in his most formative years."

Sex play in young monkeys determines whether they will become adults capable of normal sexual functioning. All young monkeys, male and female, explore one another's genitals, masturbate, and play at thrusting movements and copulation. When denied the chance to play at sex, they are seldom proficient later. For instance, a male may attempt to mount the front or side of a female.

Children, too, require normal sexual rehearsing, which is little more than witnessing and imitating normal healthy sexual behavior between their parents or older siblings and partners. A little girl may bat her eyes at a little boy, then run away giggling, as the boy chases her, also giggling. When he catches her, they kiss and giggle, and the chase starts anew. Or children find hiding places away from adults and play "show me." They strip, poke at each other's genitals, giggle, and talk "dirty"—toilet words that throw them into laughter. Discouraging these activities by telling children "it's not nice" or slapping their hands away during natural play creates a barrier to their normal sexual development.

As sexual creatures, the need for understanding our sexual nature is always with us. Ignoring childhood sexuality does not make it go away. It only produces in the child a hodgepodge of mixed feelings: curiosity about things that no adult will talk about, guilt about doing something that needs to be hidden from parents, confusion from not getting clear information, and fear of unexplainable feelings, possibly erotic, and of the unknown. All this complicates the task of piecing together a cohesive and comfortable sexual picture. Writes Floyd Martinson:

> Most parents and teachers treat children as essentially nonsexual. Even if a child is seen engaging in some activity which to adults appears as sexual, it is the unusual adult who does anything to maintain and encourage the activity or to help the child give it meaning. . . . We can say that children remain largely asexual because they do not live in environments that create sexual meanings and provide sexual scripts.

Perhaps we can learn something from native cultures where, with sexuality more open and accepted and sexual play common and sanctioned, children have the opportunity to build sex maps—templates of their ideal-ized sexual partner. Later, they traverse sexuality as familiar territory, not as an unknown and frightening experience. Interestingly, when children are free to engage in normal sexual play, as tribal children are, there is no "latency" school-aged period, as Freud termed it. Rather than sex going underground at around age seven and reemerging in full force at puberty, flirtation and boy-girl sex play continues alongside the common same gen-der pairing of eight- to eleven-year-olds.

High-Touch, Low-Touch Cultures

In high-touch cultures, as in Latin countries such as France, people seem relaxed about their sensual nature, their bodies, and sex. They also seem more affectionate with their children. In low-touch cultures, as in England, people in general appear more prudish and make more distant parents—especially those in the upper class. Prince Charles, for instance, describes how, after his mother returned from a trip abroad, he had to wait in line with everyone else for her greeting. When it finally happened, it was a mere handshake. "I was born in England," writes Ashley Montagu, "a land full of peculiar people, of people who are adults who seldom touch each other, and in which one apologizes to one's father or one's mother when one touches them accidentally."

Sidney Jourard, a psychologist at the University of Florida, noticed touching differences in multinational students, leading him to do a pilot study on "body accessibility" in 1966. Sitting casually in coffee shops in San Juan, Paris, London, and Gainesville, Florida, he counted how many times in one hour people, while conversing at a table, touched each other. The score: San Juan, 180; Paris, 110; London, 0; Gainesville, 2.

Tiffany Field recently observed teenagers at a McDonald's in Miami and in Paris. In Paris, the teens tended to congregate in groups of three—most often two females and a male and then two males and a female. All leaning against each other, until two began to kiss, it was hard to figure out who the lovers were. "They talked a little, drank a little, smoked a little, ate a little, and smooched a little," says Field. Here, in contrast, U.S. teens ate more, drank more, smoked longer, and talked and touched each other less. As if to compensate for lack of affectionate touch, the U.S. teens engaged in more self-touching: They played with their hands and hugged them-selves; the boys cracked their knuckles a lot; the girls swept their hands through their hair.

Paris is such a sensual, tactile city that even just speaking the language forms the mouth into a kiss shape. There, not only do friends touch in cafés, lovers touch freely in public, and women comfortably bare their breasts at the beach, but women walk comfortably hand-in-hand down the street and men traditionally greet each other with kisses and embraces.

Here such behavior intimates homosexuality. For men, the only exception is the burst of whole-body hugging often following athletic triumphs— winning that, in team sports, results often from violent contact between men. In the Brazilian highlands, the Kaingang tribe are so tactile that, reported Jules Henry in his book *Jungle People*, "married and unmarried men lie cheek by jowl, arms around one another, legs slung across bodies, for all the world like lovers in our own society."

For women, public show of affection—such as walking hand-in-hand in public—creates less head turning. Extended body contact, however, carries sexual overtones and may be misinterpreted. On the morning of May 28, 1995, Harvard student Sinedu Tadesse, an Ethiopian, stabbed her roommate Trang Ho, a Vietnamese, to death. Lying next to Trang was a friend, Thao Nguyen, with whom she had been sharing her bed as she had done with her little sister at home. The media later played this event as sexual. Thao was dismayed. As she explained, women in Southeast Asian cultures often share beds and are physically affectionate.

Concerned about misinterpretation, American women engage in brief, friendly, affectionate hello and good-bye hugs but generally avoid prolonged touching. But in high-touch cultures, where touch is not necessarily equated with sexuality, extended contact between women relaxes and reassures. Take the Trinidadian child-care workers to whom I recently gave a workshop: Lounging, entwined like felines, for well over an hour, *they* listened to *me* talk about the importance of touch in an infant's development. I felt absurd.

We can divide touchophobes from touchophiles by gauging how much personal space people require. Those more cautious in their contact with others, as we are in the United States, more quickly experience others as trespassing. "Waiting for a bus," wrote Ashley Montagu, "Americans will space themselves like sparrows on a telephone wire, in contrast to Mediterranean peoples, who will push the crowd together." My yoga teacher complained to a yoga teacher from Spain that she's forced to teach in a small room, where people struggle to make space between one another. The Spanish teacher described the opposite problem: She teaches in a large room, but her class squeezes close together.

For Americans, wrote Edward Hall, intimate space is about eighteen inches around the head; only pets and intimates dare venture this close. Personal space is two to four feet surrounding you; friends may enter. Social space is from four to eight feet away; comfortable distance during work and social gatherings. Public space are areas beyond nine to ten feet.

Imagine how violated we might feel if confronted with the raw tactile exploration of a Stone Age New Guinia tribe, isolated from the rest of the world for forty thousand years, as did Michael Leahy, an Australian prospector looking for gold in New Guinea in the 1930s:

> We waved to them to come on, which they did cautiously, stopping every few yards to look us over. . . . One old chap came forward gingerly with mouth open, and touched me to see if I was real. Then he knelt down, and rubbed his hands over my bare legs, possibly to find if they were painted, and grabbed me around the knees and hugged them, rubbing his bushy head against me.

The Japanese would likely have been more comfortable with this encounter. They view crowding together as a sign of warm and pleasant intimacy. In fact, in the Japanese language there is no word for privacy. Germans on the other hand, not traditionally known for their warmth, have a strong need for large areas of interpersonal space. This is telling. Touch is a language only the initiated can mutter. In Japan, the intense closeness of mother and infant carries through to an ease with later intimacy. In northern Germany, where mothers encourage physical distance and show a low level of affection toward their infants, we see a later need to keep people at arm's length.

Where do we Americans fall? Somewhere in the middle. But we're steadily becoming more and more touch conservative. Incest, the most heinous of crimes and the one for which some form of taboo exists in all human societies, is popping up in uncomfortable numbers in all strata of our population. An ominous trend, it carries along with it another affliction—the threat of accusation of perverse conduct.

Childhood Sexual Abuse Hysteria

I am watching, on TV, a true-life teleplay. In it, a man has killed his wife to collect on an insurance policy. How does he justify the murder? His wife was sexually abusing their infant, he says. Though not a juror in the room held him in anything but contempt, one seed of doubt planted in the public's mind and there's no quicker way to ruin the reputation of a parent, a friend, a relative, a babysitter, a teacher, a child-care worker, than an accusation of child sexual abuse.

A shocking 25 to 30 percent of children in the United States are sexually abused. The stuff of talk shows, movies, recent novels, and celebrity-magazine cover stories, the issue of childhood sexual abuse—largely hush-hush before the 1980s—has pervaded our culture and become a media event.

While no one questions that in the past it was underreported and that exposure has helped victims to better cope with this monstrous crime, there is backlash—the emergence of childhood sexual abuse hysteria. "Sexual allegations in divorce, involving the minor children of estranged parents, are becoming the weapon of choice in bitter divorce and custody battles across the nation. This phenomenon has become common enough that there is now a name attached to the action—the SAID syndrome (Sexual Allegations in Divorce)," writes Dean Tong, himself a SAID victim.

With the specter of child sexual abuse accusations hovering over their heads as the easiest and quickest way to ruin a reputation, and possibly even terminate parental rights, some fathers hesitate to hold and kiss their children affectionately, to sleep in the same bed with them, or to bathe with them. In the recent Russian film *Burnt by the Sun*, a father, his young daughter, and the mother are in the family's steam bath. The mother is standing with a towel wrapped around her waist, her breasts bared. The father, wearing only undershorts, lies on his stomach, while the daughter lies naked, prone across his back. The scene is clearly set up to show the strong love and affection between father and daughter, not sexuality. But in Hollywood, where most adult films contain adult sexual nudity, a scene like this would never be permitted—unless the outcome were childhood sexual abuse.

How many fathers hesitate when meting out innocent affection to their daughters? And, if they hesitate, how might this impact on their child's later development? One way is in body image. Sandra Weiss, a professor of nursing at the University of California in San Francisco, looked at quality of parental touch in relation to body concept in children aged eight to ten. In both boys and girls, the quality of the father's touch had a predictive relationship to body concept—more so than did the mother's.

As for strange men touching children, most are suspect until proven innocent. Even Victorian England was not as hysterical as are we today. Lewis Carroll, a.k.a. Reverend Charles Dodgson of Christ Church, Oxford, was inspired to write the "Alice" books by his love for a real-life prepubescent girl named Alice. Also a photographer, he requested and received from parents permission to photograph Alice and other little girls in the nude in poses that today would put him in jail. Dodgson *didn't* molest any of these young girls, and they later remembered him with affection. "Today, we would insist that any college don who wanted to take pictures of naked little girls was just a pervert, and we would drive him out of the school and into the tabloid press," writes Adam Gopnik in an article on Dodgson. "We know, or think we do, that there is no such thing as an innocent passion for the bodies of young children." More tolerant than we, "the Victorians may have been hypocrites, but they weren't hysterics."

Much of this change relates to the media's powerful influence on our attitudes. In a study in which parents and early childhood professionals rated a videotaped adult-child interaction, half of whom were first read a statement about sexual abuse and the other half about the benefits of touch, those in the first group were more disapproving of affectionate touch and favored noncontact, while the second group favored contact.

Almost all childhood sexual abuse is perpetrated by a male, most often the stepfather. Rarely does a mother, unless deranged, abuse her child, and especially an infant. But this does not mean females are immune to accusations. In a backlash maneuver, in the mid- to late 1980s men began accusing their wives of sexual abuse, says Richard Gardner, though "this retaliatory maneuver has never been widely used." Of course not: If it were as frequent as with males, it would threaten the whole sanctity of motherhood, on which civilization rests. But this doesn't stop our paranoia.

The Sensuality of Breastfeeding

One night, Denise Perrigo called a local helpline seeking information on how to contact La Leche League. Something strange happened to her while nursing her three-year-old daughter, and Perrigo wanted to find out if it was a normal event: During nursing, Perrigo became sexually aroused. But she did not get her question answered by La Leche League. Instead, she somehow got switched to the Syracuse Rape Crisis Center. A counselor there thought it "unnatural" to nurse children past infancy. Perrigo, a single mother, was accused of child sexual abuse—the words "mouth-to-breast contact" appeared on police records—and thrown in jail for the weekend, her daughter sent to foster care. It took one year to get her daughter back, as Perrigo and her lawyer battled, among other charges, the accusation that she breastfed for her own sexual satisfaction.

A naked baby suckling an unclothed mother's breast is the height of intimacy and tactile stimulation. It can be sensually pleasurable and, although mild erotic sensations are generally only felt briefly at the start or end of feedings, for some women it can be, occasionally, orgasmic. "When you suckle I am slowly moved in my sensitive groove, you in your mouth are alive, I in my womb," writes Alicia Ostriker in her poem "Greedy Baby."

During nursing, explained the late Niles Newton, former professor of behavioral sciences at Northwestern University Medical School in Chicago, similar things happen as during sexual arousal. The uterus contracts, the nipples become erect, and body temperature rises. Just as we experience a flush during sex, so can nursing mothers experience a kind of flush. The reason: oxytocin, the feel-good hormone that rises during sex and while lactating.

If you find this information a bit jolting, you are not alone. Though perfectly normal, a conspiracy of silence prevents many mothers from knowing that sensual and sexual feelings even occur. With the breast restricted to a sexual object, rather than maternal object as well, discovering that suckling combines both is confusing for mothers, explains feminist writer Alice Rossi. Moreover, emphasis on covering up the breast as a sexual object makes mothers feel self-conscious about using the breast as a maternal object. Robbed of a framework in which to place sensual arousal during nursing, mothers may perceive these feelings as unique and therefore unnatural.

In fact, the more in tune a mother is with her body and the more comfortable she is with her sexuality, the more likely she will be to experience sensual and sometimes sexual feelings, explains Rossi. In support of this, Masters and Johnson found that for the first three months after delivery, nursing mothers reported the highest level of sexual interest. Furthermore, mothers who breastfeed are more tolerant of sexual matters such as masturbation and social sex play. Nor do mothers, unless deranged, sexually abuse their infants nor, except in rare cases, their children. In fact, that she suckles her infant may account for lack of mother-son incest, suggests some anthropologists. Suckling, they say, may lay down a universal imprinting trait that leads to later mother-son incest aversion.

Easy acceptance of one's sexuality also affects how successful a mother will be at nursing. When mothers experience sensual feelings during nursing, milk ejection increases, as it does during sexual arousal. In fact, when lactating women have sex, their babies, smelling the milk, often wake. Hence, societies that permit mothers these natural feelings may have mothers who produce more milk, increasing the likelihood of success at breastfeeding.

Sexual attitudes affect the birth experience as well. In a society with relaxed sexual attitudes, like that of the South American Siriono, labor is remarkably short and painless. Among the Cuna in Panama, in contrast, who prevent young girls from learning about sexual intercourse or childbirth, it is a prolonged painful process, as it is here often.

As parallels exist between sexual arousal and nursing, so do they exist between sexual arousal and childbirth, explains Newton. During childbirth, as during coitus, breathing accelerates, the uterus contracts rhythmically, grunts and loud noises are made, women tend to become uninhibited, and there is a flood of ecstasy following delivery. In fact, Newton views coitus, giving birth, and lactation as an intertwined part of female reproductive behavior:

> In practical terms . . . what occurs on the delivery table is very pertinent to what will transpire later in the marital bed and that mother-baby relationship without enjoyable lactation is in a somewhat similar psycho-physiological position as a marriage without enjoyable coitus.

As a spouse fondles the mother's nipples during foreplay, toddlers, in all traditional cultures where breastfeeding is carried on for years, play with one nipple while nursing on the other. Writes novelist Kathryn Harrison of her eighteen-month-old, "He has recently stopped nursing, but still he touches me often and with a delight that has taught me that lust, at least in its first form, is innocent." Freud equated bliss at the breast with bliss after sex:

> No one who has seen a baby sinking back satiated from the breast and falling asleep with flushed cheeks and a blissful smile can escape the reflection that this picture persists as a prototype of the expression of sexual satisfaction in later life.

That women would find nursing a sensual experience makes evolutionary sense. The survival of the human race, after all, depended on how satisfied women were in maternity. And since babies were made to suckle frequently, the more pleasurable lactation was, the more it motivated mother to ensure frequency.

Dislike of nudity and sexuality, in contrast, which leads to aversion of breastfeeding, decreased milk production, and early weaning, defies evolution's ground rules, since it weakens the mother-infant tie and therefore the infant's survival. The commonality of these feelings in the United States reflects the degree to which forces in our culture debilitate natural maternal feelings and prohibit women from enjoying the full sensual nature of their bodies. And they help explain why some mothers do not try breastfeeding and, of those that do, why few stick with it past six months.

10

⊰⊱

Breast or Bottle?

It appears to be the fashion these days to disrupt all inherited patterns and to defy in a million small ways what nature seems bent on preserving.

—Kenneth L. Woodward (*Newsweek*, 1974)

Kelli Echagarrua of Boca Raton, Florida, nursed all four of her children, the shortest period for ten months and the longest for two years. When she went out—alone or with her spouse—a curious pattern developed. At the time she was scheduled to nurse, her nipples would start to leak. "Sometimes it was just a drop. At other times I would drip with milk. When I called home, I would often find my baby had been crying and that nothing the sitter could do would console my baby for any length of time. None of my babies would take the bottle, even though it contained breast milk. By the time I got home, my breasts were engorged and my baby's mouth was open wide like a baby bird ready to feed." Need anyone doubt that nature designed the woman's breasts first and foremost as a feeding tool?

Breastfeeding Benefits

⊱ Since mammals first roamed this earth, breast milk has literally been at the heart of our survival. An incredibly well-designed system, breastfeeding mutually regulates baby *and* mother, keeping the mother-baby system in balance both physiologically and emotionally.

For babies, breast milk is the ultimate health food, supplying their full component of nutritional needs and thirty-seven known immune mechanisms. Breastfeeding makes babies less susceptible to food allergies and is believed to promote growth of the gastrointestinal tract and to regulate digestive functions. Some evidence indicates long-term protection against at least some cancers, diabetes, and other major health problems. Since nursed babies do not overeat but instead self-regulate their feedings in tune with their physical needs, it may also help protect them against later obesity. Nursed babies also suck more vigorously than those who are bottle fed, which results in straighter, less crowded teeth and stronger jaw development. Preliminary data show breastfeeding may also improve infants' eyesight.

Breast milk may also be an IQ builder. One study showed an increase of eight IQ points in breastfed premature babies. A key ingredient, researchers speculate, may be the fat found in breast milk, known as DHA, which is part of the omega-3 family of fatty acids (derived from fish oils like salmon and tuna). If this is true, it's not coincidental that mothers throughout our evolutionary history have breastfed the first two to three years of life, when the greatest amount of brain growth occurs. Do we really want to rush weaning?

Nursed babies also swallow little air during feeding—the culprit in gas and indigestion and a frequent problem with bottle feeding (especially if the nipple is too big). Also, since infants are held vertically, on an incline, or on their side during breastfeeding, the air and milk in the baby's stomach is able to separate so that the air rises to the top and separates with ease. Incline positioning also helps prevent ear infections. In contrast, when lying flat, as bottle-fed babies frequently are, milk (full of bacteria) often seeps into the ear canals.

For babies carried throughout the day, as those in tribal societies, the continual upright positioning eliminates the need for burping or "bubbling." Writes Jean Liedloff of the Yequana, a tribe in the Venezuelan rainforest:

> The notion that nature has evolved one species to suffer from indigestion every time it drinks its mother's milk has, amazingly, not been questioned by civilized experts. . . . Yequana babies never require special treatment after nourishing themselves—any more than do the young of other animals.

As for mother, suckling not only serves to release the afterbirth but helps the mother to quickly regain her figure, completing the reproductive cycle that began with the fertilization of her egg. ("It's true," said one of my students. "When my baby was nursing, I could actually feel little tugs in my uterus.")

Psychological Benefits

Breastfeeding is the ultimate intimate experience between mother and baby. Sensual, intense, and about love, during nursing a mother holds her infant closer to her body than during bottle feeding, and tenderness exudes from her. Her baby is more turned into her mother's body than during bottle feeding and experiences greater warmth, support, relaxation, and tactile stimulation. And the baby can more easily touch her mother's body and face. Wrote Kabongo, a Kikuyu chief of East Africa, at age eighty:

> When I was hungry or thirsty [my mother] would swing me round to where I could reach her full breasts; now when I shut my eyes I feel again with gratitude the sense of well-being that I had when I buried my head in their softness and drank the sweet milk that they gave.

At birth, the newborn's suckling releases hormones in droves that elicit maternal nurturance. The first is oxytocin, the "cuddle hormone" that makes the mother want to hug and fondle her baby, strengthening the mother-baby bond. Next is prolactin, the "mothering" hormone, which rises as we nurse and hold our babies. The higher it is, the more we wish to mother.

Maternal radar, which perks up during close contact, allows mother to better sense her baby's need for a change of pace, wanting more, or being full. This increased sensitivity to her infant's cues, along with the greater physical closeness, increases the likelihood of secure attachment between mother and baby. Nursing also helps to reinstate the baby as an extension of the mother's body, mitigating the trauma of the abrupt separation from her womb and helping ease postpartum adjustment.

Human milk, free, always ready, at the right temperature, and needing no sterilization, presents virtually no delay when mother and baby are together and only minor delay when apart. Thus the nursed infant spends little time in a state of want, minimizing discomfort and frustration. Moreover, since breast milk contains less fat and protein than bottle milk— meaning babies become hungrier more often—nursing spurs more frequent mother-baby contact, which furthers bonding. Since their baby's cry creates a let-down reflex and milk drips from the mother's nipples, which makes delay uncomfortable, mothers also feel more inclined to breastfeed on demand. The result is babies who are more relaxed and less fussy.

La Leche mothers, who feed their babies more frequently than mainstream parents in this culture, can attest to this. When developmental pediatrician Ronald Barr and his colleague Marjorie Elias measured rhythmic crying in La Leche League babies, they found—to no one's surprise—that under two months of age, the more frequently fed babies of the La Leche mothers cried and fretted far less. The heart rate of breastfed babies, which is slower than those who are bottle fed, also reflects a more intact and relaxed nervous system.

Natural Feeding Frequency

How frequently was the human infant meant to feed? The answer may lie in the composition of human breast milk. In mammals with high-protein/fat content in their milk, such as deer and lions, babies are nested and fed every six to twelve hours. In mammals with low fat/protein milk content, such as apes, babies are fed frequently in short bouts, requiring continuous maternal availability. This is one of the reasons monkey babies are rarely off their mother's body the first few months of life.

A human mother, too, has milk low in protein and fat, suggesting our feeding style is more adapted to frequent snacking than gorging at a few grand meals when near starvation. Since this requires continual availability of the mother, and since the human infant suckles slowly, human infants were apparently fashioned to be carried, not nested and left to sleep alone like a baby bird with mother returning primarily to feed them.

The feeding pattern of the !Kung San infant, observed by anthropologist Melvin Konner, supports this. On the mother's body almost continuously the first few months of life and fed completely on demand, the !Kung infant suckles for a few seconds to fifteen minutes at a time, feeding up to four times an hour and several times during the night. When hungry or when wanting to suck for calming, he merely reaches out, seizes the omnipresent nipple, and suckles—no fussing, no delay, no frustration. This intense pattern continues for two years, only gradually declining until weaning, at around age three, when mothers usually become pregnant again.

This level of nursing would put most of us over the edge, but its advantages are numerous for infants in that culture, explains Konner. Frequent feeding assures frequent contact, necessary for the baby's survival in a predatory environment, and it provides the baby with essential immunities against disease. And since !Kung mothers don't have access to bottled milk nor ready-made pureed baby food, it ensures sufficient nutrition throughout the early years. And the frequent feedings and contact give infants a sense of calm and confidence they might not otherwise have, and give mothers intense pleasure, which strengthens the mother-baby bond.

Breastfeeding also provides natural family planning for cultures that rely on it. Frequent and prolonged breastfeeding releases prolactin, which suppresses the function of the ovaries and ovulation, making breastfeeding a natural contraceptive. Unlike us, !Kung women don't menstruate until they wean! Why doesn't it work for us as a contraceptive? For one, we don't feed frequently enough—Konner and colleague Carol Worthman found that the prolactin levels of the !Kung women were far above ours. Secondly, the intense physical activity of the !Kung keeps body fat low, suppressing ovulation. !Kung women not only actively forage but do so beginning shortly after birth.

This natural planning created a birth spacing of two to four years, which enabled the mother to devote her time to her infant until the child was relatively independent—nimble enough to run from a leopard in the distance, dexterous enough to reach up and pick berries off a tree for breakfast, and verbal enough to announce that daddy injured his foot and needs help. At this time, the mother weaned her child and became pregnant again.

In our culture, where planning is by choice, nature's program has been modified, and not always in the best interest of parent and child. Having infants too close together, for instance, drains parental resources—financially, physically, and emotionally. It takes a mother at least six months to physically recoup from pregnancy, and may take as long as nine months to erase all effects of an episiotomy. Getting pregnant again within the first year does not allow her body to recuperate. If mother wishes to nurse, both mother and baby will experience nutritional risk with each subsequent pregnancy. Carrying, feeding, and diapering more than one infant at a time with little help is also an exhausting physical burden that strains parental nurturing and deprives infants of necessary maternal care. Infants, left jockeying for a position on mother's shoulder, become more fussy and more demanding and often regress in behavior.

This does not mean we too should rely on natural birth control and become virtual feeding machines. We live in an entirely different ecological niche where few of us would want to spend our adult years either pregnant or lactating. Our environment requires, for survival, neither continual contact nor frequent feedings. In fact, twenty-four-hour carrying and feeding would be maladaptive in our highly mobile, fast-paced technological society. Infants are flexible enough to adapt to feeding more at one time and feeding less frequently, and the breast pump frees the mother from being sole feeder. Lacking extended family, this is important, for it means we can include the father in feeding baby.

Sucking their thumb or given a pacifier, our babies don't need to suckle our breast for non-nutritive sucking and calming. And, with the availability of baby food, we can wean early, supplementing feedings at six months of age with baby food that should assure proper nutrition. Moreover, with artificial contraception, we do not require frequent feeding for birth control.

Nevertheless, given that babies were designed to eat frequently and mothers to feed frequently, the closer we match nature's plan, the greater the benefits. Physiologically, frequent nursing, along with sucking for the sake of sucking, increases excretion of lipase (an enzyme that helps with digestion), increases how much milk the baby ingests, and increases early weight gain. Psychologically, the more we maintain closeness to our infant and minimize delay to the hunger cry, the greater the protection and comfort of our infant, as well as closeness and social exchange during feeding. Of course, for almost all of human history, mothers have had no choice *but* to nurse or give their infant to another mother to nurse. It's only since the emergence of bottle feeding that mothers have options.

The Emergence of Bottle Feeding

❧ Bottle feeding was introduced during the Industrial Revolution in order to free working mothers from needing to be continually available. With the invention of public transportation, it meant mother needn't be tied down. The pediatric community recommended it over nursing for most of this century, even hoping—falsely—that scientific formulas could improve upon breast milk. As for breastfeeding, it was equated with low status—something that the poor, immigrants, or animals do. Few of us had mothers or grandmothers, if they grew up in America in the first half of the century, who were nursed.

Mothers during the early part of the century, influenced by the early behaviorists, bottle fed on a rigid four-hour schedule, which minimized mother/infant contact and left hungry babies to cry in frustration for long periods, straining some babies and mothers beyond the limit of adaptability. Depleting energy reserves, persistent crying left some infants too exhausted to nurse once the crying stopped. This was particularly nonadaptive in the first weeks of life, when infants need to conserve energy for growth.

There were long-term consequences as well. Laying down an association of frustration preceding feeding and satiation, frustration later triggered a desire for food, sending many scurrying to the refrigerator. In the extreme, this association leads to eating disorders, the scourge of our modern affluent society. Interestingly, anorexia nervosa and bulimia nervosa are found primarily in Western industrialized societies.

Predictably, pockets of resistance emerged against artificial feeding and rigid scheduling (most notably La Leche League) and turned the tide back in favor of breastfeeding. After a fifty-year decline, the American Academy of Pediatrics since 1978 has sanctioned breast milk as the best food for every newborn. Today, most nurse practitioners, obstetricians, and pediatricians encourage mothers to try nursing before bottle feeding.

Of course there's no harm in bottle feeding, if we find this a more comfortable arrangement than nursing, or if we have no choice. Whole generations of infants *have* grown up on bottle milk and survived well enough. Nevertheless, it makes good sense that if breastfeeding fits into our life, it's the best choice. Why then is it not more successful?

Breastfeeding Obstacles

🌱 Only one half of all American mothers breastfeed postbirth, and since 1984, the numbers are dwindling. Moreover, though 85 percent of all human cultures breastfeed two years or longer, of those mothers that begin nursing in the United States, only one in five will breastfeed for at least six months, and a full 29 percent stop by two months. And mothers wean early even though former U.S. Surgeon General Antonia Novello recommends that mothers nurse for at least one year, ideally two, and the La Leche League advises mothers to not set an age limit but to let babies wean themselves. In fact, mothers who nurse past infancy are looked down upon as weak hanger-ons and must brave ridicule—"You're *still* nursing?" Many become "closet nursers," doing so behind closed doors.

What's to blame for these statistics? Not modernization, necessarily. In Sweden, 98 percent of women giving birth leave the hospital breastfeeding, 80 percent are still breastfeeding after four months, and 60 percent after six months. But in Sweden, nudity and intimate touch are not associated with sexuality. Here, our shame about our bodies, along with a culture that encourages detachment of our baby from our body as early as possible, makes mothers feel uncomfortable about intense intimacy with their babies and with their bodies. The 1963 edition of the U.S. Department of Health book *Infant Care* states, regarding nursing:

> You may feel some resistance to the idea of such intimacy with an infant who, at first, seems like a stranger. To some mothers it seems better to keep the baby at arm's length, so to speak, by feeding plans which are not so close.

In Sweden, mothers also stay in the hospital as long as they feel necessary and a parent-friendly social support system provides all health benefits for mother and baby and a yearlong, at least partially paid, maternity leave.

But in the United States, the cards are stacked against the nursing mother from the onset. A mother's let-down reflex is influenced by her state of mind; any preliminaries to immediate breastfeeding postbirth, such as cutting the cord and washing and dressing the baby, which prohibits intimate skin-to-skin contact between mother and baby, can impede the let-down reflex for colostrum. Furthermore, postpartum complications (medical or postpartum blues), inadequate education regarding breastfeeding, and insufficient supports make many a mother too anxious to even start nursing. And mothers who must soon return to work may feel it's useless to begin.

Even if mothers get past those first barriers, sometimes infants just don't seem to latch on and suckle away. Mothers, fearful of starving their babies, give up and turn to the bottle. Infants, however, who come with mouths wide open, always know what to do. It's mothers, likely not to have observed a nursing mother, who don't necessarily know what to do; with a lactation consultant and patience, this can turn around (see the Resource Guide for more information).

Postbirth separation also impedes nursing success. Permitting the newborn to suckle within the first hour or two following birth latches mother and baby into the nursing lock and increases the likelihood of nursing success. But too often babies are taken away from their mothers after only a few minutes. If a mother was apart from her baby more than 40 percent of her hospital stay, one study found she was more likely to stop nursing before her child reached four months of age. Rooming-in should solve this problem. But since many hospitals separate the baby the first hours postbirth and during the night, rooming-in often occurs for only 40 percent of hospital stays.

Insufficient milk supply is another common problem, commonly related to lack of social supports. Anxiety inhibits the production of prolactin and oxytocin, which interferes with lactation. The less support, the more anxious the mother and the greater the likelihood of failure-of-milk-flow.

Other mothers succeed at nursing but discontinue it as too inconvenient and incompatible with their lifestyle. Others do not begin nursing or stop soon after beginning because they can't tolerate the intense closeness.

And then there's the make-up of the human breast. Made to function !Kung style, repeated suckling works best. With less frequent feedings, the breasts can become engorged. As overloaded breasts try to disgorge their milk, they can flood the baby, who then vomits the milk up.

Furthermore, babies, if kept waiting, may be unduly ravenous, and may continue to suckle at the breast after the milk supply is gone. This causes damage to the breast and cracked nipples. In other words, the more spaced out the feeding, the greater the likelihood of the baby getting too much milk at once and then not enough afterward. Causing both physical discomfort for the mother and worry that her milk supply is deficient, some mothers feel too discouraged to continue breastfeeding.

Uncomfortable engorgement is especially common in the first two to four days after birth. With our short hospital stays and lack of postpartum guidance, some mothers, easily discouraged, give up quickly. And even if they make it through this period, cracked and sore nipples and nipple pain turn breastfeeding into agony rather than ecstasy. One mother I know spent two weeks crying in the shower as she washed her painful nipples. After four weeks, she gave up nursing.

If mother turns to the experts for advice on how frequently to feed, she meets varying opinions. La Leche League advocates feeding on demand. Dr. Benjamin Spock advocates establishing a four-hour feeding schedule almost immediately, as do many pediatricians. Advice like this can leave the inexperienced mother unprepared for just how often nursed infants *can* get hungry and lead the mother to *expect* her nursed baby to eat only every three to four hours. If her baby cries "in between" feedings, she may dismiss hunger as the cause, or else recognize that her baby is hungry but worry there might be a problem, throwing further doubt into her lactation competence.

And there's a further nursing deterrent—our separate sleeping policies. Because breastfeeding mothers feed more often, this means more trips during the night to the nursery and less sleep. Unless, of course, the mothers sleep with their infants. But this, in our culture, is not encouraged.

11

Co-Sleeping Taboos

To love the tender
heart hath ever fled
As on its mother's breast the
infant throws
Its sobbing face, and there in
sleep forgets its woe.
—Mary Tighe, Irish poet

In the summer of 1970 I was on my way to a youth hostel in Paris when I was stopped by a small, sprightly woman. It's unsafe in the hostel, she said: I should come home with her. Intuitively, I trusted her. Her small walk-up apartment on the third floor consisted of a kitchen, a living room, one bathroom, and two bedrooms—one for her and her seven-year-old granddaughter, and one for her daughter and son-in-law and their other two children, a two-year-old and four-year-old. Her teenaged son slept on the couch in the living room.

Where, I wondered, was I to sleep? With her, of course. Her granddaughter, who usually shared her bed, would sleep in the room's little daybed, too small for me.

Before going to bed, we chatted in the living room, they patiently listening to my college French. All three grandchildren stayed with us, the older daughter near her grandmother and the two little ones next to their parents. No one insisted the children go to bed. There were no interruptions, no tantrums. While we spoke, they sat quietly staring at me, leaning against their parents. Slowly, the two little ones drifted into sleep. When we retired for the night, the parents lifted them up and carried them to their, the parents', bedroom.

Years later at a conference, I asked a leading developmental psychologist from Harvard, who had done field work in Africa, what he thought of co-sleeping. "It's okay if you're enmeshed," said he. This family was enmeshed—in kindness, in warmth, in generosity, and in humanity.

The Co-Sleeping Taboo

↜ The Swedes do it, the Japanese do it, the Africans, Mexicans, and Eskimos do it. In fact, in most of the world, mother and baby co-sleep and always have. But when a baby is born in this country, she generally goes directly home to her beautifully decorated nursery. Some newborns will sleep alone in their crib from day one; others will sleep in a bassinet next to their mother's bed for the first few months or so before being transferred to their own room. A small proportion of babies will sleep with their mother; she will usually not advertise it.

In the United States, co-sleeping is taboo, discouraged by almost all the leading child care experts as "unnatural"; most advise a "holding curfew" for after 11 P.M. In Benjamin Spock's 1985 edition of *Baby and Child Care*, he recommends never allowing your baby to sleep with you. If your baby cries when put to bed, the cure is to "walk out of the room, and don't go back." After a few nights of crying "furiously" for ten to thirty minutes, the baby will tire and stop. If unable to tolerate the crying, parents "can muffle the sound by putting a rug or blanket on the floor and a blanket over the window." Also, "It's important not to tiptoe in to be sure the baby is safe or to reassure her that you are nearby." If the baby vomits while crying, this may be deliberate, the result of anger, and "it is essential that parents harden their hearts to the vomiting if the baby is using it to bully them."

T. Berry Brazelton, a strong contemporary influence on parents, also views separate sleeping as necessary to develop self-reliance. He encourages parents to allow their infant "to develop his own pattern for getting himself to sleep." It may take time to get baby to sleep independently, "but it's worth it."

Not only are parents discouraged from co-sleeping, they are discouraged as well from holding and rocking their baby to sleep. "What is best for almost all children after the first few months of life," writes Richard Ferber in his popular book *Solve Your Child's Sleep Problems*, "is to learn to fall asleep in a crib or bed alone in a room that is fairly dark and quiet. They should not be held, rocked, or nursed. . . ." Allowing children to fall asleep in your arms, Ferber contends, is the core of all sleeping disturbances: When the infant awakens during the night, he is unable to fall back to sleep on his own.

Should the infant be unable to manage separation while awake, Ferber offers charts that map out a general decrease over seven nights of how many minutes to let your child cry before soothing her, how many minutes a night to close the door if your child will not stay in bed. If you give in to your tendency to take your child into your bed, you are "taking the easy way out."

By implication, co-sleeping is potentially anxiety-producing for our children, leading to dependency and psychological damage. If we as parents engage in it, we are wimps. Little wonder most mothers feel compelled to persist in getting their infant to sleep alone until the infant (and they) "adjust." If baby does not, he will be labeled as having a sleeping problem. If a mother is too weak to let her baby cry it out alone in a crib and sneaks baby into bed, *she* will be labeled the problem. Why such drastic measures to do what infants, if they're tired and in their parent's arms, will do instantaneously?

The crib may be tailor-made for the needs of modern parents, but by dividing infants from their source of physiological stability and psychological protection, it is an evolutionary misfit. Since no organism adapts easily to something perceived as inherently unsafe, babies protest unwillingness to sleep in the crib because it is out of proportion with their basic need for protection. In this sense, separate sleeping, not social sleeping, is deviant.

Co-Sleeping Is Universal

Our assumption that solitary sleeping is the norm and "natural" for infants is cultural myopia. For two million years, human beings and their hominid ancestors co-slept. In 136 societies sampled around the world, mother and infant shared a bed in two thirds of them; in the remaining societies, the babies were placed in the same room with their mothers. All babies regularly slept with their mothers until weaning. The sleeping arrangement we accept as routine—an infant in his or her own nursery—exists nowhere else!

In Bali, an infant sleeps and wakes without moving out of the parent's arms. In Alaska, the whole Inuit Eskimo family traditionally slept cuddled naked. In Cuna in Panama, infant and mother sleep together in a hammock. In Ngoni, infants, parents, and other children sleep together on a reed mat. In Korea, couples do not think of buying a two-bedroom home until their child is six to seven years of age. In Japan, the infant sleeps with his mother until age five, after which the child sleeps usually with a sibling or a grandparent. The only time the Japanese sleep alone is during adolescence. They think of our separate sleeping practices as heartless. Guatamalan mothers, when told of our separate sleeping arrangements, expressed pity. In fact, up until almost sixty years ago, explains anthropologist James McKenna of Pomona College in Claremont, California, we would have considered isolating a baby during the night tantamount to child abuse.

Born with Innate Fears

Co-sleeping has always had survival value, both physical and psychological. In the past, if mother and infant shared a bed, a hammock, a cot, or a nest, the baby was better protected from predators, and both stayed warm. (Witness how baby animals never sleep alone but sleep curled up beside, on top of, underneath, and pressed against mother, brothers, and sisters.) With baby at her side, mother could then sleep better knowing her baby was safe; baby could sleep better knowing mother was protecting him.

After millennia of co-sleeping, how do we tell our nervous system and our baby's just to "relax" when sleeping alone? We can't. When we sleep alone, the night seems darker, the room colder, the thunder louder, the shadows dancing on the wall more sinister. Says a 1970 cartoon by Ketcham showing a young child standing at the foot of his half-sleeping parents' bed, "It's easy for you to say, 'Don't be afraid of the dark' . . . You got somebody to sleep with!"

Children are born with innate fears of things that can harm: darkness, which makes us less aware of danger; being alone, in which we lose protection from another; loud, close, and sudden noises, which indicate possible predators; loss of physical support, leaving us vulnerable to falling; and fear of strangers, who might harm us, and of heights, from which we could fall. Our brain interprets any of these conditions as a disaster waiting to happen.

The more clustered these conditions, the more anxious the infant and the more urgent the need for body contact. An infant in her own room is both alone and in the dark, sufficient conditions for her nervous system, if she's awake, to flag "danger." Add loud noise, like a thunderstorm, and all her survival reflexes go on red alert.

Nor is this response avoidable since infants periodically awaken during the night. In the first four months of life, they cycle in and out of light and deep sleep about every three hours. As they come into light sleep, they easily awaken due to noise or their own movements, often crying, sometimes startling. If they don't feel us as the cap of darkness covers them, there's no consolation. They perceive themselves as invisible and are too young to know we are sleeping in another room. Left feeling alone and unprotected, they must get themselves back to sleep in a condition in which they feel inherently unsafe. "Protect me!" says their cry.

That cry also says "put me back together," for separation is more than a psychological feeling of vulnerability for the young, immature infant. It means they also must achieve physiological stability independently—a daunting task. Night awakenings and the distress that accompanies them signal their inability to do so unassisted by their mother's body.

But if infants feel our presence, they feel safe from feelings of isolation, vulnerability, and disorganization and resettle easily. Writes Jean Liedloff of the Yequana infants of the Venezuelan rainforest:

> Happenings that would frighten an unprepared adult are barely noticed by an infant in arms. Figures loom close above his eyes, treetops spin high overhead. Things go dark or light without warning. Thunder and lightning, barking dogs, deafening roars of waterfalls, splitting trees, flaring fires, surprise dousings in rain or river water do not perturb him.

After four to five months, sleep states stabilize for the average American infant, and many now sleep through the night—or at least they seem to. In truth, they're still awakening once or twice, but two-thirds—the "self-soothers"—return to sleep without alerting the parent. The others—the "signalers"—are considered to have sleep problems. That the majority of infants adjust to sleeping alone attests to the supreme adaptability of the human species. But it does not mean infants *prefer* to sleep alone. Rather, it likely means they've learned that their cry will not bring a pick-up.

In the second year, discomfort with sleeping alone often intensifies, as children become more capable of using their imagination. At this time, nightmares start. Now able to crawl out of bed, they're also able to crawl into the parents' bed. In fact, it's not unusual for infants to appear to cope with separate sleeping only to begin co-sleeping with their parents in the second year of life.

Sleep Disturbances

In seconds I am washed, powdered, clean-clothed, and brought to
secret smiles in the dark. I ride, the young prince, in her arms to
their bed, and am welcomed in the blessed dry warmth between
them. My father gives me a companionable pat and falls back to
sleep with his hand on my shoulder. Soon, they are both asleep. I
smell their godlike odors, male, female. A moment later, as the
faintest intimation of daylight appears as an outline of the window
shade, I am wide awake, blissful, guarding my sleeping parents, the
terrible night past me, the dear day about to dawn.

                —E. L. Doctorow, *World's Fair*

❧   Of all childhood memories, is any more poignant than slipping into
sleep locked safely in our mother's or father's arms? And is any more frightening than those long nights alone? Child psychologist Bruno Bettelheim
once said that children look forward to summer camp not so much because
of all the fun and games but because it's a summer-long pajama party—a
break from nightly fears!

Solitary sleeping can be a time of separation, loneliness, anxiety, and
fear of sleep that breeds uncertainties and insecurities in our children and
explains why many behave at bedtime as if banished to a dungeon. Even T.
Berry Brazelton, who readily admits his discomfort with co-sleeping as a
personal bias from his own childhood, says that being alone in a bed is a lot
to ask of a child. Yet, most parents do ask just that.

Solitary sleeping, which defies our need to feel protected in inherently
unsafe circumstances, results in a plethora of sleep disturbances: difficulty
falling asleep, difficulty staying asleep, and frequent nightmares. Suffered by
some 30 to 40 percent of all American children, Brazelton calls sleep problems *the* major problem in American childhood today. Behaviors like teeth
grinding and bed-wetting may also relate to solitary sleep.

Trying to cope with a child's nighttime distress puts a strain on families
and has spawned a burgeoning business on how to help overwrought parents modify their children's sleeping habits. Books and numerous articles
tell us how to get our child to sleep and most major cities have special sleep
clinics.

We have our props as well. To counteract darkness, we have the nightlight. To counteract loneliness, we have the teddy bear. To counteract
potential danger, we use the baby monitor. To counteract fears and separa-

tion anxiety, we enact rituals at bedtime: a song, a story, or a dance. And all help, but they cannot replace the security of a warm, live body nearby. This is why the rituals continue ad nauseum—to give children the needed proximity to their parents, their source of security (which they require to relax into sleep). We can prevent their nocturnal sojourn to our rooms by locking our doors and theirs, but we can't lock away the fear inside.

Sleep disturbances in infants occur as both bedtime protest and night awakenings. Both a casualty of separate sleeping in Western industrialized nations, they scarcely exist in most traditional cultures. To begin with, there is no bedtime. Since children will not have separate sleeping quarters, babies and young children stay with their family and fall asleep wherever they are, when sleepy. In Japan, parents stay with their children until they fall asleep. If the child is not ready to sleep, the parent, rather than create anxiety, will let the child fall asleep and then move the child. This eliminates transitioning to sleep as a painful form of separation and the hullabaloo that often accompanies it, and it eliminates forcing babies and young children to fall asleep before they're ready. Not surprisingly, there's little report of sleep problems in Japanese infants.

Not needing to transition from being with others to being alone, children do not require the bedtime rituals, transitional objects, or self-soothing techniques that our children do. Thumb-sucking, for instance, has been noted as practically nonexistent in co-sleeping cultures from Africa to Tahiti, Japan to Mexico. Psychologist Gilda Morelli found no babies who sucked their thumb among the co-sleeping Mayan in Guatemala. Nor did any require the "lovies" our children lug into bed with them. The exception was one little girl who took a little doll to bed. This child was the only one who had had a bed for a time by herself.

Slumbering away within a protective environment, nighttime arousals are not a trauma, as with our children, but an occasion for momentary pats of reassurance and quiet words, neither of which need disrupt parent or child's sleep.

Feeling more secure and accepted, co-sleeping children learn to associate sleep with closeness and comfort, instead of abandonment and anxiety. Learning that comfort comes from people, not from objects, they have greater trust in human relationships. "At night when there was no sun to warm me, her arms, her body, took its place," wrote the African chief Kabongo at age eighty of his mother, "and as I grew older and more interested in other things, from my safe place on her back I could watch without fear as I wanted and when sleep overcame me I had only to close my eyes."

Maternal Separation Anxiety

Infants and children are not the only ones to suffer from separation anxiety at bedtime; mothers do as well. Unsuited to leave her baby to slumber away from the immediate protection of her body, rest comes with a perpetual soldier's readiness to pop up at the slightest rustle of the crib, turning mothers into zombies. According to the National Commission on Sleep Disorders Research and other experts, parents of young children are among the highest groups at risk for sleep disorders. When babies sleep in a separate room, a mother, upon hearing her infant cry, jolts out of sleep, dashes out of bed, and makes her way to her baby's bed. This means that both mother and baby are likely to become fully awake and that baby is more likely to cry. If the crying persists, the baby may be difficult to calm.

Even if babies, as they cycle into light sleep, only move or whimper, which may not require mother getting up to check on baby, mothers arouse from sleep. A new mother's hearing is extraordinarily sharp, primed to remain vigilant of her baby's safety; the slightest sound awakens her. Even if baby successfully gets herself back to sleep, mother, now fully awake, may not immediately nod off. Moreover, mothers wake to check on their babies even when not awakened by a noise.

Loss of sleep probably has much to do with the high incidence of postpartum blues and depression in new mothers. Wake up someone every three hours, as mothers can be, and they don't make it to rapid eye movement (REM) sleep in a qualitative way. People deprived of REM sleep begin to cry and get disorganized. With mother emotionally on edge, her infant's cry becomes more grating, affecting her mothering capacity. The spousal relationship suffers as well.

During co-sleeping, on the other hand, often neither mother nor baby are fully awake. If baby is in bed with mother, when baby transitions into light sleep mother may sense it through a stir or a whimper. Pulling her baby into the protection of her body, the comfort of the mother's touch settles baby and neither need to awaken fully. Knowing that her baby's cry won't keep her up, mother is more relaxed and sleeps better, as does father.

Breastfeeding and night sleeping make especially good bed partners. Since nursed babies feed more often and will wake during the night for a longer period of time than will bottle fed babies, making awakening once or twice during the night to feed baby unavoidable, having baby in bed is convenient. In fact, when co-sleeping, a mother often anticipates a feed, awaking around 30 seconds before her baby and offering her breast before baby begins crying and fully awakens both. Not surprisingly, nursing mothers tend to take the baby into their bed more so than those that bottle feed.

Nevertheless, most do so with some reservation, as cultural ghosts beneath the covers whisper all the untoward things that could happen during the night.

Co-Sleeping Myths

Threat of Suffocation

"Each year approximately 273 infants [age] one year and under suffocate," writes Heather Paul, in *Parents* magazine "and sadly, some of those deaths are caused by seemingly harmless things. For example, a mother takes her infant into her bed to nurse her, then lets the baby spend the night in the adult bed. The baby turns her face toward the pillow and can't breathe." The article continues: "There is also the danger of the baby's rolling and getting trapped between the mattress and the headboard or between the bed and the wall." To protect your infant, "always put your baby in her crib for sleep."

Co-sleeping does have the risks mentioned above, such as soft bedding or the possibility of the baby getting caught between the mattress and the headboard. It is also recommended never to sleep with your baby on a waterbed. But the implication in this article is that *taking* your baby into your bed is dangerous.

The real deterrent to co-sleeping is a pervasive fear that the mother could roll over and suffocate her baby. In the seventeenth century, laws were passed in England, Germany, and France threatening parents with jail should they be caught in the same bed with their infants. The reason? Infanticide. Poor people, unable to feed their families, were killing their infants by "accidentally" rolling over on them as they slept. Without means of contraception, infanticide has been practiced throughout history to rid parents of babies they couldn't take care of; it's still practiced in many parts of the world.

Should we be concerned today about smothering our baby? Probably about as concerned as our baby strangling himself by getting caught between the crib slats. In other words, it happens, but in normal circumstances rarely and parents can take cautions to minimize those risks.

Our fear of rolling over on our babies and suffocating them is out of proportion with the facts. When we sleep, our proprioceptive sense—our awareness of ourselves in space—remains active. This is why we do not fall out of bed or tend to roll over onto our dog or cat. Most incidents of rolling over occur because parents are under the influence of drugs or alcohol.

If we did roll over on our babies, they would likely protest. Born with strong survival reflexes, newborns have from birth a strong gag reflex and will squirm and cry if uncomfortable. "One can hardly choke or smother a newborn," says T. Berry Brazelton. (If fathers, because they are bigger, worry more, they may feel more confident if mother sleeps between them and baby.)

To Sleep, Perchance to Touch

Some parents don't co-sleep because of a concern it could lead to incest. Just as an equation of sexuality with touch can interfere with successful breastfeeding and the freedom with which parents fondle their naked baby, so too can it send babies off to the crib. T. Berry Brazelton lists "strong fears in our culture that co-sleeping could lead to sexual abuse" as one of the reasons he does not recommend co-sleeping. Social workers today often voice the same concern, and adoption agencies, in qualifying prospective parents, often require the parents to have a separate bedroom for the baby. Richard Ferber really appears to sexualize co-sleeping, writing that it is not good for a toddler to displace his father in the parental bed and to sleep "on top of the mother" or to be "allowed to twirl her hair or scratch her face as she falls asleep."

These attitudes have historical roots. In the seventeenth and eighteenth centuries, tales of incest between pubescent daughters and their fathers began to make their way into the Catholic confessionals. This, along with the fear of the repercussions of observing the sexual act, led the Catholic Church to advocate separate sleeping arrangements for parents and children.

Additionally, parents worried that children might interfere with the marital relationship, especially with sexual relations. Infants and children suddenly perceived as competitors that might threaten the sanctity of the marital bond, the family bed converted into the marital bed. This view was reinforced in the twentieth century with the introduction of the Oedipus complex into the family psyche.

Why We Emphasize Self-Reliance

If the Oedipus complex is a universal phenomenon, it does not seem to have affected sleeping arrangements in Japan, where it is tradition for the baby to sleep between mother and father on their futon. They call this sleeping arrangement *kawa*, or "river." The mother is one bank, and the father is another, while the infant is the river itself. Sleeping in this tactile sandwich leads to harmony and interdependency, the qualities Japanese culture strives for. When there is more than one child, the father moves out of the bed to make room.

In our culture, striving not for interdependence but independence, we fear that co-sleeping not only wrecks our sex life but creates "enmeshment," everyone entangled in everyone else's business, emotional and otherwise. This concern stems from the view that independence needs to be taught. And since sleeping with us acts as a reward, we worry that our children will be unable to wean themselves from the family bed.

But there's a fundamental flaw in this thinking. Autonomy is not taught but built into the organism. What interferes with autonomy is not co-sleeping but anxious attachment or extreme stress. Co-sleeping children, if not prematurely forced out of the parental bed, will generally leave on their own. Some, by age two or three, start desiring their own private space for belongings. Playing musical beds, they spend one night in their own bed, one night with a sibling, one night back in bed with the parents, one night on a mattress on the floor next to the parental bed. By age four or five, the time when children start closing the bathroom door for privacy, they usually sleep independently by choice, returning to the parental bed only during times of stress.

But readiness varies. One mother I know has only recently weaned her six-and-a-half-year-old—described as "easygoing and well adjusted"—from her bed. At night, she would put him in his own bed. In the morning, she found him lying placidly next to her. "He got very good at being able to creep in without waking us," she says. Now he sleeps some nights alone, some nights with his brother, and occasionally with his parents.

In Thailand, some children regularly sleep with their parents until puberty. In certain cultures, even adolescents slip between the covers of the parental bed from time to time. When I taught in the Head Start program in Chicago, my aide, a loving, warm, and kind Mexican American, told me that both her boys, one aged ten and one aged fourteen, came into bed with her at night occasionally. She thought nothing strange about this.

Other Hispanic parents began to reveal similar stories to me, without embarrassment.

Most child development specialists would see this as a clear case of dependency. T. Berry Brazelton worries that the circumstances of some mothers in our culture lead to dependency. For instance, single mothers may use co-sleeping to assuage their own loneliness. Working mothers may use it to reweave at night the unraveling of the long separation of the day. But it's equally the case that, in father-absent homes, increased closeness between mother and child may comfort both. And sleeping with their child may give working parents the closeness they need to bond better with their children, as well as lessening the guilt of long separations.

There's little evidence that co-sleeping creates the dependency that so vexes American child development specialists. In fact, noted Abraham Wolf and Betsy Lozoff, "if leaving children to fall asleep alone truly fosters independence, it is perhaps surprising that during historical periods in the United States in which 'independence' was most vividly demonstrated, such as the colonial period or the westward movement, children were not likely to fall asleep alone." Actually, separate sleeping, which elicits strong needs for an attachment figure, could ultimately further dependency by leaving the child forever seeking the thwarted closeness. Lacking the needed security at night, children may have more difficulty separating during the day. In this respect, separate sleeping can actually impede autonomy.

Spacing Considerations

To a large extent, co-sleeping exists out of necessity; the Japanese and most of the rest of the world do not have the luxury, as we do, of large dwellings with extra rooms for separate sleeping. But, though a consideration, space holds less weight than cultural values. Mayan mothers, for instance, appear to co-sleep because of the kind of relationship they want with their children, not because of space limitations. And in a study of sleep patterns in the United States, working-class families living in homes with many rooms still kept their infants with them, while professional-class families with small living space kept their baby separate, even if it meant putting a crib in the kitchen.

Consider my friend Sarah. Living in a two-bedroom apartment in Chicago, she felt the nursery was too cold for her baby in winter. So this very concerned and loving mother put the crib in her bedroom. Where did she and her husband sleep? In the living room. She felt it necessary to inconvenience herself to assure her baby's well-being. Co-sleeping was not a consideration.

In the Appalachian region of the United States, we find unusual family solidarity. The children, desiring the benefits of an extended family, often build homesites next to their parents. Susan Abbott, a professor of anthropology at the University of Kentucky in Lexington, credits co-sleeping for the increased attachment in adulthood in this community. There, more than 65 percent of infants sleep with or near their parents through the first two years of life: Space does not seem to enter into the equation. She quotes Verna Mae Slone, a seventy-five-year-old Knott County, Kentucky, woman, in her 1978 autobiography, *Common Folks:* "How can you expect to hold on to them later if you begin their lives by pushing them away . . . ? These new mothers are losing two of the greatest blessings that God gave mothers—the pleasure of sleeping with your child, and letting it nurse. A closeness that cannot be understood unless you have experienced it."

Long-Distance Baby

One reason for the large number of infants today who sleep in separate rooms is the invention of the baby monitor—the answer to loss of maternal night protection. Should baby begin to cry, cough, or sneeze, mother is able to hear and decide if a quick response is needed without having the inconvenience of having baby in bed with her.

At the heart of this practice is the notion that our infants *can* go it alone at night, making it all right to replace our presence with the baby monitor. But this is incorrect from an evolutionary perspective, explains anthropologist James McKenna of Pomona College in California. "Rather than pump the baby electronically into the parent, we need to pump into the baby the parent's sounds, air, smells, movements, and warmth."

During co-sleeping, parent and baby don't share just bed, they share oxygen, noises, smells, temperature, touches, pressure against the skin, movements, radiant exchanges, arousals, and sleep patterns. This sensory richness, explains McKenna, affects each of them continuously in the most fundamental ways and may "confer certain physiological and psychological advantages on infants that solitary sleep environments do not provide."

Temperature exchanges are a good example of this. If baby sleeps in the mother's arms, the mother's body regulates the infant's thermoregulation needs. If lying next to mother, the mother can usually immediately detect, by movements or frets, any change in temperature needs. If mother and baby sleep nude and mother nurses, awareness and thermoregulation are at their height.

Other things happen as well when huddling together. Mother and baby have more frequent arousals. Sleep stages and waking periods are synchronized about 45 percent of the time between mother and baby. When the baby is restless, mother is likely to be in light sleep. When baby wakes, mother is likely to wake and vice versa, and they will stay awake together for at least fifteen seconds. This synchronization begins in the womb, where maternal REM periods and fetal activity often match one another. Synchronization of sleep cycles helps account for the co-sleeping nursing mother's ability to anticipate a feed and awaken before her baby. Further, it means mother is less likely to awaken from a deep sleep state when baby starts to stir or cry.

For babies, it means they arouse more often and spend less time in deep sleep or NREM sleep. Babies who sleep separately, in contrast, sleep longer and more deeply, allowing them to sleep through the night earlier than those who co-sleep, the average being between four to five months of age. In our culture, this appears an advantage. The sooner a baby sleeps through the night "all by himself," the more grateful the parents for having such a "good" baby. If he does not sleep through the night independently by four to five months of age, the parent will worry their baby is off schedule. In a parenting magazine, a renowned parenting educator, as her advertisement professes, offers "expert" newborn care. With her help, your infant "will sleep through the night by three weeks!"

But are young babies neurologically mature enough to handle long periods of uninterrupted sleep? Though conventional wisdom says they are, McKenna points out a fundamental flaw in this thinking. The four-to-five-month milestone is derived from infant sleep studies done on solitary, bottle fed, sleeping babies. This misleads American parents to believe that all infants should be sleeping through the night at this age.

In fact, babies who co-sleep, and especially those nursed, do *not* begin to sleep through the night until around eight months of age. Since co-sleeping is the evolutionarily correct pattern of sleeping, McKenna wonders whether all babies are biologically capable of handling early prolonged and uninterrupted sleep. Our insistence that they do so prematurely may be unrealistic, putting unnecessary pressure on them and accounting for at least some of the complaints of sleep disturbances. Changing our expectations and viewing these night awakenings as normal and expected may aide parents in better coping with them. Furthermore, arousals have survival value, particularly during co-sleeping.

Following these arousals the baby's breathing and heart rate change. For instance, babies who are aroused breathe more rhythmically. This is important. Respiration, like other physiological systems, is immature during infancy. Human infants breathe quickly; sometimes they have apneic episodes and stop breathing altogether for several seconds. When co-sleeping, infants hear and feel the parent breathe. Entraining to these rhythms, they respond by breathing in synchrony with the parent, which helps stabilize their own breathing.

Likewise, the vestibular stimulation felt from the up-and-down movement of the parent's chest creates similar entrainment. For example, if you place a "breathing bear" set at a normal neonatal rate inside the incubator of a preterm infant, the infant will scoot close to the bear, which provides a similar constant source of rhythmic vestibular input, and will entrain to the rhythm of the breathing bear.

The baby's breathing is tied to its mother's rhythms even before birth. As if to practice for the outside world, the fetus breathes in amniotic fluid in utero. This breathing pattern responds to changes in the mother. For instance, the fetus's breathing increases between 4 to 7 A.M., when mother's glucose levels are falling. In other words, there is continuity from pre- to postnatal in the mother's physiological regulation of her baby. Other mammals, such as whales, also synchronize their breathing with their young's.

Lacking sensory cues from the parent's breathing, the baby must learn to readjust breathing independently. For a small group of especially vulnerable infants, this may make them more susceptible to a variety of disorders, including, as some have speculated, sudden infant death syndrome (SIDS).

SIDS

❧ At the start of the film *Terms of Endearment*, Aurora stands over her newborn baby Emma's crib, fearful she's stopped breathing and is dead from crib death. To allay her anxiety, she pinches the baby who, to her great relief, lets out a wail. This is a scene most new mothers identify with: What parent has not gotten up at least once during the night to check if their baby is breathing? We laugh at our own hysteria when we find our baby alive and well, but our fears are not entirely unwarranted. In the United States, approximately 5,000 to 7,000 babies less than one year of age die each year of sudden infant death syndrome (SIDS), sometimes called crib death.

No one knows what causes SIDS, and little is known about how to prevent it. What factors predispose an infant to SIDS? Everything from sleeping position to room temperature to bedding to how a child is fed, and, yes, whether the child sleeps alone or with his mother.

In urban societies where mothers and babies sleep separately, as in the United States, United Kingdom, Canada, and New Zealand, incidents of SIDS are the highest. In urban societies where mothers and babies co-sleep, as in Hong Kong, Stockholm, Tokyo, and Israel, incidents of SIDS are low. In Hong Kong, incidents are 50 to 70 times less common than in Western societies. In the U.S., Asian immigrants report fewer SIDS deaths, but the longer they live in the United States, the higher their rate of SIDS.

Sleep Position

When researchers began looking at commonalities among SIDS victims, one thing really stood out: They are twelve times more likely to be found lying on their stomach than on their back. This evidence initiated an aggressive campaign from pediatricians to get babies to sleep on their back or side, rather than their stomach, and it's made quite a difference. For the first time in twenty years, SIDS is decreasing worldwide. In England, the "back to sleep" campaign has reduced SIDS by 91 percent. And in Japan, where infants are traditionally put down on their backs, SIDS rates are the lowest.

Now for the critical question: In what position do babies tend to sleep when next to their mothers? When James McKenna and his researchers watched mothers and babies in a sleep lab, they found the answer. Babies position themselves next to their mothers on their sides, or backs, diagonally, within just a few inches of her face. Mothers, primed by evolution to protect their infants, almost always faced their infants during sleep. In other words, mother and baby were in the position least associated with SIDS and the one that maximized sensory exchanges.

In a sense, this is a mystery. Almost all mammals other than humans sleep prone. On his back, the infant is likely to startle, throw out his arms and legs, become upset and cry. Newborns sleep more in the prone position than in the supine and sleep better—there is less movement, more deep sleep, more regular breathing, less crying, and less apnea. If on their stomach when they come into light sleep and awake, the resistance of the bed generally subdues the infant's disorganized activity. Apparently, prone sleeping in and of itself is not the problem. Rather, it's prone sleeping in combination with other factors, such as overheating.

Heatstroke (hyperthermia), due to overwrapping, has been identified as a cause in many SIDS deaths. While on their stomach, babies lose less heat than when lying on their back, making them more vulnerable to overheating—especially if overbundled or swaddled. During co-sleeping, this risk is minimized: Were the infant to become overheated, the parent might feel the baby perspiring and make the necessary adjustment. But during separate sleeping, parents may be unaware of overheating, especially since babies may stay passive when hot (infants will cry when cold, which helps warm them) and therefore not alert the parent to a problem.

Furthermore, gauging the appropriateness of the room temperature by how comfortable they feel, separate sleeping parents err often in the direction of overdressing their babies when putting them to sleep. But a baby's body temperature is higher than ours, and babies are usually covered as well as warmly dressed (the room temperature generally recommended for a clothed newborn is 75 degrees). This helps explain why SIDS occurs more in the winter months, when babies are more likely to be overdressed and heavily covered. Cold weather is an additional risk factor since infants are sick more often in winter and SIDS episodes are often preceded by illness. In premature infants, increased room temperature has also been associated with increased apneic episodes.

While lying prone, babies are also more at risk for having their airway occluded by bedding, such as soft pillows or blankets, sheepskin mattresses, beanbags, or the changing mattress of a waterbed. If they stop breathing, they may be unable to turn their head far enough to resume respiration. Or they may take in the same air, which has more carbon dioxide and less oxygen, which can lead to death.

Nighttime Arousals

Part of the reason that people sleep better alone, explains Richard Ferber, is that movements and arousals of one person cause the sleeping partner to awake more frequently and thus sleep less well. However, says James McKenna, these arousals may be one of the very best reasons *to* sleep with your baby—especially those infants at risk for SIDS. Bed-sharing infants awake more frequently (for short transient arousals) than do solitary sleeping infants, even when they sleep alone. This suggests that co-sleeping encourages babies to sleep in a way more conducive to the infant's survival.

Some SIDS babies may die because of a failure to awake and breathe. While short breathing pauses, or apnea, are quite normal in infants, with SIDS victims, the hypothesis is that they stop breathing and their brains fail to tell them to begin to breathe again. In other words, SIDS victims may have a normal apneic episode but, in a deep sleep, then have difficulty in waking up. This makes solitary sleeping, in which infants learn to sleep longer without sensory interruptions from parents, undesirable for those infants at increased risk for SIDS. "If the infant's physiology enables it to sleep efficiently but does not yet enable it to arouse efficiently, these long uninterrupted sleep bouts could prove dangerous," writes McKenna.

But how do the frequent arousals that occur during co-sleeping reduce the risk of SIDS? McKenna feels they permit babies to rehearse responding to challenges by practicing learning to breathe again after an apneic episode. Since kangaroo care infants, asleep 50 to 75 percent of the time while lying on their mother's body, would be co-sleeping in a sense, Gene Anderson suggests that the fourfold decrease in apnea and bradycardia reported in these infants may relate to increased arousals and decreased deep sleep as compared to preemies sleeping alone in an incubator.

When we look at sleep cycles, we can further appreciate the usefulness of increased arousals. Newborns, who don't die of SIDS, spend 50 percent of sleep time in REM sleep. This lessens as they grow (although less quickly for nursed babies), and non-REM, or deep sleep, increases. SIDS peaks between two to four months of age, the time when infants are reorganizing their sleep cycles and moving away from sleep states dominated by REM and beginning to sleep longer in deep sleep. During this time, there's also a shift in breathing control. While young infants breathe reflexively, at this age a move begins toward greater interdependence between higher brain cortical structures that permit voluntary control of breathing and the lower brain stem structures that control automatic reflexive breathing. When intermediate NREM sleep replaces REM sleep or when infants dream, there may be a back and forth between voluntary and involuntary breathing. If infants are no longer entirely under the control of reflexive breathing and not yet capable of voluntary control, during an apneic episode, and especially in deep sleep, they may fail to resume breathing. Having a cold further increases vulnerability for babies who have not yet mastered efficient voluntary control over their breathing.

Co-sleeping might reduce the risk for SIDS in other ways. The vestibular stimulation received through the up-down movements of the parent's chest, as well as the little kicks, stirs, pushes, and turns of the parent's body against the infant's, may help stabilize the infant. Rocking and other types of movement also reduces incidents of apnea.

Then there are the gases exchanged while co-sleeping. The increased carbon dioxide from the parent's breathing, registered in the infant's upper nasal chemoreceptors, may fuel inspiration. Thus, during an apneic episode, merely breathing the same air as the parent might trigger the infant's breathing.

Feeding style may also relate to SIDS vulnerability. More bottle-fed babies die of SIDS than those breastfed. At the same time, a larger percentage of co-sleeping nursing mothers sleep with their infant than do those who bottle feed. And breastfeeding helps ward off respiratory infections. Furthermore, during co-sleeping, nursed infants feed twice as often as they do if they're nursed and sleeping alone, and they feed for longer periods. This elicits more mother-baby contact and increases sensory exchange and arousals. The !Kung, whose infants feed an average of four times an hour, report no incidents of SIDS.

Babies who sleep with their mothers also don't get into crying jags. This may be significant. Prolonged or exhausted crying during the night could compromise respiration in babies already at risk, explain anthropologists Melvin Konner and Charles Super. In infants whose glucose reserves are marginal, "long crying could conceivably deplete them to dangerously low levels." And if long crying is habitual, chronic hypoxia (insufficient oxygen intake) can occur. Moreover, the stress associated with crying also increases apneic episodes.

Should All Parents Co-Sleep?

It's not that solitary sleeping is a cause of SIDS, James McKenna is careful to point out. Rather, certain deficits in the infant collude with environmental factors to increase the risk that a certain class of infants could die of SIDS. For those, the protective physiological regulation that parental contact confers may substantially reduce the risk of "adaptive failure" that occurs as a result of the infant's immaturity, at least (potentially) for a small subclass of SIDS victims.

Mothers need not feel compelled to sleep with babies because it may decrease the chances for SIDS. Though rates are lower in co-sleeping mothers and babies, SIDS exists under all conditions, including co-sleeping, even when it lacks other risk factors.

Mothers should sleep with their babies because they want to, and many do. In fact, in spite of our taboos, surveys indicate that some 25 to 30 percent of parents confess to routinely sleeping with their children for at least part of the night. Some parents start out by the book but switch to co-sleeping as other children come along and, parenting less daunting, increased confidence allows them to follow their gut feelings.

But for those parents who don't wish to, forcing social sleep will benefit neither parent nor infant. If parents find themselves too aware of their baby or that their baby is too restless, both will sleep worse, and exhausted parents cannot take adequate care of their infants. Though co-sleeping is what babies want, the secret is to find the best fit to both baby's and parent's needs. If a mother slept with her baby under coercion, the baby would sense it and both would suffer.

On the other hand, for those parents who wish to co-sleep, there is nothing unnatural or dangerous about bedding with baby. Few of us adults, given the choice, would opt to sleep alone. Why, then, should a tiny baby?

12

Crybabies

But what am I?
An infant crying in the night:
An infant crying for the light:
And with no language but a cry.
—Alfred, Lord Tennyson

When I began my doctoral studies, I was unsure what area of infant development I wanted to investigate. Then I attended a lecture by T. Berry Brazelton. He spoke of his work with the Zinacanecto Mayan Indians of Mexico, and how impressed he was that the babies, wrapped most of the day inside a rebozo on the mother's back, rarely cried. I decided then that touch would be my doctoral focus. I hate to hear babies cry, and in our culture babies cry *too much*.

Imagine the all-American baby: We picture a mouth in a wide "waaah!" Marc Weissbluth, director of the Sleep Disorders Center at Children's Memorial Hospital in Chicago, writes, "When my first son was born, he cried and cried for hours on end. Neither my wife nor I thought this was strange. We assumed that all babies behaved this way."

They don't. We assume they do because prolonged crying is common in our culture. In most other cultures, where babies remain close to their mothers, it's not. Much of the crying we consider normal baby behavior may be a separation distress call in response to stress.

The Crying Myth

☙ For prolonged crying to be normal and expected for infants, it would have to meet at least two conditions. It would have to be a universal characteristic of infants, which it isn't, and it would have to serve some important survival function, which it doesn't.

Accustomed to perceiving babies as crybabies, anthropologists studying carrying cultures—Brazelton with the Mayans, Melvin Konner with the !Kung San in Africa, Margaret Mead with the Balinese and Samoans, Richard Sorenson with the Fore in Papua, New Guinea, and Jean Liedloff with the Yequana of the Venezuelan rainforest—were all struck by how seldom the babies cried. Of course, it's not that carried babies never cry. Whether born in the Amazon jungle, the mountains of Tibet, or in Seattle, *all* babies cry and do so with some consistency. The difference between cultures lies in duration.

The !Kung baby, for instance, begins to cry as frequently as does the Western infant—about eleven times an hour for babies less than three months of age and seventeen times an hour after twelve months of age. But because of the mother's immediate response—within six seconds!—the duration is short. Thus, the !Kung baby cries about twenty-eight minutes a day. Our babies, in contrast, cry twice as long. I'm not sure this is in our infant's best interest.

Imagine the child's felt experience during crying. There is a visceral response, as the gut tenses up; an autonomic response, as breathing becomes labored and the heart pounds; a motoric response, as arms and legs stiffen and flail out into space and as facial muscles tense up; and a metabolic response, as stress hormones are released into the bloodstream. The longer the crying episode, the more stressed the baby and the more alarmed and stressed the mother. In the newborn period, it's especially stressful, and, as some have postulated, potentially harmful.

But it's more than bodily distress that makes prolonged crying undesirable. Extended crying expends energy and calories, draining an infant and particularly a newborn who must conserve energy to gain weight. It interferes with nursing and in our culture may discourage a mother from continuing to nurse.

Persistent crying can also affect sleep patterns. After crying for long periods, babies tend to cry themselves into a stupor. Bypassing light sleep, they go directly into deep sleep and, to conserve energy, sleep deeply for long periods—a primitive response to stress. "After crying furiously all night, my baby finally fell asleep and wouldn't wake up till the afternoon," one mother told me of her baby. Following routine circumcision, infant boys commonly fall into a long period of knocked-out sleep.

Long crying bouts even affect learning. For one, it takes time away from babies examining their world. Second, babies remember less when learning is followed by crying. For instance, let's say we put a new mobile in our two-month-old baby's crib and attach a string from the mobile to her left toe, so that when she kicks, the mobile moves. If we present the same mobile to her two weeks later, she's likely to remember how the animals bobbed up and down and automatically begin to kick her left leg in anticipation of the colorful show. But if, after the first time we presented it, she lay in her bed crying for five minutes after she tired of kicking, two weeks later she's less likely to remember the mobile. Thus, the more time spent crying, the less time spent learning.

Nor do exhausted babies interact with their parents; instead they go to sleep, minimizing time for parents and babies to get to know each other. The more a baby cries, the greater the risk of setting up a negative feedback cycle of difficult-to-calm babies and exhausted, drained, and resentful parents. Since this can cause parents to withdraw nurturance, which threatens the infant's well-being and, in extreme circumstances, leads to child abuse, letting the baby cry it out is indefensible from an evolutionary perspective.

In our ancestral environment, regular crying and mothers ignoring their babies' cries would have been a catastrophe, as anthropologist Wenda Trevathan notes. To begin, lustful crying would have been a dinner invitation to prowling lions and tribal enemies, placing vulnerable mothers and babies at risk. Moreover, to survive persistent crying, parents learn to tune out the cry. This means that, like the boy who cried wolf, a cry that needed immediate attention, like one of pain, might get ignored and imperil survival.

And crying grates on a mother's nerves, particularly if she is rarely separated from her infant. In cases of child abuse and infanticide, it is the cry that often causes the parents to snap. Evolution would have weeded out inconsolable babies, as well as mothers who let their babies cry without attention. In short, prolonged rhythmic crying is an evolutionary mishap, a defiance of the initial purpose of crying—to elicit caregiving.

What Does Crying Mean?

The cry, as any parent intuitively knows, is first and foremost a fine-tuned communication system to convey that something is amiss and needs to be changed. Before infants can talk, walk, cling, or gesture, it is their only means for communication. As such, it literally assures the infant's survival.

The newborn's cries indicate a need (feed me; change me; cover me; remove the covers; hold me; give me something to suck; put me to sleep; relieve my gas) and the primitive fears "I'm going to fall" or "too loud!" By three to four months of age, emotions become part of the infant's behavioral repertoire and "play with me, I'm bored or lonely" gets added to the list, as does fright. In the second six months of life, babies cry when confronted with a stranger: *"You're not my mommy."*

By four to six months of age, babies begin to make an association between what they do and what happens to them. Now capable of behaving intentionally to bring about a desired effect, they can now cry to get what they want. For instance, if they want to be picked up, they will hold out their arms. If refused, their mouth will pucker and tears will start to roll down the face; if received, they will reward you with a broad smile and gurgle. Before this time, they lack the mental maturity to behave intentionally; the notion that the cry could be a demand, as some parents perceive it, is alien to their brain.

To aide the parent in decoding their baby's messages and to respond on target, nature designed the cry with different sound nuances. The basic cry—which usually says "food!"—starts out with soft whimpers but, if unanswered, soon becomes a loud, full-throated rhythmic wail. When mothers hear this, they feel some tension and concern but not anxiety or dread. But when they hear a loud ear-shattering shriek and energetic gasping sounds—the nonequivocal "hurt!"—they scurry, prepared to go to any length to protect their infant.

A cry starting out with two or three long, drawn out cries without long periods of holding the breath says "frustrated," while a rhythmical but energetic cry says "mad!" At least that's how we interpret it; in truth, young infants don't get mad but rather disorganized or overwhelmed. That's why, suggests developmental psychologist Evelyn Thoman of the University of Connecticut, it's better to call it the "out of control" cry. Unless the infant is in pain, the prolonged rhythmic crying that we consider routine infant behavior is this "mad" cry.

Cracking the Crying Code from a Distance

When mothers are able to read their baby's cues and turn off the cry, they feel powerful. When they don't, they feel ineffective and often blame themselves. But cracking the crying code is not always easy, and especially not for new and inexperienced parents of young infants, who often tend to assume the cry to indicate primarily hunger or need for a diaper change. If both needs are satisfied, parents may be baffled as to the cause. And though a mother who is tuned in to her baby's signals begins to distinguish her baby's cries by two weeks of age, the most sensitive mother will, at times, be unable to decipher the cry and prevent uncontrollable crying.

Separation has much to do with this. As we are frequently apart from our infants, we must overrely on the cry sound as our Morse code. But when in touch with our babies, we not only hear the cry, we *feel* what our babies need, which allows us to respond before crying becomes necessary. If hungry, the baby wriggles, gives out little grunts, and mouths like a guppy, signaling her mother to feed her before crying begins. In contrast, on-demand feeding here means feeding as soon as the first cries are heard. If the baby starts to mouth when satiated, which indicates she wants to suck for self-soothing, mother can give the breast, help her find her hand, or offer a pacifier. If tired, her mother's rhythmic movements often lull her to sleep. If cold, her mother's body will warm her.

If baby needs a diaper change, mother knows instantly. Tribal mothers, as we recall, know beforehand when their babies need to urinate or defecate and hold them away from their bodies to do so.

The baby is never lonely nor, in the protection of her mother's arms, need she fear losing her balance, which eliminates the "hold me" and "I'm going to fall" cries. Nor is the baby likely to cry as a result of under- or overstimulation. Her mother's ongoing touch and intermittent stroking, rocking, and motherese talking keeps her brain titillated enough to prevent boredom, while being low-key enough not to overstimulate.

And as for the out-of-control cry: Since the cries of carried babies are immediately quelled, this cry would be uncommon, which leaves pain as the primary reason for a carried infant to cry for any length of time. In other words, secure that they will get suckled if hungry, rocked if sleepy, warmed if cold, protected if in danger, talked to if bored, and contained if jumpy, these infants learn to have little reason to feel threatened and, therefore, little reason *to* signal distress.

But when put down, the infant's sense of protection is lost, and life becomes potentially more dangerous. Enter the cry—nature's way of flexing her muscles to trigger maternal behavior to correct the distance by reestablishing contact, and thus restoring equilibrium. This is why babies generally stop crying when picked up: The sensation of warm arms enveloping them signals that help has arrived. When we delay answering the cry with a pick-up, we extend the time the baby feels in danger—both from what triggered the cry and from the consequences of crying itself.

Nor, once the cry starts, does it take long before it's out of control—ninety seconds on average. After this, babies become hard to soothe. Yet parents often wait for longer than ninety seconds. In fact, research shows that American mothers tend to wait an average of four to five minutes before picking up their infants—*even* crying newborns.

It's not unusual to witness babies crying and parents ignoring them. Preoccupied with other activities, parents often offer other interventions before picking up their babies: They put pacifiers or bottles in their babies' mouths, turn them over or place them on their side, pat their back, or shake, wheel, and frantically rock the buggy back and forth. Not until all these fail do many parents reach down and gather up their baby, who—to no one's surprise—usually quiets.

Were a hunter-gatherer mother to witness this commonplace scene, she would be dismayed. To a !Kung mother—her baby usually in her arms or nearby and her response immediate—our delay smacks of child neglect. In response to Dr. Spock's recommendation to not "spoil" babies by rushing to their side when they cry, one replied, "Doesn't he understand it's only a baby, that's why it cries? It has no sense yet, so you have to pick it up. Later, when it's older, it will have sense, and it won't cry anymore."

Of course, we don't need to respond to our baby's cry immediately. Nevertheless, our delay is far from nature's design of keeping our babies close and offering immediate comfort. Causing babies to cry more than they need to, and causing parents undue frustration and irritation, why *do* we tend to wait so long?

The Delay

In New Guinea, when a baby cries, the natives often remark in pidgin English *pikinini i cri.* It means the baby is crying to be close to his mother's skin, literally "skin to skin." In this country, when a baby cries, mothers are often dissuaded from holding their children close to their skin too soon or for too long. Instead, cultural values tend to encourage a mother to delay responding.

Viewing the infant as relatively physiologically independent and therefore capable of extended separation on the one hand, and on needing to learn psychological independence on the other, our battle cry for the first half of the century was "Let them cry it out." The cry was considered a complaint, a demand, or a manipulation for attention. (Such devious wiles for something so immature!) Giving in except at feedings times, parents were warned, would spoil their baby, who would then take control. Even Dr. Spock said, "The more parents submit to the baby's orders, the more demanding the children become." Consequently, babies cried and cried. Not to fear, reassured the experts, all that crying is just how babies behave.

Research backed up this contention. But there was an inherent bias here: They were done on Western infants. Since our standard care differs from that of most other cultures, they reflected not the biological nature of the infant but a cultural artifact. Consider two classic studies. The first, done in 1945 at the Mayo Clinic, concluded that newborns cry an average of two hours a day. But they looked at newborns in the nursery. Since we now know that newborns kept with their mothers in rooming-in rarely cry, these statistics represented not normal newborn behavior but a stressed response to a baby removed from its normal ecology—its mother's body.

The next extensive study was done in 1962 by T. Berry Brazelton, who found newborns to cry an average of two hours a day. This increased to about three hours per day at six weeks of age and then declined thereafter. By three months, babies averaged about one hour a day crying.

But look at the care provided. Mothers were encouraged to delay comfort—told to pick up their babies "every twenty to thirty minutes during crying periods." When they did pick up their infants, they managed to quell the cry, but unable to continue holding their children, the cry often quickly resumed. In other words, crying occurred while the baby was separated from mother, ceased when the baby was picked up, and resumed when the baby was separated again. The following is a "typical" description of a "fussy period":

> At one point each day, usually after a feeding, the baby would wake from a sound, contented sleep. Then he would begin to fuss in a whimpering discontented fashion. . . . Nothing [the mother] did helped. He was not hungry, wet, or dirty, would not accept a pacifier or his thumb. He would stop briefly if she held him or rocked him, but when she had to put him down to attend to one of the other children, he would start all over again.

Next, though initially advised to begin with a demand feeding schedule, most mothers quickly instituted "a more reliable but flexible three- to four-hour schedule." Since the unanswered hungry cry can quickly escalate to out of control, some extended crying was likely due to hunger. In a study of La Leche League mothers, who feed their infants more frequently and respond more promptly to their fretting than we do in standard American baby care, the babies cry far less frequently.

The statistics from the Brazelton study have become gospel and are widely quoted today. And though Brazelton would be the first to caution against generalizing them beyond the American infant, carefully stating that they reflect normal crying behavior for babies in our culture, they nevertheless perpetuate the myth that routine daily crying is business as usual. This reinforces the mother's impression that it is expected baby behavior, particularly in the newborn period. Not only is this erroneous but these findings do not necessarily generalize to all Western infants. They didn't to La Leche babies, nor did they to some lucky Canadian babies. Urs Hunziker and Ronald Barr of McGill University Faculty of Medicine in Canada asked mothers to carry their three-week-olds in their arms or in a soft body carrier for at least three hours a day, until the babies were three months old. The babies who received more carrying—four and a half hours compared to a little over two and a half for the control group—cried an amazing 43 percent less than the control group. And they cried 51 percent less in the early evening when babies are presumed most fussy.

Furthermore, contrary to Brazelton's findings, they found that infant crying did *not* peak at six weeks of age in the babies who were held more. At six weeks of age, the babies cried for a little over an hour a day, versus just over two hours a day for the control group and Brazelton's figure of three hours as the average for the Western infant.

Of course, it's not that modern mothers *want* their babies to cry. On the contrary, they want to make their babies as happy as they can. But the realities of modern life make this hard. Alone and lacking extended family and close community, mothers need breathers from the all consuming task of providing care to an infant. And so we place our infants in carts while we shop, and in cribs and playpens, divided from us for part of the day when home.

When we hear our baby cry, we're likely to be occupied washing baby clothes, answering the phone, helping another child with homework, or cooking dinner. This makes it easier to wait and hope it will stop on its own. And, at a distance, the cry is less piercing and thus less compelling. Moreover, physically and emotionally exhausted and overwhelmed with responsibilities, we are not always up to consoling our infant. "One day when Mickey was a baby," a friend told me, "I lost it. I dropped everything, sat down in the middle of the floor, stared at the undone laundry, stared at the unmade bed, and cried along with Mickey. We must have both cried for at least an hour until I finally dragged myself up from the floor."

Anxious Mother/Anxious Baby

When babies cry, mothers feel it in their gut—as they're supposed to. If inexperienced or, as we saw when talking about attachment, if a mother has her own issues about unresolved loss, she may get anxious. Consequently, rather than tone down stimulation, she may rev up her baby.

For instance, while waiting for her husband at the check-out counter of a busy hardware store, a new mother is trying to console her howling three-week-old infant. Holding him like a football, she swings him discordantly—three seconds; bounces him up and down—five seconds; pulls him into her body and pats him—five seconds; swings him again in a football hold—four seconds. Suddenly she begins to sway him slowly and rhythmically. Relief—it seemed she finally locked into his need for calming touch. But that lasted only ten seconds and then back she went, pacing back and forth in a frenzy, rapidly patting his back, and anxiously muttering and looking as agitated as her screaming infant. In five minutes, she used no fewer than thirty changes of strategy. As a result, her touch came across not as calming but as negative and produced negative behavior in her infant, who left the store screaming.

Depending on how we mix the different palette of sensations that make up our tactile sense, we can excite, calm, irritate, or cause pain:

* *Force*—our brain registers touch at the *slightest* indentation of our skin (remember "The Princess and the Pea"): too light can be annoying; too deep can be painful
* *Timing*—as a rule, slow soothes, while fast excites
* *Interval*—continuous and steady (static touch) calms, while intermittent (vibratory touch) arouses; (the skin is able to pick up a break of about ten thousandths of a second in a steady mechanical pressure or tactile buzz, explaining why we are bothered by the tiniest ant crawling along our arm)
* *Tempo*—rhythmic (da dum, da dum) comforts, while arhythmic (da dum, dum de dum) stimulates
* *Duration*—quick excites, while prolonged calms
* *Quality of sensation*—whether something is dull or sharp, soft or hard, smooth or rough, dry or wet, hot or cold, prickly or slimy, gritty or greasy affects our response

When our baby is tense, exhausted, or hyperaroused, we soothe him to sleep with slow, repetitive, prolonged, rhythmic strokes. When he's tuned out, we arouse him into alertness with fast, staccato, short strokes. But if anxious, we tend to soothe with arousing stimuli: staccato touch rather than a rhythmic beat; alerting sounds (an intense "shu shu" rather than a soft "shshsh"); and bouncy movements rather than smooth, steady ones.

A working mother, anxious all day to see her baby and play with her, can be especially at risk to use touch to arouse rather than calm. Excited when she gets home, she wants to turn on her baby's world. But about 80 percent of American babies, estimates Brazelton, are fussy at the end of the day. This means they need mother to turn the world off—to calmly withdraw stimulation rather than increase it.

Fathers, especially, have a tendency to overstimulate their babies. First, males tend to touch to excite for play, and second, the end of the day may be their only time with their baby. And, fathers tend to be less polished than mothers in picking up the baby's signals, both because most spend less time with their babies than mother and because the mother's brain is wired to allow her to more easily pick up her baby's cues. This can make the first few months of life particularly frustrating for the father—especially if he has a difficult or colicky infant.

Colic: How Universal Is It?

🌱 Two-month-old red-headed Claire is sweet, adorable, and alert—when she's quiet. But that seems rare. Mostly, her face is as red as her hair, and she writhes in pain and screams her head off, especially in the evening when daddy gets home and during the night when daddy wants to sleep. Her sleep-deprived parents are ready to jump off a cliff, their only consolation the knowledge that this nightmare presumably ends in another month: At three months, says her pediatrician, the crying will subside.

Few things make a parent more anxious than having a colicky infant: babies between two weeks and three months of age who cry inconsolably for more than three hours a day, especially at night, for at least three days a week and continuing for at least three weeks. One in five American babies will suffer from colic; thus, 20 percent of American babies are born irritable and more vulnerable to distress.

But are these statistics universal, or are they culturally determined? There's some evidence they may be specific to Western cultures. Colic is almost unheard of in more child-oriented cultures where babies are rarely separated from their mother. !Kung infants do not become colicky, nor do the Yequana infants of Venezuela. Nor has colic been reported as a problem in Japan, although this has not been studied scientifically. Since colic is likely an expression of sensory defensiveness (see chapter 8), and since a major part of the intervention for sensory defensiveness is deep-pressure touch, extended holding likely prevents colic, as parents quickly discover.

Colicky infants, we know, easily get out of control. Regardless of what techniques parents institute to calm them, it literally may take hours before some quiet. Nevertheless, once calm, they will remain so if held. But if not in a sound sleep, they often will resume crying when put down. Writes Marc Weissbluth, author of *Crybabies* and an expert on infant colic, of his colicky firstborn:

> Calming him down always took an hour or two of rocking. Once he began breathing deeply and regularly in my arms, I could put him down in his crib. But if I was impatient and tried to put him down before this deep sleep developed, he would arch his back, open his eyes wide, and start to cry once again.

There are several reasons why holding has this lulling effect. For one, the warmth transpired from tummy to tummy during holding. Writes actress Liv Ullmann of her baby daughter:

> Linn is four weeks old. She has colic and cries and cries. Ingmar [film director Ingmar Bergman] sits with her in bed. He undresses her—then himself; places her tiny body, stiff with cramps, against his bare stomach. She quiets down and in each other's warmth they fall asleep.

Another possible explanation is the pressure against the belly when the baby is held tummy to tummy. Our thin-skinned abdomen is sensitive to pain; in infants this sensitivity is twenty times more than in their fingers. This is why if you touch a particular spot during a colic episode—frequently around the belly button—the infant writhes and screams. For relief, infant-massage therapists "walk" their fingers across the baby's abdomen from left to right, often feeling bubbles release under their fingers. Similarly, when parents carry their infant belly to belly, the movement of the adult's belly against the baby's may stimulate the digestive system, thus explaining why parents of colicky infants hold their baby tight and walk the floors at night.

Positioning may also prevent colic. Carried babies eat while upright, allowing gravity to help the food go down. Cached babies, in contrast, and particularly those who are bottle fed, tend to be fed lying down. Furthermore, the gas that accompanies a colic episode may occur as a result of swallowed air during long crying episodes. Since carried infants don't cry for long periods, they're less likely to swallow air. And carried infants are likely breastfed, which means less delay when hungry than those bottle fed, and thus less time crying from hunger and less possibility to swallow air.

If we never let crying get out of hand, but prevent it by responding quickly (within ninety seconds) and accurately, can we eliminate those long colicky episodes? To find out, pediatrician Bruce Taubman divided babies into three groups, with thirty babies in each. In one group, parents were told to put the baby in the crib and let the child cry up to half an hour. Then, if still crying, to pick up the baby for a minute or so to calm her, then return her to the crib, and repeat the same protocol until the infant falls asleep or three hours have passed. After three hours, parents were instructed to feed the baby.

In the second group, parents were told to attempt to decide why the baby was crying—hunger, fatigue, boredom, need to suck, or desire to be held—and do what was appropriate. In other words, they were to respond quickly and accurately to the infant's needs—in psychological jargon, with "contingent responsivity." If crying continued for more than five minutes with one response, try another. Parents were told not to be concerned about overfeeding baby or spoiling the baby. The third group was a control group, not given any specific intervention.

The results? Neither the control group nor the let-them-cry-it-out group showed a decrease in crying. The second group, however, cried 70 percent less, from 2.6 hours to 0.8 hours per day. Predictably, speed and accuracy proved the reliable keys parents needed to turn off their infant's cry. In other words, it appears colic *can* be manageable.

This is because crying, even when it's excessive, is still communication! Figure out the message, and the problem goes away. What makes colicky babies different, says Taubman, is that they slip more quickly into uncontrollable crying if their needs are not more quickly met, and they persist with a ferocious will until they're pacified or exhaust themselves into sleep. Since babes-in-arms are unlikely to get into a crying jag to begin with, colic is likely an extreme response to separation in an especially vulnerable class of babies.

Maternal Tug-of-War

❧ Many times parents will worry their babies are colicky when they're not. Pediatricians reassure them that all babies cry a lot. This assumption—false, as we've seen—has resulted in several negative outcomes. For one, it sanctioned separation from mother throughout infancy under the premise that if it's all right for babies to cry extensively, it's all right to leave them alone—especially at night, when they cry with a fury.

It may even have helped condone the practice of circumcising newborn males without anesthesia. During the procedure, the newborn screams his lungs out. But possibly due to recovery from maternal anesthesia and his general state, the newborn takes a second or so to react to pain. (Two months later, in contrast, there's an almost instantaneous yell when given his first DPT injection.) This delay led to the assumption that the cry indicated not pain but overstimulation, making crying presumably harmless. It was not until cry analysis revealed the cry to have all the qualities of the pain cry that physicians began to consider the newborn to experience pain during circumcision. Mothers, driven to a frenzy, knew this all along.

Prolonged crying is agony for the mother. The cry's piercing sound (twenty decibels louder than ordinary speech, and approaching the intensity of busy street traffic) causes the mother's body to erupt with urgency: Oxytocin is released; her heart rate goes up; her blood pressure rises; and, in preparation for nursing, her breast temperature increases, as does the rate of blood flow in her breast, and her nipples become erect and ooze milk. Mothers feel an urge, as one mother said, "to go and grab the baby." Nor does this tension let up until, reunited, the mother feels assured her baby is safe.

Clearly, the mother is ill-suited by nature to ignore her infant's cry. Consequently, though pediatricians and child-care experts may encourage her to delay, it's hard to convince her hormones to do so. When we ask a mother to delay response, we ask her to deny her own biology, to violate her protective function, and to forfeit her baby's right to a natural state of well-being. This leaves a mother tugged in one direction by her biology and in the other by her culture's reasoning. If she takes the visceral route and darts for her crying baby, she chastises herself for being weak. If she takes the cerebral route and, to not spoil her baby, waits, she feels she's deserted her infant. What confusion!

To Wait or Not to Wait

⚜ Some experts, Dr. Spock for instance, give a rubber stamp of approval to let the baby cry it out (although he recommends this only for infants over three months of age). Others recommend a quick response, while T. Berry Brazelton warns to neither let the baby cry it out nor to respond quickly. Whose approach to follow? I suggest that which will give our child both roots and wings.

During infancy, adaptive patterns are laid down that have potential life-long consequences for self-organization. For later emotional well-being, we want our infant to learn to tolerate distress. One approach that will not accomplish this is to do all three: Arbitrarily delay at times, rush at times, and let the baby cry it out at times. Such inconsistency, leaving the infant unable to predict that he will get comfort, leads to insecure ambivalent attachment and all its ramifications.

If parents follow the advice of those in the let-them-cry-it-out camp, they run the risk of creating frequent rhythmic crying in their baby which, in addition to the negative consequences already noted, will make the baby feel that crying is an ineffective signal to get her needs met. This will force her into too much self-soothing before she has the capacity. Overwhelmed with bad feelings that will keep her anxious all the time, she will learn to inhibit her need for comfort, which leads to insecure avoidant attachment and mistrust in relationships. Lacking terra firma, we will rob her of roots, and the wings she acquires will give her only a false sense of freedom.

If, on the other hand, a mother hovers and does not permit her infant to learn to self-soothe, the baby will not learn self-regulation. Instead of taking off to discover the world, distress will overwhelm her and defensive behavior patterns will emerge as protection from intolerable excitation: overdependence on us; overdependence on her own body in the form of excessive thumb-sucking, hair twirling, ear pulling, masturbation, etc.; and overdependence on things such as excessive pacifier sucking, blanket chewing, overeating, etc. Ambivalently attached, she will be robbed of wings, and the roots she develops will be unhealthy dependency.

Furthermore, if a mother responds to the cry *"before* the infant can build up an expressed need, feel the importance of it, make a demand, and then find it gratified"—the pattern Brazelton observed with the Mayans—Brazelton worries that though our babies will cry infrequently, they will become passive. And this would be nonadaptive in our culture.

In our ancestral environment, and in nondeveloped cultures that exist today, survival was and is precarious. Among the !Kung San, half of all babies die before adulthood. Continual carrying and an immediate response to the cry was and is necessary for physical survival. Further, since work is largely agricultural or hunting and gathering, all hands are needed for survival, making cooperation among family members essential for the viability of the family. A Mayan child who took her own initiative and decided she preferred reading to doing her part in caring for baby or tending the goats would be a liability, as would a child who relinquished her chores to go off to summer camp. Consequently, compliance to parental wishes is valued over independent decision making. To achieve this, says Brazelton, the Mayan mother seeks to reinforce quiet passivity and little movement in her infant.

But in a concrete jungle, where the issue is no longer physical survival but psychological, we have the opposite goal. We want to enforce a pattern, he says, for later self-initiation and reinforced independence—the qualities we deem necessary in our society to ready our children for the dog-eat-dog world in which we live. Therefore, we allow tension to build, often to the point of frustration, before our infants experience gratification. In this way, we allow our infant "to find his own sources of comfort, to find his own ways of waiting for and of demanding a feeding, and to establish independent sleep patterns and rhythms of sleep that are optimal for receiving stimulation when it will be available." Thus, it's best to soothe our infants only to the extent they cannot manage it on their own, with the intent of having self-regulation come increasingly from them, as they can manage it.

But, as Brazelton warns, there are risks in this pattern. There's a fine line between a demand-response pattern that will create mild frustration and lead to independence and one that thwarts needs and culminates in much of the demandingness we've come to associate with the American child. Far from autonomy, these demands are the exaggerated emotions typical of coercive children in their quest for continual parental attention.

Furthermore, though a demand-response pattern may toughen up some babies it throws others over the edge. How much crying a baby can tolerate before becoming overwhelmed depends on factors such as age, time of day, temperamental differences in irritability and soothability, internal state, the intensity of the particular cry, and repertoire of available behaviors.

Some "happy" infants seem to self-soothe easily. They cry rarely and get consoled quickly when they do, making the parent's job a snap. For others, the whimper quickly becomes a howl that turns into a storm of angry, red-faced screams, tense little hands clenching and unclenching, and frantic arms and legs flying, throwing their whole system into a tailspin. Unless a parent wants to put up with possibly hours of screaming, they need to react quickly. Into this category fall many high-risk infants, such as preterms, those neurologically or medically compromised, "difficult" infants who are hypersensitive to stimuli, and especially colicky infants who, in addition to hypersensitivity, appear to have also gastrointestinal involvement. In other words, how much delay, if any, comes down in large part to infant temperament. For some infants it's okay to dawdle a bit to let the infant self-calm; for others, mother must run.

Nevertheless, the notion that an immediate response interferes with self-regulation leaves an unanswered question. How do we explain that, though most infants in other parts of the world are immediately comforted, they grow up to function as self-regulated adults and, as we've seen, become self-reliant *earlier* than do our children. And, in fact, if any culture is considered unregulated, it would be ours.

One possibility is that because carried babies don't get especially fussy and are quickly pacified when they do, the mother keeps her baby's emotional thermostat within the comfort zone. This makes self-soothing unnecessary for the most part, at least in the young infant. For instance, thumb-sucking hasn't been noted in carrying cultures.

When mature enough to take over, the baby possesses a well-calibrated instrument to achieve relaxed self-regulation. The !Kung infant, for instance, gets rather harshly weaned at age two or three, quickly thrusting them into independence. Though they go through an initial period of protest and fussiness, they quickly make a transition to their peer group and accept the loss of the breast to a new baby brother or sister.

But for our babies, who may lack their mother at hand, and for whom soothing sources are often external—the pacifier rather than the thumb; the bottle rather than the breast; the crib rather than the parent's chest— achieving self-regulation can present a daunting challenge. This makes them more fussy, which makes self-soothing more imperative, especially since mothers can't always drop what they're doing to answer the cry. In other words, for infants in our culture, some delay to encourage them to find their own means of comfort seems appropriate. It's then satisfying when they succeed in quieting themselves.

Mothers in indigenous cultures, as Brazelton found with the Mayans, also tend to remain calm when their infants get distressed, and do not further arouse their babies. Here, however, mothers, and especially inexperienced ones, often get anxious when their infants cry, rushing to them and overwhelming them with their own anxieties.

As for Brazelton's concern that an immediate response will create passivity, as in the Mayan infants, this may be more temperamental than cultural. Brazelton himself discovered the Mayan infant to have low-key modulated responses and a placid nature at birth. The highly indulged Aboriginal infant, in contrast, is described as possessing "boundless joy, exhuberance, and independence."

Does Crying Beget Crying?

The belief that a quick response to the cry interferes with autonomy reflects our image of the infant as needing to learn independence. Part of this comes from a concern that a quick response to the cry will act as a reward. Consistently doing so will train our baby to cry to be picked up; as a result, our babies will cry all the time to be held, increasing their dependency on us for self-soothing. Ignoring the cry, in contrast, which is punishment (it fails to remove the distress and can increase it), should decrease the number of times baby cries.

Interestingly, in Okinawa, Japan, where mothers wish to create interdependence rather than independence, they rush to their infants because they believe immediate comfort *prevents* the bad habit of crying, which is believed to form in the first four months of life. Who's right?

Ignoring an infant's cry does seem to decrease it, at least temporarily. But since crying indicates a need, there's also the risk that ignoring it over the long run will teach the infant to inhibit this need—needs that do not disappear but merely go underground. Thus, the short-term gain of decreased crying may, over the long run, prove a developmental disaster. And indeed, when we studied attachment theory, we saw that young infants left to consistently cry in frustration developed not true autonomy but a false independence to cover up deeply unsatisfied dependency needs.

As attachment theory would predict, what leads to true autonomy is the opposite—promptly removing the need that the cry signals. This protects the baby from overwhelming discomfort and increases confidence that someone will protect the baby in time of need, all of which increases the baby's capacity for survival. As such, contrary to the spoiling theory's predictions, several studies have found that a quick response *diminishes* rather than increases crying—La Leche mothers, as we recall, had babies who cried less frequently at two months of age.

The classic study supporting this hypothesis was done by Sylvia Bell and Mary Ainsworth. After spending a year closely observing twenty-six infant-mother pairs in both a laboratory setting and at home, they found that when mothers responded promptly to their baby's cry in the first six months of life, babies cried less in the second six months. The "spoiled" babies—that is, those who increased their demands—were those who experienced the delayed response. Moreover, rather than becoming demanding tyrants, infants whose cries were quickly answered requested less holding, enjoyed being held more and protested less when put down, and cooperated more with parental demands than did infants of less sensitive mothers.

Infants do of course learn they can use the cry to get a pick-up. But if they learn that a smile, a coo, or a pre-cry pucker or holding out their arms brings a response, babies utilize these more effective modes of communicating, rather than resorting to the cry, which would explain Bell and Ainsworth's findings.

Promptly answering the cry allows the baby to begin to make an association between his actions and the needed response: When I cry, Mommy comes and my tummy stops gnawing at me; when I cry, Mommy comes and I don't feel wet anymore. This gives the baby a feeling that what he does gets him what he needs.

Delay has the opposite effect. It fails to allow the baby to make a connection between his plea for help and subsequent comfort, and it gives the baby the message that he's incapable of getting his needs met. As he develops, this lack of control makes him feel he has little voice in what happens to him, causing him to associate frustration with his actions. When a parent delays routinely, the baby's trust in people is eroded. Since basic trust is at the heart of the baby's attachment to the mother, consistent delay is nonadaptive.

PART *3*

Getting in Touch

Caresses, expressions of one sort or another,

are necessary to the life of the affections

as leaves are to the life of a tree.

—Nathaniel Hawthorne

13

❧

The Self-reliant Supermom

The greatest source of terror in infancy is solitude.
—William James

Isolation of the Nuclear Family

❧ "Defenseless as babies are, they have mothers at their command, families to protect the mothers, societies to support the structure of families, and traditions to give a cultural continuity to systems of tending and training." So wrote Erik Erikson in *Insight and Responsibility*.

Well, not always.

In the United States, half of all mothers with infants work, half of all families break up, and the extended family is usually too spread out to offer assistance. We lack communities to fall back on, and we do not offer the programs that other countries have to support families: postpartum care for all mothers (including nursing visits at home for the first week or two of life); parental leave of absence with at least partial pay for the first year of life; readily available health insurance; and affordable and easily accessible high-quality child care (including corporate care). And modern culture makes the tending and training of infants stressful and frustrating. None of this supports building intimate family relations.

Many experts see the increase in working mothers at the heart of parent burnout and wayward, uncontrollable children. If we restructured our society to allow mothers to stay home for at least the first year, they claim we would eliminate much woe. False. The issue is not the working mother—women have always worked and most wish to. At issue is this: For the first time in human history, nurturing and work are mutually incompatible.

The modern mother with an infant falls largely into two categories, unique to our evolution: Those who stay home and mother full-time, or nurturers, and those who work outside the home full-time, or workers. Both cultural casualties, they leave many mothers with a split identity. If I work, am I mother? If I don't work, am I a person?

In my view, the solution is to replicate the basic patterns of adaptation inherent in our ancestral environment and apply them to modern life. A close primary attachment figure is needed to respond promptly to the infant's physical and emotional needs. This is usually the mother, since she's most invested in her infant's survival, but it need not be. Add to this an array of other attachment figures to support her efforts, including a father, grandparents, sisters, brothers, nannies, or other surrogate caregivers. Then, fill both the mother's and infant's day with camaraderie, and create a baby-friendly society to support parenting efforts. To the extent our lives follow these patterns, mothers and babies thrive; to the extent our lives deviate, mothers and babies suffer.

Home Alone with Baby

"The worst thing is just having the mother boxed up with her baby twenty-four hours a day, which nobody ever meant to have happen in the whole history of the human race." So lamented Margaret Mead.

Though staying at home gives a mother the opportunity to devote herself fully to her infant's care, especially in the early months, and to enjoy those tender moments where the whole world is captured in a toothless smile and a gurgle, many mothers are dismayed at how unsatisfied they soon come to feel.

Throughout history, women have spent the day with other women—for company, friendship, advice, guidance, and help. But ours is the lonely generation. Our nearest neighbor is probably at work, on the tennis court, or overwhelmed with her own responsibilities. This is no small problem. Biological evolution, having designed us to live in an ensemble, did not fashion a contingency plan for a mother-baby solo act.

The mother-infant relationship is meant to function within a social system, embedded like Russian stacking dolls in the spousal relationship, the extended family, the community, and, in recent history, the society at large. In other words, as the old African proverb says, "It takes a village to raise a child." With the loss of the extended family and the tight-knit community, we are asked to do, as Margaret Mead said, "what an entire clan used to do." This leaves many voids.

To start, it warps the mother's nurturing capacity, draining her emotionally, causing resentment and mother burnout. "I put her in bed and ten minutes later she was up. One hour, I thought, just give me one hour alone," one mother bewails to another.

Bereft of female companionship a good part of the day, mothers lack direction and overworry they are not parenting right. Though some can turn to their own mothers for advice, others find that their mothers, often from the you'll-spoil-them school, offer advice out of touch with their more nurturant tendencies and create more conflict than comfort.

And so mothers put their faith in parenting experts and their pediatricians. Often helpful, this can also be confusing, since there's little consensus among experts on the important issues. This doctor says, "Pick up your baby when he cries." Another warns, "Wait to see if your baby will stop crying on his own." One psychologist cautions, "Don't get into the habit of putting your baby in your bed." Another says, "Babies feel insecure sleeping alone."

Lacking other women at hand, women can't easily depend on someone to give them a helping hand. This is quite stressful. A mother's ability to manage has always depended on the availability of other women to help relieve her of caregiving responsibilities. The Tarong women of the Philippines, for instance, consider child care a community affair. No mother takes exclusive responsibility for her children, and the women like to feel that "we all take care of our children." Some mothers even nurse each other's children.

Lacking helping hands, mothers cope by turning to helping things. Not only because they feel overwhelmed with responsibility, but also because with no one during the day to settle *them* down, it's harder for them to settle their babies down. For mothers, too, need affection during the day to keep their own nurturance reservoirs full. Consider this story relayed to Harvard psychiatrist Robert Coles by the mother of an African-American child coping with desegregation in 1961:

> My child comes home from school, and she's heard those white people shouting. . . . And the first thing she does is come to me, and I hold her. Then she goes to get her snack, and then she's back, touching me. I'll be upset myself, so thank God my mother is still with us, because I go to her, and she'll put her hand on my arm, and I'm all settled down again, and then I can put my hand on my daughter's arm. When my mother puts her hands on me, and I put my hands on my child, it's God giving us strength.

Clearly, mothers must avoid social isolation and maximize social supports, such as "mommy and me" classes, which ultimately become mommy social hours. (For more information, see the Resource Guide.) Replacing the neighborhood doorstep, these classes help mothers to release tension, to gain moral support by sharing notes, and to observe one another. They also strengthen community bonds and expose babies to others. Currently, they encompass only a small part of the average stay-at-home mother's week. This needs to change. Ideally, mother-baby drop-in centers should be as common as the neighborhood beauty shop. And mothers need to augment their caregiving with other caregivers.

Multiple Caregivers

Nature has two laws: Multiply, and keep your offspring fit enough for them to multiply. Multiple caregiving, explains Harvard developmental psychologist Edward Tronick, accomplishes this better than exclusive parenting.

Multiple caregivers provide increased investment in the infant, expanding resources; increase the likelihood for adoption should mother fall seriously ill or die; help compensate if mother provides inadequate care; relieve mother of some caregiving chores, helping her to ultimately give better care and thereby increasing the likelihood of secure attachment; enhance the infant's sense of security by decreasing the chances of the infant being alone; and give the infant wider and more varied social exposure. For mother, other care allows her to feel more free and less controlled by her infant's continual needs and thus less resentful and ambivalent. It's hard to enjoy parenting if you're doing it twenty-four hours a day, seven days a week! Not surprisingly, abuse occurs most often when mothers seldom get a mothering break.

Furthermore, a bored, frustrated, stressed, exhausted, lonely, or self-involved mother cannot easily nurture someone else, and especially one who needs constant care. Nor are our babies sympathetic to our problems. They know only what their bodies tell them: When they're comfortable, life is good; when they're uncomfortable, life is bad. And life is best when their needs are quickly and lovingly met by someone who gives them full attention, something a mother too stressed or unfulfilled to satisfy her own needs cannot easily provide. In other words, babies require full-time mothering—but not necessarily their *mother* full time.

An outside caregiver is one solution, but in wealthy United States live-in help is a luxury for the few and infrequently employed by the nonworking mother. Imagine the following ad, written by child psychoanalyst Selma Fraiberg:

> WANTED: Mature woman; care for six-month-old of employed mother. Light housekeeping; live in; must love children; more for home than wages.

Alas, said Fraiberg:

> This devoted nanny will not be found. I believe she was last employed by David and Agnes Copperfield, London, circa 1850, having been the childhood nurse since the untimely death of his father. For a modest wage this cheerful, red-cheeked woman performed all household duties, consoled and advised the widow, and mothered the orphan child. This goodly woman burst with maternity. Her hearty embraces . . . caused the buttons of her bodice to fly off in all directions.

Even if we could afford a nanny, it is not without drawbacks. We have a natural distrust of strangers—a survival instinct that begins with the eight-month-old's stranger anxiety—and we value our privacy. We also fear jealousy, creating competition between mothers and nannies: "What if my baby loves *her* more than *me?*"

This concern isn't entirely unrealistic. Until around six to seven months of age, infants play the field. Oh, they bat their eyes more at mother, but in the first six months of life, any warm, cuddly body could take her place. It is not until babies start to crawl at around eight months of age that, now officially bonded, they scamper close to mother at any hint of danger. If infants form an insecure attachment to their mother and a secure one to their nanny, the infant *will* turn to nanny when distressed.

We also worry that only we can keep our babies safe and that care that differs from our own may have an ill effect on our baby's development. And we feel guilty if we don't do it all, as if sharing caregiving implies irresponsibility. "I wanted help," said one mother, "but felt *I* was supposed to do it all myself." This puts enormous pressure on mothers.

Ideally, as Margaret Mead once suggested, babies ought to have about six people consistently caring for them. In this way, someone is always available, and babies have the opportunity to adapt to different caregiving styles, which increases flexibility. And, in fact, in our ancestral environment, babies would have been cared for by about six people—mother, father, older sister, two grandmas, and maybe an aunt or two.

Although today we may lack extended family, there are still ways to invent one. We could create "aunts" by setting up co-babysitting, which would increase community support and socialization. We could assertively pursue "grandmothers" by putting up a sign at our local church or synagogue for a retired woman to spend a few hours a week with our baby.

For "sisters," we could establish a relationship with a trusted neighborhood adolescent to stop by a few afternoons a week. If a mother uses young girls to help her (boys rarely want to baby-sit), in addition to increasing her baby's social circle, she helps to prepare these girls to become mothers. Before we lost the extended family, observing birth and breastfeeding and caring for babies was a natural rite of passage for young girls. Now, rare is the mother who's had previous experience caring for an infant.

As for father, to better adapt to our lack of supportive extended family and the large influx of women into the labor force, society has been redefining his role as necessary co-caregiver and psychological support of mother: Dad's become our biggest helper. This explains why our spouse, rather than our mother, has become our primary companion during labor; why some fathers request parenting leave to play, as they say, "Mr. Mom," or arrange their work schedule to care for baby while mommy works; why "daddy and me" classes are offered along with mommy and me classes; and why many fathers demand sharing in feeding their baby.

By removing some of the caregiving burden from mother, father as co-caregiver strengthens the mother-infant relationship and the family bond as well. But that's not all. When a father learns how to care for his baby—diapering her, feeding her, bathing her—he more quickly bonds to her. This has long-term effects: She's less likely to be afraid when left with a stranger and likely to grow up more kind, sensitive, and smarter. And, says Kyle Pruett, a professor of psychiatry at the Yale University Child Study Center, she's unlikely to be sexually abused by her father. Moreover, when mothers leave their babies with daddy as babysitter, or as co-caregiver when they go to work, they feel more relaxed and confident that their infant will receive adequate care, which makes separation easier.

Utilizing other caregivers, including those fathers with flexible hours, gives mother more time for self-nurturing, the freedom to work part time, and time to refuel her emotional energy. The more mother works, the more resources she will have for her infant and the more she can satisfy her personal need for identity and for the stimulation of adult company.

The Working Mother

❦ Since the beginning of human history, women have worked. But with work and nurturing integrated, work took place in a relaxed spirit of social exchange with other women and was considered an essential part of the economy.

For !Kung San women, work was part time, leaving much time for play. Every two to three days, they went in groups into the bush to forage for food, their nursing babies snuggled into a sling on their hip. Older children were left at the village, taken care of by kin invested in their care. When not foraging, the women spent an average of two to three hours a day on chores and meal preparation. Much of their work done in a community of chattering women and playing children, the !Kung women worked at their own pace, shared their food with whom they chose, enjoyed a good deal of leisure, and did not suffer social or emotional isolation. Contributing around 70 percent to their family's meal, they were the primary bread-winners. They had power.

When humans shifted from hunting-gathering to farming, women spent many hours in the fields, tended animals, or produced material resources from the fruit of their labor. Part-time work became full-time work. As the women picked apples, sowed wheat, tended sheep, or weaved mats, their babies slept peacefully on their back or hip or next to them. Older, more active infants were often left at the village with grandmother or an older sister and fed by a wet nurse. The women, like their foraging ancestors, remained an important part of the agrarian income, and still do in many parts of the world.

But industrialization, urbanization, and affluence changed all that, split-ting mothers into two groups: the at-home mother and the laborer. A woman's place was now considered in the home, and unless she had to work, she was expected to tend children and home as an unpaid laborer, her work not considered a part of the labor force. Economic life suddenly separated from home and immediate community and women lost contact with the wider society. For many, home became a prison. Those who could not afford to stay home trudged off to factories, offices, and shops, separated from their babies and, though with other women, were discouraged from socializing except at break time. Work and child care became incompatible, as did work and socializing. Work became drudgery.

In the affluence of the period after World War II, the number of women able to stay home increased, as did the taboo of leaving your children and going to work. Even in the 1960s, leaving home to work was barely an option for a mother with an infant. "If the car broke down," my friend Cynthia told me, "I didn't have a car. It never occurred to us that I should go to work to increase our income and look for a babysitter for Michael." No longer. Now my friend Cynthia would likely take a six-week to three-month maternity leave, leave her child with a sitter or in day care, and return to work.

Today's women are entering the work force in droves—some out of necessity, many out of choice—and this is not likely to change. Work allows women to restore the balance between life at home and society-at-large. It brings home a paycheck which, by contributing to the family's economic viability and to society, creates independence and a feeling of self-worth. It confers status and, for many women, adds interest and meaning to their lives. For some, their job largely defines who they are—to not work means giving up a huge chunk of their identity. Furthermore, work means spending their day in the company of adults.

Being a housewife, in contrast, can mean being a second-class citizen. Not receiving wages for their labor, women are financially dependent on their husbands, which gives them less status and negotiating power in the marital relationship. And society, though it considers them good mothers for opting to fill their day with diaper changes and burps rather than memos and coffee breaks, nevertheless accords mothering low status, presuming stay-at-home mothers to lack strong identity, intelligence, or ambition. All this leaves many housewives feeling unsatisfied and powerless.

Housewives, however, at least have their children. Work, in contrast, means relinquishing your mothering role for a large part of the day. And herein lies the rub: Our work structure puts mothering and work at cross purposes. Unlike our foraging or farming ancestors, our babies are unwelcomed at our workplace, and doubly so suckling at our breast. Lacking kin to watch them, we must pay strangers to do so, who may or may not parent to our satisfaction. We work long hours and spend much time commuting, including the time it takes to drop our infants off at other care. Returning home exhausted, with chores and child care awaiting us and sometimes nary a sole to commiserate with, we may feel too exhausted to spend much quality time with our baby, or else try to fit a whole day's love into a few hours.

Having to let go of our child each day, we feel emotionally tormented, with a vague longing as if a part of us is missing, worried about whether our baby is okay and comfortable. These feelings are our evolutionary heritage reasserting itself, whispering "stay in touch." For though we may wish to leave our maternal side at home when we leave for the office, in reality we are cavewomen in business suits, programmed to perceive separation from our infants as threatening to our infant's well-being. "I can't bear to think about it," says a mother whose job requires she return when her baby is two months old. Some mothers get an actual physical reaction in their gut to separation, especially when it's prolonged.

This guilt is furthered by the fact that, though many mothers must work out of economic necessity, many also choose to work. This may intensify a mother's feelings of negligence. "What kind of mother *chooses* to leave her baby?" we ask ourselves, dripping with guilt. When problems arise from separation—increased fussiness in our infants, eating or sleeping problems, illness—these feelings magnify. This guilt further reduces the mother's caregiving capacities and job performance, leaving many a mother filled with doubt about her choice.

Knowing she must soon return to work and that loss is inevitable, some mothers may resist (often unconsciously) behaviors that incur intense intimacy, such as frequent and exclusive breastfeeding, sleeping with their infant, and prolonged holding and carrying. Furthermore, if a mother comes home, cooks dinner, feeds and bathes her baby, and then collapses, work drains her of necessary resources rather than helping her regroup and furthering her nurturing capacities. Anything that makes a mother *less* able to adequately care for her infant decreases her infant's survival chances, psychologically if not physically.

From the mother's perspective then, full-time work—and particularly when an infant is under six months of age—often creates undue stress that does not support optimal parenting. On the other hand, if mothers—accustomed to a career, coworkers to share and commiserate with, a salary, and an on-the-go lifestyle—give up their profession to stay home with a baby, they find themselves bored with the tedious chores involved in caring for an infant, lonely without the stimulation of adult company, frustrated with being bogged down, and often depressed. In other words, staying at home may also not support optimal parenting. Neither does it meet all of their infant's needs.

No Friends for Our Babies

If mothers are bored home alone with baby, the infant—who spends long periods without a soul in sight other than mother—is bored as well.

Older sisters and brothers, if any, are in school, daddy's at the office, and grandmas and aunts cannot be counted on to visit. This limited exposure to adults and other children restricts the infant's opportunities to observe, to become familiar with, to socialize with, and to attach to other people. It also sets up a mind-set of aloneness as a common state.

Furthermore, mother, involved in housework and drained from all her responsibilities, often spends little time playing with her child. One national survey found that, though working mothers average only eleven minutes and fathers eight minutes per weekday in child-centered activities with their children—reading, conversing, playing—homemaker mothers did not fare much better, devoting only an average of thirty minutes per day to such activities.

Nor is playing with babies and repeating the same game ad infinitum a role mothers were made to relish. Siblings and other children, on the other hand, adore playing with babies. In a !Kung village, the infant holds court, as a line of extended family—both big and little—wait to hold or play with the baby. This gives the infant endless opportunities to babble, to flirt, to gesture, and to imitate others, which widens their capacity to adapt to different people's rhythms and styles of interacting. When old enough, infants crawl over and toddlers toddle over to play groups, periodically relieving the mother of intensive caregiving throughout the day.

This early fraternizing preps babies for later fraternizing and frees mother to care for another baby or to pursue her own interests. Babies unused to other caregivers, in contrast, tend to show greater stranger and separation anxiety. Grandparents who visit occasionally are often mystified when their eight-month old grandchild, who two weeks earlier laughed and gurgled when picked up, now wails when taken from her mother's arms. When intense, this anxiety renders later transition to day care and to a playmate group more difficult, leaving children frantic when mother tries to depart. Exclusive care and isolation, then, can interfere with the later autonomy we so value.

On the Israeli kibbutz, where infants live in groups that stay together throughout childhood, babies start to make "friends" by five months, observed anthropologist Melford Spiro, by laughing, babbling, waving arms and legs, and touching each other. Spiro recounts a typical interaction among older babies:

> Uzi (ten months) and Yaakov (nine months) are on the porch, looking at each other. . . . Uzi touches Yaakov with his hand, they touch each other's hands and jabber.

As children mature, the group experience becomes the norm, and kibbutz children are rarely if ever alone. "A child alone in his room watching TV would be considered pathological," a kibbutznik once told me.

Between twelve and eighteen months of age, some babies who have been with a group of playmates on an ongoing basis choose a special "buddy." They smile and giggle when seeing their best friend and repeat his or her name when they go to sleep. Infants also "teach" each other, as this article from the *New York Times* tells us:

> It was during the blustery days of last March that ten-month-old Russell Ruud taught the other babies in his day care group a lesson their parents may have wished he hadn't: how to unzip the Velcro chin straps of their winter hats.
>
> "One day I went to pick Russell up and his teacher told me that the other mothers were complaining that their children had learned from him how to take off their hats," said Dr. Judith Ruud, Russell's mother.

His mother said she never showed him how to unzip the Velcro. He learned it by trial and error, and the other children learned it by observing him. In fact, toddlers show a remarkable ability to learn from one another and they retain this information outside the group setting. Children who do not get early socializing, in contrast, take longer to learn social skills. If seriously deprived, they may never adequately catch up.

Fathers also offer a crucial role in socializing. Their playful interactiveness, filled with humor and verve, along with a tendency to stand back and let their child take risks, pushes the child to cope with the world outside the comforting mother-baby bond. The ability to manage frustration, a willingness to explore new things and activities, and persistence in problem solving have all been linked to the quality of the father-child interaction. Play with father also sets up babies for play with their siblings, which later gets transferred to playmates.

Full-time Other Care

❧ If staying at home has its drawbacks for mother and baby, what about other care, particularly for full-time working mothers?

One to One

If a grandmother, nanny, or father assumes full-time care for the baby, the infant should receive ample nurturance and intense bursts of love-play periodically throughout the day and will have an opportunity to form an intense attachment to another loving caregiver. On the down side, babies will miss out on socialization. Though not a problem for the infant less than six months old, it becomes increasingly so as the baby matures and gains greater interest in the outside world. But there are ways around this, such as daily walks to the park and by providing a "friend" or two for baby. Or the caregiver may take care of another child as well, which would have the bonus of making a full-time caregiver more affordable. Or, parents could hire a caregiver who has her own children. If she has an older child, this adds baby-sitting to socialization. Margaret Mead hired an English nanny who brought her adolescent daughter along—another helping hand. In the summers, they moved in with a family who had six children of their own—more helping hands. Says Mead:

> In the summer months I had an opportunity to realize what it had been like to bring up a child in a household in which there were many willing hands ready to hold the baby and someone to do the endless chores and to sleep with the baby at night, so that the mother's contacts with her child were both intense and relaxed.

Family Day Care

A second option is family day care, either by giving the baby to another nurturant woman who is home with her own children, or to licensed family care, where the baby will have the benefit of a caregiver with some training and supervision. If the home environment is safe, sanitary, and stable, with only a few other children, and provides sufficient interesting objects for play, the baby should receive adequate care and social and mental stimulation and, again, will have the benefit of another attachment figure than mother.

Family care has numerous other advantages: The infant is in a familiar environment—a home with a mother figure and only a few other children. And he is with children of mixed ages, giving him varied social exposure and an opportunity for observing and modeling the older children. Children are exposed to less illness than in day care, and home situations usually offer more flexible hours.

The downside? The baby will get less of the intense love-play and physical closeness that takes place between a baby and a mother—that wide-eyed, open-mouthed enthusiasm that can't be bought. There's also concern that infants, especially very young ones, will be left alone while the caregiver chases after older children. Another negative is the lack of backup care should the provider become ill. In spite of these negatives, many parents feel confident in home care and find it a workable solution.

Infant Day Care

A third option is infant day care. On the plus side is the social and intellectual stimulation lacking in one-to-one home care. Surrounded by other babies, lots of colorful toys, and people hired to entertain baby, day care is rich in interesting things to see, touch, listen to, and fiddle with. This eliminates much of the boredom that babies at home, dependent on mother for entertaining and for chasing elusive toys, experience.

But day care has distinct disadvantages. Babies may not get enough individual attention—especially young ones. Though child-care experts recommend an adult/infant ratio no larger than one to three, as of 1992, only three states met this. Nine states still allowed a one to six ratio for infants. In Florida, where I live, we have a one to four ratio. Holding, feeding, burping, diapering, consoling, and playing with four or more infants at once can be a juggling act for caregivers, who are often unable to get to all needy infants at once. Therefore, propping bottles is common and infants spend much time in cribs, playpens, walkers, infant seats, swings, or on the floor. When more than one baby cries at a time, one infant often has to wait for care.

Even the best day care offers less personal contact than babies need, especially those infants under six months of age. Tiffany Field observed infants and their caregivers in a model infant day care located at a major university and teaching hospital. She found relatively little holding and affection toward babies.

In 1990, the National Institute of Child Health and Human Development initiated an ambitious long-term ten-site study of other care for infants. Among their first findings: Infants get the highest quality care, based on sensitivity to the child's needs, when one person cares for them. Nor does it matter who cares for the baby—father, grandparent, or in-home caregiver—as long as baby has one-to-one care. Child-care centers provided the lowest quality care. In other words, though wonderful for social and intellectual development, the average infant day care falls short of supplying the baby's emotional needs, and especially for infants under six months of age whose primary object of interest is their caregiver. These results, not surprisingly, match nature's baby care manual, where a one-to-one ratio evolved for the first two to four years of a baby's life to ensure sufficient attention to the infant's needs.

Other day care conditions reduce nurturance. Caregivers receive low pay, making turnover high—close to 50 percent as of 1990. If a baby makes an attachment to a special caregiver who leaves, change creates instability, which disorganizes an infant, who can become clingy and irritable.

Illness is another problem. Babies kept close to their mother and nursed receive immunities from her milk. Since mother and baby are exposed to the same germs, babies do not have to fight germs to which they've not built up immunities. But kept far from the mother, babies both lose this immunity and get exposed to a large number of germs which, combined with the stress of separation and adaptation to a new environment, presents an ideal culture for microbes. Consequently, babies in day care get sick frequently. Agonizing for the mother, each sneeze reinforces her feeling that she has failed to adequately care for and protect her infant.

All this indicates that infants, especially those under six months of age, benefit best in family care or one-to-one care in the home. Psychologist Sandra Scarr in her book *Mother Care Other Care* concurs, "Our own research on day care centers, homes, and sitters found that, on the average, babies and toddlers are better off with sitters or in day care homes, because centers do not usually provide sufficient adult interaction for the really little ones."According to *Zero to Three*, a publication of the National Center for Clinical Infant Programs, which has a board of directors that includes many leading child development experts—T. Berry Brazelton, Robert Emde, Stanley Greenspan, Joy Osofsky, Arnold Sameroff, and Edward Zigler, among others—until the infant is at least six months of age, parents should not even be confronted with the choice of other care. Among the recommendations they put forth in 1992 for day care reform was a six-month work leave of absence for new parents to help promote responsive caregiving.

This does not indicate that day care in and of itself is bad. In high-quality centers that meet a low adult/infant ratio and have low turnover of staff, many older infants can and do thrive.

Impact of Infant Day Care on Later Development

If infants, particularly those under six months of age, benefit best from one-to-one care, why has day care become so popular? Out of necessity, of course, but also because of our view of the infant as a competent, quickly self-reliant being who, if no one comes to pick him up, will learn to lick his own wounds and be that much more independent.

How does an emphasis on early independence impact the child's adjustment? Some researchers have found that children who begin day care as infants get along better with their peers in preschool, play more cooperatively, and seem happier, which makes sense. Day care children get much practice socializing and children who have friends are the most happy. Other studies have found that the children are more aggressive, noncompliant, less tolerant of frustration, less cooperative with grown-ups, less happy, and more likely to be withdrawn or clingy—which also makes sense. Missing out on nurturing and individual attention leaves a child with needs unmet and thus less happy, more angry, and less capable of empathy and altruism—the basis of getting along with other people.

Does day care affect security of attachment? This is an important question and has fueled much debate. In 1985, psychologist Jay Belsky of Pennsylvania State University announced, after reviewing much data, that more than twenty hours a week of day care in the first year of life placed infants at increased risk for insecure attachment and later behavioral problems. Overnight, he became a pariah: mothers felt guilty about going to work; researchers were furious that his announcement could mean less government funding for quality day care. Theoretically, Belsky's concerns had some backing. As attachment researcher Alan Sroufe pointed out, daily separations could water down the infant's confidence in maternal availability, and mothers would have less opportunity to fine-tune their interactions with their infants. A combination of the two could leave the infant more needy.

But, according to the latest findings from the National Institute of Child Health and Human Development study, infant day care does not necessarily affect infant-mother attachment. When mothers are sensitive to their infant's needs, their relationship holds up against the long separation; the infants, remember, have an "internal working model" of mother—as John Bowlby called it—as someone who is always watching over them. The highest rates of insecurity were, predictably, when infants received insensitive care from mother combined with poor quality, unstable, or more than minimal amounts of child care.

Additional research has found a relationship between how mothers perceive returning to work and separating from their infants, and the quality of attachment. Stress, lack of social supports, and increased anxiety about leaving their infants can overwhelm the parenting capacity of some working mothers, causing them to be less sensitive to their infants' needs. Some mothers, for instance, concerned their absence will adversely affect their babies, experience strong separation anxiety. To make up for lost time when they return home, they overwhelm their infants with excitement. For instance, in one study that looked at infants at ten months of age in a free-play session, these overly anxious working mothers were highly intrusive, stimulating their babies too much, taking away objects while the baby was still interested, and not letting the baby influence the pace and focus of the play. Many of these babies, as expected, became avoidantly attached to their mothers. How do we know these mothers would have been less controlling were they not employed? Interestingly, these same mothers were also described as sensitive toward their infants. In other words, their intrusiveness may have been at least partly linked to their anxiety about working and leaving their babies.

Is it possible for babies to be insecurely attached to their mother and securely attached to their caregiver? Yes, and it can help compensate for some deficits that occur from insecure attachment, particularly in the areas of social and language skills. This does not indicate, though, that infants become more strongly attached to their caregivers. Except in those cases where mothers are emotionally removed from their infants, strength of attachment is not based on who logs more hours with baby. Mother love, the strongest force in all our lives, carries a power not measured in minutes. Both in full-time day care here and on the Israeli kibbutz where the metapelet (nurse) cares for the children most of the day, in normal circumstances children make the strongest attachment to their parents, not their caregivers. For instance, if both the caregiver and mother are in the room when baby hurts himself, the baby will toddle to his mother for help. He will also stay closer to mother and lie on *her* lap when tired, bored, or unhappy. And he will greet her with a brighter smile upon return at the end of the day than he greeted his caregiver with in the morning.

Furthermore, mothers tend to stay, while caregivers come and go—first, because caregiver turnover is high, and second, because the overwhelming majority of day care centers segregate ages, moving infants to a different room and a different caregiver when they become toddlers, and again at 18 months, 2 years, 3 years, and 4 years of age, which continually forces the child to undergo attachment and separation.

This is not to say that the amount of time an infant is separated from mother is inconsequential. Whether a baby spends six hours in day care versus nine, or whether mother comes at lunchtime to feed her baby versus nine straight hours of separation, could impact on how well the mother gets to know her baby and on closeness. "If I hadn't been able to nurse her at lunch," says a mother who, beginning at two months, put her baby in a day care center close to her office, "I don't think I would have been able to tolerate the separation. Being able to nurse her once a day allowed me a necessary feeling of connection."

There are also individual differences in how babies cope. Some infants weather the storm of separation easily and seem to flourish in day care. Usually of easy temperament and social butterflies, they adapt easily to change and go readily to other caregivers, welcoming the opportunity to be with lots of different people, both little and big. In fact, these babies may be more fussy at home, where they can be bored with the same day-to-day scene.

My neighbor's gregarious eleven-month-old was like this. When I held my arms out to Marisol, she freely left her mother's arms and went to me, even when she barely knew me. The first time I took her into my house, she did not look back at her mother waiting outside. When I put her down, she squealed and ran around, excitedly exploring. When her mother put her in day care, she went eagerly.

Other infants are cautious, taking time to adjust to change. Often hard to comfort, they have a strong need for the special care their mother provides and suffer when separated for long hours. Ten-month-old Kareem was like this. In day care, he spent much time crying and fussing. "He's like this all the time," the caregivers told me. But with his solicitous mother, he was all smiles. When I show my child development classes a videotape of him with his mother, they rate him as a quiet, easy, and happy baby, securely attached. When shown in day care, they rate him as difficult, miserable, and insecurely attached.

Age of onset into day care may relate also to how easily a baby—and a mother—negotiate attachment and separation. If babies begin day care at less than four months of age, they may go more easily to another, but mother and baby may not have had an opportunity to become sufficiently attached. If, on the other hand, mother puts the baby in day care at seven to eight months of age, when attachment proper is just beginning for the baby, they are more likely to cry and cling. And, though most will cease crying soon after the mother leaves, infants of more sensitive temperament like Kareem often adjust poorly and remain fussy throughout the day, their adaptive capacities pushed to the limit.

But what of mothers who do not have a choice of when to return to work? I think it's important to evaluate other care as to how much each meets their infant's social, emotional, cognitive, and physical needs, and weigh this with the mother's own level of comfort for each choice. Or mothers can do what mothers have always done—combine work and nurturing, at least for babies under six months of age. If mothers feel at ease having their infants with them at the office, work and caring for young babies don't have to be incompatible. Young babies, content to be held for long periods, cry little unless in pain. Cashiers can punch, typists can type, receptionists can greet, leasing agents can tour, stockers can stock, telemarketers can dial, computer operators can input, and beauticians can cut hair with a three-month-old asleep on their back or happily cooing away. One mother I know cashiered in a health food store with her baby on her back until he was seven months old. I never saw him cry or fuss. He was too busy flirting with the customers. This situation is, of course, not ideal, but for many mothers, it beats trying to slip in and out of the mothering mode.

Nor need the presence of babies interfere with productivity. In fact, the opposite should occur. Having their baby with them, and especially nursing them, can prevent much stress and illness for both mother and infant, keeping both happier and healthier. This means less days missed and greater worker efficiency. Furthermore, mother will feel a deeper commitment to the workplace.

Nor must mothers necessarily work far from home. With a computer, a modem, and a fax, bookkeepers, journalists, editors, secretaries, telemarketers, accountants, auditors, even attorneys can do much of their work at home—full time if they must, part time if they can. Able to earn income, mothers can more easily afford home help, which gives the mother both helping hands and adult company. As their infant gets older, they can insure sufficient social and cognitive stimulation for the baby by putting their babies in other care part of the day, which still leaves the mother sharing an important part of her baby's life for much of the day.

14

‧ ‧

Finishing Touches

When I studied the Mayan Indians in Southern Mexico for their childrearing patterns, I longed for the revival in our society of at least two customs that we as a culture have given up. I longed for mothers to allow themselves more continual physical closeness with their infants and for the cushioning of the extended family for all young parents.

—T. Berry Brazelton

Civilization and its discontents: Freud thought they were inevitable, our effort to tame the savage within. Perhaps so, but the savage within isn't just rampant id. It speaks of a certain primitive design, one quite harmonious with modern civilization: a close mother-baby bond to protect the stability of the baby; a family structure to protect the stability of the mother; a community to protect the stability of the family; and a social framework to protect the stability of the community.

The more a society matches this basic ancient pattern, the less stressful. Unfortunately, though, our society has evolved away from this design, creating little rips and tears in the social fabric. Our emphasis on supreme self-reliance, our lack of social supports, our increasing isolationism—all leave many parents feeling vulnerable and inadequately protected. The more parents get absorbed in reducing the threats to their own safety, the less they are able to assure their infant's psychological and, sometimes, physical safety. Since this is antithetical to the mother's desire to promote her infant's survival, conflict results.

To restore balance, societies enact changes to create a better fit with our basic biological pattern. Witness our own recent history. Since the 1920s, the height of touch minimalism, we've seen a steady decline in the rigid parenting recommended by the behaviorists and a cultural shift toward more intimate parenting. By the 1970s, infant care underwent a revolution. We saw a re-emergence of breastfeeding and greater demand feeding, postpartum contact for bonding, more natural childbirth, the invention of the Snugli, a quicker response to the cry, the introduction of infant massage, and a slight lift of the longstanding taboo against co-sleeping. By the 1980s, Dr. Benjamin Spock was considered a hard-liner, forced to slug it out with the new kids on the block, people such as William Sears and Penelope Leach who advocated more indulgent parenting. By the 1990s, Richard Ferber modified his views never to rock or nurse a baby to sleep and T. Berry Brazelton began to modify his stance against mother and baby bed-sharing. Moreover, interdependence is becoming a bit more fashionable. Use of nannies and au pairs, for instance, is becoming more acceptable for even nonworking parents.

This gives us reason for optimism, but there's also pause for concern. Though mothers feel freer to indulge their infants' need for closeness, a voice still taunts us not to "spoil" our baby. This is unfortunate. As we've learned, touch has power.

At the heart of secure attachment, vital touch is our best ticket to increase our babies' chances for a smoother ride through life. Secure within our arms, crying is minimal, minimizing frustration and anger and making distress manageable. Physical safety is at its maximum, making babies more confident in their movements. Sensory stimulation is optimal—especially when flesh touches flesh—cutting down on boredom or overexcitement. And closeness is desired and available, making our babies feel understood, valued, and loved. Feeling protected, our babies eagerly explore the world when put down, knowing that if danger lurks, open arms await. Loved, the world becomes loving.

But when maternal envelopment is not guaranteed in times of need, the child is undermined from the start with a resumé that reads "easily threatened." The more this faulty perception mingles with other risk factors—losses, tragedies, failures, emotional reactivity, or sensory defensiveness—the more coping becomes an ongoing challenge and the more the world frustrates, disappoints, rejects, and, for some, overexcites. From our first breath to our last, how content we will ever be comes down to the degree to which we feel we can assure our own survival.

Touch reduces threat in other ways. It creates wonderful biochemical changes that relax us and makes coping easier. And the more in touch, the more sensory nourishment our babies' brains receive. This doesn't mean we should turn "native" and carry our babies all day. But we also can't allow ourselves to become tools of our tools, in Thoreau's words. Rather, we need a hybrid: buggies *and* slings. And we need to stop making mothers feel guilty for *wanting* intimacy with their infants.

Restricting touch adds nothing to our humanity. Affection is what makes us most human. Decreasing it makes us more prone to anxiety, depression, disease, violence, and general human misery. If we start out touch conservative with our infants and young children, and, as a result of touch's bad press in this current climate of sexual abuse hysteria, discourage human intimacy, we run the risk that our children will grow up touch malnourished. This is a disquieting thought. As it is, there's little touch in this society. Even before sexual abuse hysteria, we felt the need to advertise touch—"Have you hugged your child today?" asks the bumper sticker. Moreover, children whose need for intimacy was satisfied in infancy and early childhood do not grow up to sexually exploit others as an outlet for physical closeness. Nor do they become violent. By restricting good touch to avoid bad touch, we throw out our very best deterrent. Ultimately, we increase the very thing we wish to eliminate—unhealthy touch.

Even a little touch can go a long way. In the still-faced situation, when mothers transform from playful and loving to "still-faced" and unresponsive, their babies start to fall apart. They slump, drool, hiccup, pale, clench and unclench their fists, and look horrifically sad. But if mothers are touching their baby even slightly—a hand on their baby's leg—babies smile more and grimace less.

This has all sorts of implications. Because we lack more time for ourselves, we often shoo our little ones away—when company comes or the phone rings, for instance. But this only increases their need for us. But if we let them lean against our leg when on the phone or hug our knee when talking to our neighbor, thereby satisfying their skin hunger, they usually quiet and we see less of the brazen attention-getting that parents find so annoying.

As for concern that indulging our infant's need for close contact will lead to dependency, we can lay this worry aside. It is the children whose mothers answered their cry inconsistently (leaving them unable to predict safety) or those whose mothers did *not* promptly answer their cry with close bodily contact (leaving them doubtful of adequate protection) who end up with strong dependency needs. Some, fearing abandonment, treat each separation as a trauma, clinging and begging to not be left alone. Others *seemingly* separate with ease but live inside with perpetual *unease*, racked with desire for unmet nurturance they feel compelled to conceal. Many grow up maintaining this facade lest, by becoming intimate, they open up a Pandora's box of longings to share a synchronous closeness with someone who appreciates them and understands how they feel—longings that leave them, when disappointed, dangerously vulnerable to rejection, to despair. Self-reliance as a defense: Such is the legacy of nonsynchrony in our first relationship.

For this, we've paid our pound of flesh by becoming a nation of social solitaries, as Allan Bloom noted, governed by a psychology of separateness. This has created a pathology peculiar to Western civilization—alienation. It takes little imagination to see its roots in the failure of our first attachments to adequately satisfy early dependency needs.

How much affectionate touch do babies need? Probably more than the average American baby in a container much of the day receives. As for the individual infant, she should receive as much touch as it takes to keep her content. On the other hand, parents should not feel compelled to assume an intimacy that feels uncomfortable. A mother who breastfeeds her infant grudgingly—"It was like a business," admitted one mother—will translate her feelings to her baby and do more harm than good. Likewise, a mother who sleeps with her infant to prevent SIDS but who tosses and turns all night as a result will be too exhausted to care for her infant. Similarly, a mother who stiffens when holding her baby naked against her body will only cause her infant to draw back.

Yet, I can't deny that this book is a call to arms and that the victory parade I envisage will be a march through the malls with more babies strapped on our hips, our backs, our fronts, or shoulders. I believe this will be good for all babies—and especially those content only when held. Each tender touch buys love stock kept in a permanent reserve, always there to be drawn from. What better future security could parents offer?

To make this a reality, I envision a society that becomes more in tune with our human nature and offers a protective halo of support for parenting from the beginning: widespread use of a doula for birthing; minimal separation of infant and mother postbirth; full-time rather than part-time rooming-in; the abolishment of drive through births; guaranteed nursing visits for at least the first week of life; and a developmental consultation as part of wellness visits to the pediatrician.

I would like to see social policies become more parent friendly: extended work leave and at least partial pay for the first six months of a baby's life; more on-site day care; a federally mandated caregiver and infant ratio of no greater than one-to-three for caregivers of infants; flexible work arrangements, including more part-time work, working at home, and bringing young babies to the worksite. In addition, mommy drop-in centers should be a part of every neighborhood and should include daily "mommy and me" sessions, and housing should be designed in a more family friendly way.

Touching a baby is an epiphany—the essence of life! Neither baby *nor* parent should be deprived of it for a moment.

❧

Notes

The numbers at left refer to page and line numbers respectively.

v   Margaret Mead and F. C. Macgregor, *Growth and Culture* (New York: G. P. Putnam's Sons, 1951).

INTRODUCTION

4:9–11   Betsy Lozoff and Gary Brittenham, "Infant care: cache or carry?" *Journal of Pediatrics* 95, 3 (1979): 478–83.

6:14–20   H. Troyat, *Tolstoy*, trans. Nancy Amphous (Garden City, N.Y.: Doubleday, 1967).

25–26   Rod McKuen, *Alone* (New York: Pocket Books, 1975).

1. PARENTING IN THE MACHINE AGE

13:4–5   Lionel Tiger, "My turn: a very old animal called man," *Newsweek* (September 4, 1978), 13.

23–26   Cited in D. M. Schneider and G. C. Homans, "Kinship terminology and the American kinship system," *American Anthropologist* 57 (1955): 1206.

37–40   John B. Watson, *Psychological Care of Infant and Child* (New York: W. W. Norton, 1928).

14:1–5   Ibid.

7–15   Cited in Ashley Montagu, *Touching: The Human Significance of the Skin* (New York: Harper & Row, 1986).

21–28   U.S. Children's Bureau, *Infant Care*, Care of Children Series No. 2. (Bureau Publication no. 8, rev., 1924), 44.

40   John B. Watson, *Behaviorism* (Chicago: University of Chicago Press, 1924), 104.

15:1–6   Ibid.

10–19   For a review of evolutionary psychology, see David Barash, *The Whisperings Within: Evolution and the Origin of Human Nature* (New York: Penguin, 1979) and *Sociobiology and Behavior* (New York: Elsevier, 1982).

16:11–24   Cited in Montagu, *Touching*, p. 98.

18:6–7   Margaret Mead, *Male and Female* (New York: William Morrow and Co., 1949), 154.

7–26   Robbie E. Davis-Floyd, "The technological model of birth," *Journal of American Folklore* (October–December 1987): 479–95.

27–29   Wenda Trevathan, *Human Birth: An Evolutionary Perspective* (New York: Aldine de Gruyter, 1987).

38–40   Michel Odent, "Newborn weight loss," *Mothering* (Winter 1989), 72–73.

19:1–3 Ibid.

6–15   Betsy Lozoff, "Birth in non-industrial societies," in *Birth, Interaction and Attachment*, Pediatric Round Table 6, eds. M. Klaus and M. O. Robertson (Skillman, N.J.: Johnson & Johnson Baby Products Company, 1982).

22–40   Marshall H. Klaus, John H. Kennell, and Phyllis H. Klaus, *Mothering the Mother* (Reading, Mass.: Addison-Wesley, 1993).

20:1–4 Ibid.

9–11   Ibid.

36–37   Michel Odent, "The milieu and obstetrical positions during labor: A new approach from France," in *Birth, Interaction and Attachment*.

21:3–4 R. Caldeyro-Barcia et al. "Effects of position changes on the intensity and frequency of uterine contractions during labor," *American Journal of Obstetrics and Gynecology* 80 (1960): 284–86.

9–10   A. Flynn and J. Kelly, "Continuous fetal monitoring in the ambulant patient in labour," *British Medical Journal* 2 (1976): 842–43.

17–21   Odent, "The milieu and obstetrical positions during labor."

22–31   Dora Henschel, "The milieu and obstetrical positions during labor: a new approach from France—commentary," in *Birth, Interaction and Attachment*.

22:16–17 Robin Fox, *The Red Lamp of Incest* (Notre Dame, Ind.: University of Notre Dame Press, 1980).

24:4–6 T. B. Brazelton, "Implications of infant development among the Mayan Indians of Mexico," in *Culture and Infancy*, eds. P. Leiderman, S. Tulkin, and A. Rosenfeld (New York: Academic Press, 1977), 287–328.

10–12   J. Schreiber, "Birth, the family and the community: a southern Italian example," *Birth and the Family Journal* 4 (1977): 153–57.

13–16   S. Rodell, "Memo to Hillary: please have a look at Australia's system" (Editorial Notebook), *New York Times* (25 July 1993), 16.

23–25   Hideo Kojima, "Becoming nurturant in Japan: past and present," in *Origins of Nurturance*, eds. Alan Fogel and Gail F. Melson (Hillsdale, N.J.: Lawrence Erlbaum Associates, 1986).

30–36   Lozoff, "Birth in non-industrial societies," 2.

25:4–9 Quoted in *Motherhood* (Philadelphia: Running Press, 1991).

24–27   Penelope Leach, *Children First* (New York: Alfred A. Knopf, 1994), 50.

28–32   Michel Odent, *Birth Reborn* (New York: Pantheon Books, 1984).

2. NEWBORN HARMONY

27:17–26 M. M. Haith, "Sensory and perceptual processes in early infancy," *Journal of Pediatrics* 109 (1986): 158–71.

27–30   Marshall H. Klaus and John Kennell, *Maternal/Infant Bonding* (St. Louis: C.V. Mosby Co., 1976).

31–33   Martin Greenberg and Norman Norris, "Engrossment: The newborn's impact upon the father," *American Journal of Orthopsychiatry* 44 (1974), 526.

28:1–5 Margaret Mead and Niles Newton, "Cultural patterning of perinatal behavior," *Childrearing: Its Social and Psychological Aspects*, eds. S. A. Richardson and A. F. Guttermacher (Baltimore: Williams & Wilkins, 1967).

10–11 K. Robson and R. Kumar, "Delayed onset of maternal affection after childbirth," *British Journal of Psychiatry* 136 (1980): 347–53.

29:10–12 Ashley Montagu, *Touching: The Human Significance of the Skin* (New York: Harper & Row, 1986).

21–26 Martin Reite and John P. Capitanio. "On the nature of social separation and social attachment," in *The Psychobiology of Attachment and Separation*, eds. Martin Reite and Tiffany Field (New York: Academic Press, 1985): 223–55.

27–29 C. R. Carpenter, "Societies of monkeys and apes," *Biological Symposium* 8 (1942): 177–204.

30:3–7 A. M. Widström, A. B. Ransjö-Arvidson, K. Christensson et al. "Gastric suction in healthy newborn infants: effects on circulation and developing feeding behavior," *ACTA Paediatrica Scandinavica* 76 (1987): 566–72.

35–40 Gene C. Anderson, "Risk in mother-infant separation postbirth," *Image: Journal of Nursing Scholarship* 21 (Winter 1989), 196–99.

31:1–13 Ibid.

20–32 P. Karlberg, "The adaptive changes in the immediate postnatal period with particular reference to respiration," *Journal of Pediatrics* 56 (1960): 585–604.

32:8–11 C. C. Lambesis, D. Vidyasagar, and G. C. Anderson, "Effects of surrogate mothering on physiologic stabilization in transitional newborns," in *Newborn Behavioral Organization: Nursing Research and Implications*, eds. G. C. Anderson and G. Raff (New York: Liss, 1979).

15–20 Ibid.

13–14 Anderson, "Risk in mother-infant separation postbirth."

22–26 K. Christensson, C. Siles, L. Moreno et al., "Temperature, metabolic adaptation and crying in healthy full-term newborns cared for skin-to-skin or in a cot," *Acta Paediatrica Scandinavica* 81 (1992): 488–93.

30–31 Maureen Keefe, "The impact of rooming-in on maternal sleep at night," *Journal of Obstetric, Gynecologic, and Neonatal Nursing* 17 (1988): 122–26.

37–39 J. F. Sassin, A. G. Frantz, E. D. Weitzman, and S. Kapen, "Human prolactin: 24-hour pattern with increased release during sleep," *Science* 177 (1972): 1205–07.

33:24–28 Christensson, "Temperature, metabolic adaptation and crying in healthy full-term newborns."

31–40 Judith A. Färdig, "A comparison of skin to skin contact and radiant heaters in promoting neonatal thermoregulation," *Journal of Nurse-Midwifery* 25, no. 1 (1980): 19–28.

34:1–8 Ibid.

35:4–9 S. Ludington-Hoe, A. Hadeed, and G. C. Anderson, "Maternal-neonatal thermal synchrony during skin-to-skin contact," *Abstracts of Individual Papers*, Research Conference of the Council of Nurse Researchers, Chicago 1989, 286.

10–29 Gene C. Anderson, "Current knowledge about skin-to-skin (kangaroo) care for preterm infants," *Journal of Perinatology* 11 (1991): 216–26.

36:2–7 Anderson, "Current knowledge about skin-to-skin (kangaroo) care."

24–26 Ashley Montagu, *Growing Young* (New York: McGraw Hill, 1981).

30–32 K. Mizukami, N. Kobayashi, H. Iwata, and T. Ishii, "Telethermography in infant's emotional behavioral research," *Lancet*, vol. II, no. 8549 (4 July 1987), 38.

37:16–23 Saul Schanberg and Tiffany Field, "Sensory deprivation stress and supplemental stimulation in the rat pup and preterm human neonate," *Child Development* 58 (1987): 1431–47.

21–23 Michael Leon, "Touch and smell," in *Touch in Early Development*, ed. Tiffany Field (Mahwah, N.J.: Lawrence Erlbaum Associates, 1995).

34–40 Frank Scafidi, Tiffany Field, Saul Schanberg et al., "Effects of tactile/kinesthetic stimulation on the clinical course and sleep/wake behavior of preterm neonates," *Infant Behavior and Development* 9 (1986): 91–105.

38:1–5 Ibid.

5–7 Elvidina Adamson-Macedo, "Very early tactile stimulation and later cognitive development." Paper presented at the International Conference on Infant Studies, Paris, 1994.

16–27 Tiffany Field, "Massage therapy for infants and children," *Developmental and Behavioral Pediatrics* 16, no. 2 (1995): 105–11.

28–30 T. Field, D. Lasko, P. Mundy et al., "Autistic children's attentiveness and responsivity improved after touch therapy," *Journal of Autism and Developmental Disorders*, in press.

33–39 Proverb in an article on the genealogical origin of T. Wirepa's wife, in *Te Toa Takat Magazine* (New Zealand, 1925–26). Quoted in Amelia Auckett, *Baby Massage* (New York: Newmarket Press, 1989).

39:1–5 Cassie Landers, "Child-rearing practices and infant development in South India," in *Advances in Touch*, Pediatric Round Table: 14, ed. N. Gunzenhauser (Skillman, N.J.: Johnson & Johnson Baby Products Company, 1990), 42–53.

11–21 Tiffany Field, "Massage therapy for infants and children."

23–25 Julie A. Hayes, Elvina Adamson-Macedo, Shantha Perrara, "Secretory immune responses of ventilated preterms to gentle/light and systematic stroking," Abstract from International Conference on Infant Studies (Providence, R.I., April 1996).

27–35 Caroline S. Koblenzer, "Cutaneous manifestations of psychiatric disease that commonly present to the dermatologist: diagnosis and treatment," *International Journal of Psychiatry in Medicine* 22, no. 1 (1992): 47–63.

37–39 Michael J. Meaney, David H. Aitken, Seema Bhatnagar, and Robert M. Sapolsky, "Postnatal handling attenuates certain neuroendocrine, anatomical, and cognitive dysfunctions associated with aging in female rats," *Neurobiology of Aging* 12, no. 1 (1991): 31–38.

40:1–5 Ibid.

3. HOLDING HOLDS BABIES TOGETHER

43:17–22 Michel Odent, *Birth Reborn* (New York: Pantheon Books, 1984).

22–29 Dora Henschel, "The milieu and obstetrical positions during labor: a new approach from France—commentary," in *Birth, Interaction and Attachment*, Pediatric Round Table 6, eds. M. Klaus and M. D. Robertson (Skillman, N.J.: Johnson & Johnson Baby Products Company, 1982), 31.

31–36 Frederick Leboyer, *Birth without Violence* (New York: Alfred A. Knopf, 1975).

44:6–7 R. H. Woodson, "Newborn behavior and the transition to extrauterine life," *Infant Behavior and Development* 6 (1983): 139–44.

7–8 V. Yu, "Effect of body position on gastric emptying in the neonate," *Archives of Diseases in Childhood* 50 (1975): 500–504.

14–17 Patricia Wilbarger and Patti Oetter, "Sensory defensiveness and related social/emotional and neurological disorders." Workshop given in Panama City, Fla. January 1994.

37–39 T. B. Brazelton, "Development of newborn behavior," in *Human Growth 2*, eds. F. Falkner and J.M. Tanner (Plenum Publishing Corporation, 1986), 531.

45:1–4 Ibid.

46:6–11 John B. Watson, *Psychological Care of Infant and Child* (New York: W. W. Norton, 1928), 138–39.

21–28 Ann Garrould and Gail Belburd, eds., *Mother and Child: The Art of Henry Moore* (Hempstead, N.Y.: Hofstra University, and University of Pennsylvania Press, 1987), 21, 23.

48:13–15 Sandra Day, "Mother-infant activities as providers of sensory stimulation," *American Journal of Occupational Therapy* 36, no. 9 (1982): 579–85.

20–22 Margaret Mead and F. C. Macgregor, *Growth and Culture* (New York: G. P. Putnam's Sons, 1951), 42–43.

25–27 Heinz Prechtl. "Problems of behavioral studies in the newborn infant," in *Advances in the Study of Behavior*, vol. 1, eds. D. S. Lehrman, R. A. Hinde, and E. Shaw (New York: Academic Press, 1965), 75–99.

32–36 J. S. Chisholm, *Navajo Infancy: An Ethological Study of Child Development* (New York: Aldine, 1983).

49:1–4 Ashley Montagu, *Touching: The Human Significance of the Skin* (New York: Harper & Row, 1986).

6–15 Jean Liedloff, *The Continuum Concept* (Reading, Mass.: Addison-Wesley, 1977): 14.

32–36 Chisholm, *Navajo Infancy*.

50:23–28 H. R. Schaffer and P. E. Emerson, "Patterns of response to physical contact in early human development," *Journal of Child Psychology & Psychiatry* 5 (1964): 1–13.

29–40 Daniel G. Freedman, *Human Infancy: An Evolutionary Perspective* (Hillsdale, N.J.: Lawrence Erlbaum, 1974).

51:1–6 Ibid.

12–19 T. B. Brazelton, "Fetal observations: could they relate to another modality such as touch?" in *Touch in Early Development*, ed. Tiffany Field (Mahwah, N.J.: Lawrence Erlbaum, 1995), 11–18.

52:15–17 T. G. Hartstock, "Maladaptive behaviors of piglets weaned at 12 hours postpartum," *Journal of Animal Science* 49 (1979): 147.

18–20 Harry F. Harlow, "Love in infant monkeys," *Scientific American* 200 (1959): 68–74.

32–40 Heidilise Als, "Individualized behavioral and environmental care for the very low birth weight preterm infant at high risk for bronchopulmonary dysplasia: Neonatal intensive care unit and developmental outcome," *Pediatrics* 78, no. 6 (1986): 1123–32.

53:1–7 Ibid.

12 Sigmund Freud, *The Ego and the Id*, in *The Complete Psychological Works of*

Sigmund Freud, vol. 19, ed. and trans. J. Strachey (London: Hogarth Press, 1923/1961), 26.

15–20   S. Wapner, The Body Percept (New York: Random House, 1965).

21–26   S. M. Jourard, "An exploratory study of body-accessibility," British Journal of Social and Clinical Psychology 5 (1966): 221–31.

4. THE FIRST CONNECTION

54:38–40   John Bowlby, Attachment & Loss, Vol. I: Attachment (New York: Basic Books, 1969).

55:1   Ibid.

7–8   K. M. Robson and R. Kumar, "Delayed onset of maternal affection after childbirth," British Journal of Psychiatry 136 (1980): 347–53.

20–40   Harry F. Harlow, "The nature of love," American Psychologist 13 (1958): 675.

56:1–5   Ibid.

10–12   Sigmund Freud, An Outline of Psychoanalysis (New York: W. W. Norton, 1940).

16–21   L. A. Sroufe, E. Carlson, and S. Shulman, "The development of individuals in relationships: from infancy through adolescence." Unpublished manuscript, Institute of Child Development, University of Minnesota.

37–40   Mary D. S. Ainsworth, Patterns of Attachment: A Psychological Study of the Strange Situation (Hillsdale, N.J.: Lawrence Erlbaum, 1978).

57:1–20   Ibid.

25–37   Ibid.

58:13–20   Ibid.

59:8–12   R. St. Barbe Baker, Kabongo (New York: A. S. Barnes & Co., 1955), 18.

26–28   Mary D. S. Ainsworth, Infancy in Uganda: Infant Care and the Growth of Love (Baltimore: Johns Hopkins University Press, 1967).

28–33   Alice A. Honig, "Recent infancy research," in Infants: Their Social Environments, eds. B. Weissbourd and J. Musick (Washington, D.C.: National Association for the Education of Young Children, 1981), 5–46.

36–40   Bowlby, Attachment.

60:1–10   Ibid.

21–23   Michael Lamb, "Effects of stress and cohort on mother- and father-infant interaction," Developmental Psychology 12 (1976): 435–43.

28–29   Michael E. Lamb, "Father-infant and mother-infant interaction in the first year of life," Child Development 48 (1977): 167–81.

29–30   Tiffany M. Field, "Interaction behaviors of primary versus secondary caretaker fathers," Developmental Psychology 14 (1978): 183–84.

30–31   M. Yogman, S. Dixon, E. Z. Tronick, H. Als, and T. B. Brazelton, "The goals and structure of face-to-face interaction between infants and fathers." Paper presented at the biennial meeting of the Society for Research in Child Development, New Orleans, March 1977.

36–40   D. W. Winnicott, The Child, the Family and the Outside World (Reading, Mass.: Addison-Wesley, 1987), 198.

61:1–4   Ibid.

6–8   M. A. Easterbrook and W. A. Goldberg, "Toddler development in the family: impact of father involvement and parenting characteristics," Child Development 55 (1984): 740–52.

28–36   Justina C. Ray and Robert M. Sapolsky, "Styles of male social behavior and their endocrine correlates among high-ranking wild baboons," *American Journal of Primatology* 28, no. 4 (1992): 231–50.

62:2–5   Roger Kobak, "Attachment, affect regulation and defense." Paper presented at the biennial meeting of the Society for Research in Child Development, April 1987.

6–9   Cited in Robert Karen, *Becoming Attached* (New York: Warner Books, 1994).

39–40   Ibid.

63:1   Ibid.

11–12   Patricia Crittenden, "Quality of attachment in the preschool years," *Development and Psychopathology* 4 (1992): 209–41.

35–40   Patricia M. Crittenden, "The effect of early relationship experiences on relationships in adulthood," in *Handbook of Personal Relationships*, 2nd ed., ed. Steve Duck (Chichester, Eng.: John Wiley & Sons, 1997).

64:11–17   Lynn Murray and Colwyn Trevarthen, "Emotional regulation of interaction between two-month-olds and their mothers," in *Social Perception in Infants*, eds. T. M. Field and N. A. Fox (Norwood, N.J.: Ablex, 1985).

35–36   I. C. Kaufman and L. A. Rosenblum, "The waning of the mother-infant bond in two species of macaques," in *Determinants of Infant Behavior*, vol. 4, ed. B. Foss (London: Methuen, 1969): 37–59.

39   Personal communication from Patricia Crittenden, Delray, Florida, summer 1993.

65:1–2   Ibid.

13–28   Crittenden, "Quality of attachment in the preschool years."

66:35–36   Ainsworth, *Patterns of Attachment.*

36–39   Mary Main and Donna Weston, "Avoidance of the attachment figure in infancy: Descriptions and interpretations," in *The Place of Attachment in Human Behavior*, eds. C. M. Parkes and J. Stevenson-Hinde (New York: Basic Books, 1982): 31–59.

67:9–10   Mary Main and Donna Weston, "The quality of the toddler's relationship to mother and to father as related to conflict behavior and readiness to establish new relationships," *Child Development* 52 (1981): 932–40.

11–14   Patricia M. Crittenden, "Compulsive compliance: the development of an inhibitory coping strategy in infancy," *Journal of Abnormal Child Psychology* 16, no. 5 (1988): 585–99.

29–31   E. Waters, J. Wippman, and A. Sroufe, "Attachment, positive affect, and competence in the peer group: two studies in construct validation," *Child Development* 50 (1979): 821–29.

68:2–4   Alan Sroufe and Everett Waters, "Heart rate as a convergent measure in clinical and developmental research," *Merrill-Palmer Quarterly* 23 (1977): 3–27.

12–18   Crittenden, "Quality of attachment in the preschool years."

38–40   Mary Main, "Parental aversion to infant-initiated contact is correlated with the parent's own rejection during childhood: the effects of experience on signals of security with respect to attachment," in *Touch: The Foundation of Experience*, Clinical Infant Reports #4, eds. K. E. Barnard & T. B. Brazelton (Madison, Conn.: International Universities Press, 1989).

69:1–9   Ibid.

20–35   Mary Main and J. Stadtman, "Infant response to rejection of physical contact by the mother," *Journal of the American Academy of Child Psychiatry* 20 (1981): 292.

70:18–27 Erma Bombeck, *All I Know About Animal Behavior I Learned in Loehman's Dressing Room* (New York: Harper Collins, 1985).

71:4–5 Marvin E. Wolfgang, "Violence and human behavior," in *Proceedings of the Annual Conference of the American Psychological Association*, Washington, D.C., August, 1969.

5–6 M. A. Strauss, "Family violence in American families: Incidence, notes, causes and trends," in *Abused and Battered: Social and Legal Responses of Family Violence* (New York: Aldine de Gruyter, 1991): 17–34.

6–8 R. E. Sears, E. Maccoby, and H. Lewin, *Patterns of Child Rearing* (Evanston, Ill.: Row, Peterson, 1957).

15–30 James W. Prescott, "Body pleasure and the origins of violence," *The Futurist* (April 1975): 64–67.

32–40 Margaret Mead, *Sex and Temperament in Three Primitive Societies* (New York: William Morrow, 1965).

72:1–7 Ibid.

8–11 Margaret Mead, *Male and Female* (New York: William Morrow, 1949, 1975), 54.

15–19 Patricia M. Crittenden, "Internal representational models of attachment relationships," *Infant Mental Health* 11 (1990): 259–77.

39–40 Cited in Karen, *Becoming Attached*.

73:1–4 Ibid.

7–10 Crittenden, "Compulsive compliance."

74:12–13 Main, "Infant response to rejection of physical contact by the mother."

21–24 Mary Main and Jude Cassidy, "Categories of response to reunion with the parent at age six: predictability from infant attachment classification and stable across a one-month period," *Developmental Psychology* 24 (1988): 415–26.

27–29 Patricia M. Crittenden, "Relationships at Risk," in *Clinical Implications of Attachment*, eds. J. Belsky and T. Nezworski (Hillsdale, N.J.: Lawrence Erlbaum, 1988), 136–74.

75:3–5 Jack Panksepp, "Substitute bonds—drugs as family," *Brain/Mind Bulletin* 5, no. 12 (1980): 3.

28–29 P. Fonagy, H. Steele, and M. Steele, "Maternal representations of attachment during pregnancy predict the organization of infant-mother attachment at one year of age," *Child Development* 62 (1991): 891–905.

76:25–28 E. E. Perris, N. A. Myers, and R. K. Clifton, "Long-term memory for a single infancy experience," *Child Development* 61 (1990): 1796–1807.

77:19–21 David McClelland and Joel Weinberger, "Childhood antecedents of conventional social accomplishment in midlife adults: a 36-year prospective study," *Journal of Personality and Social Psychology* 60, no. 4 (1991): 586–95.

22–39 Edward Z. Tronick, "Interactive mismatch and repair: challenges to the coping infant," in *Zero to Three* VI, no. 3 (February 1986): 3.

78:1–2 Ibid.

3–12 Edward Z. Tronick, Margaret Ricks, and Jeffrey E. Cohn, "Maternal and infant affective exchange: patterns of adaptation," in *Emotion and Early Interaction*, eds. Tiffany Field and Alan Fogel (Hillsdale, N.J.: Lawrence Erlbaum, 1982), 88.

15–21 Crittenden, "Compulsive compliance."

22–26   Allan Schore, *Affect Regulation and the Origin of Self* (Hillsdale, N.J.: Lawrence Erlbaum, 1994).

35–36   M. E. Phelps et al., "PET: A biochemical image of the brain at work," in *Brain Work and Mental Activity: Quantitative Studies with Radioactive Tracers*, ed. N. A. Lassen et al. (Copenhagen: Munksgaard, 1991).

79:3–8   L. A. Sroufe, B. Egeland, and T. Kreutzer, "The fate of early experience following developmental change: longitudinal approaches to individual adaptation in childhood," *Child Development* 61 (1990): 1363–73.

14–18   Main and Weston, "The quality of the toddler's relationship to mother and father."

24–27   Mary Main, Nancy Kaplan, and Jude Cassidy, "Security in infancy, childhood and adulthood: a move to the level of representation," in *Growing Points in Attachment Theory and Research*, eds. Inge Bretherton and Everett Waters, *Monographs of the Society for Research in Child Development* 50, nos. 1 and 2 (1985): 66–104.

27–29   B. Egeland, D. Jacobvitz, and L. A. Sroufe, "Breaking the cycle of abuse: relationship predictions," *Child Development* 59 (1988): 1080–88.

30–32   A. F. Lieberman, D. Weston, and J. H. Paul, "Preventive intervention and outcome with anxiously attached dyads," *Child Development* 62 (1991): 199–209.

80:3–5   A. Thomas and S. Chess, *Temperament and Development* (New York: Brunner-Mazel, 1977).

30–33   H. R. Schaffer and Peggy E. Emerson, "Patterns of response to physical contact in early human development," *Journal of Child Psychology and Psychiatry* 5 (1964): 13.

81:13–14   S. Mangelsdorf, M. Gunnar, R. Kestenbaum et al., "Infant proneness-to-distress temperament, maternal personality, and mother-infant attachment: associations and goodness-of-fit," *Child Development* 61 (1990): 820–31.

27–28   Robert A. Hinde and Y. Spencer-Booth, "The effect of social companions on mother-infant relations in rhesus monkeys," in *Primate Ethology*, D. Morris, ed., (Chicago: Aldine, 1967)

30–32   Michael E. Lamb, R. A. Thompson, W. Gardner, and E. L. Charnov, *Infant-Mother Attachment: The Origins and Developmental Significance of Individual Differences in Strange Situation Behavior* (Hillsdale, N.J.: Lawrence Erlbaum, 1985).

32–34   Beverly Fagot, "Attachment: infancy to preschool." Paper presented at the International Conference on Infant Studies, Paris, 1994.

82:15–40   Mary Martini, "Parent-toddler interactions in Hawaii: learning social and psychological preferences." Paper presented at the International Conference on Infant Studies, Miami, May, 1992.

83:1–4   Ibid.

5–10   Vidal S. Clay, "The effect of culture on mother-child tactile communication." Ph.D. diss. Teachers College, Columbia University, 1966.

25–30   B. B. Whiting and C. P. Edwards, *Children of Different Worlds* (Cambridge: Harvard University Press, 1988).

84:24–25   Lamb et al., *Infant-Mother Attachment.*

35–39   Irven DeVore and Melvin J. Konner, "Infancy in hunter-gatherer life: an ethological perspective," in *Ethology and Psychiatry*, ed. N. White (Toronto: University of Toronto Press, 1974).

39–40   O. Schaeffer, "When the Eskimo comes to town," *Nutrition Today* (November–December 1971): 8–16.

85:1–2   Ibid.

3–15   Elizabeth Anisfeld, "Does infant carrying promote attachment? An experimental study of the effects of increased physical contact on the development of attachment," *Child Development* 61 (1990): 1617–27.

16–22   Elizabeth Anisfeld, "Effects of a carrying intervention on the development of attachment in premature infants." Paper presented at Society for Research in Child Development Biennial Meeting, Kansas City, April 1989.

40   M. M. DeVries and A. Sameroff, "Culture and temperament: influences on infant temperament in three East African societies," *American Journal of Orthopsychiatry* 54, no. 1 (1984): 83–96.

86:1–10   Ibid.

21–28   Melvin J. Konner, "Maternal care, infant behavior, and development among the !Kung," in *Kalahari Hunter-Gatherers, Studies of the !Kung San and Their Neighbours*, eds. R. B. Lee & I. DeVore (Cambridge: Harvard University Press, 1976): 218–45.

32–35   Whiting and Edwards, *Children of Different Worlds.*

87:10–20   Abraham Sagi, Michael E. Lamb, Kathleen S. Lewkowicz et al., "Security of mother-infant, -father, and -metapelet attachments among kibbutz-reared Israeli children," in Growing Points of Attachment Theory and Research, eds. Inge Bretherton and Everett Waters, *Monographs of the Society for Research in Child Development* 50, nos. 1 and 2 (1985): 257–75.

21–39   K. Grossmann and K. E. Grossmann, "Maternal sensitivity and newborns' orientation responses as related to quality of attachment in northern Germany," in Growing Points of Attachment Theory and Research: 233–56.

88:1–2   Ibid.

8–17   K. Grossmann and K. E. Grossmann, "Attachment quality as an organizer of emotional and behavioral responses in a longitudinal perspective," in *Attachment Across the Life Span*, eds. C. M. Parkes, J. Stevenson-Hinde, and P. Marris (New York: Tavistock/Routledge, 1991).

14–16   Cited in Karen, *Becoming Attached.*

22–24   Tiffany Field, "Child abuse in monkeys and humans: a comparative perspective, in *Child Abuse: The Non-Human Primate Data*, eds. M. Reite and N. Caine (New York: Liss, 1983).

28–30   Deborah L. Vandell, Margaret T. Owen, Kathy A. Wilson, and V. Kay Henderson, "Social development in infant twins: peer and mother-child relationships," *Child Development* 59, no. 1 (1988): 168–77.

32–40   Hideo Kojima, "Becoming nurturant in Japan: past and present," in *Origins of Nurturance*, eds. Alan Fogel and Gail F. Melson (Hillsdale, N.J.: Lawrence Erlbaum, 1986).

89:11–12   Lamb et al., *Infant-Mother Attachment.*

26–32   A. Sagi, M. H. van IJzendoorn, O. Aviezer et al., "Sleeping away from home in a kibbutz communal arrangement: it makes a difference for infant-mother attachment," *Child Development* 65 (1994): 988–1000.

5. ROCK OF LOVE

91:31–32   Diane Ackerman, *The Natural History of the Senses* (New York: Random House, 1990).

32–36   A. Ambrose, *Stimulation in Early Infancy* (New York: Academic Press, 1969).

92:11–17   Ashley Montagu, *Touching: The Human Significance of the Skin* (New York: Harper & Row, 1986).

93:8–11   R. N. Emde, R. J. Harmon, D. R. Metcalf et al., "Stress and neonatal sleep," *Psychosomatic Medicine* 33 (1971): 491–97.

23–26   A. B. Roberts, D. Lille, and S. Campbell, "24-hour studies of fetal movements and fetal body movements in normal and abnormal pregnancies," in *The Current Status of Fetal Heart Rate Monitoring and Ultrasound in Obstetrics*, eds. R. W. Beard and S. Campbell (London: Royal College of Obstetricians and Gynaecologists, 1977).

32–38   Jean Liedloff, "The importance of the in-arms phase," *Mothering* (Winter 1989): 17.

94:15–18   Annelise Korner and Evelyn B. Thoman, "Visual alertness in neonates as evoked by maternal care," *Journal of Experimental Psychology* 10 (1970): 67–78.

24–28   T. Bower, J. Broughton, and M. Moore, "Infant responses to approaching objects: an indicator of response to distal variables," *Perception and Psychophysics* 9 (1970): 193–96.

29–40   Patti Oetter, E. W. Richter, S. M. Frick, M.O.R.E. *Integrating the Mouth with Sensory and Postural Functions* (Hugo, Minn.: PDP Press, 1993).

95:23–26   W. A. Mason, and G. Berkson, "Effects of maternal mobility on the development of rocking and other behaviors in rhesus monkeys: a study with artificial mothers," *Developmental Psychobiology* 8, no. 3 (1975): 197–211.

27–32   A. F. Korner, C. Guilleminault, J. Vanden Hoed et al., "Reduction of sleep apnea and bradycardia in preterm infants on oscillation waterbeds: a controlled polygraphic study," *Pediatrics* 61, no. 4 (1978): 528–33.

33–38   D. Clark, J. Kreutzberg, and F. Chee, "Vestibular stimulation's influence on motor development," *Science* 196 (1977): 1228–29.

97:26–35   Elizabeth Marshall Thomas, *The Harmless People* (New York: Random House, 1955), 90.

99:8–9   Emmy E. Werner, "Infants around the world: cross-cultural studies of psychomotor development from birth to two years," *Journal of Cross-Cultural Psychology* 3, no. 2 (1972): 111–34.

13–21   Sandra Edwards, "Babes in arms," *OT Week* (22 June 1989): 18–29.

23–29   James R. De Boer, "The Netsilik Eskimo and the origin of human behavior." Cited in Montagu, *Touching*, 297.

34–37   Heinz Prechtl, in *Stimulation in Early Infancy*, ed. A. Ambrose (New York: Academic Press, 1969), 98.

100:4–7   M. Geber, "The psychomotor development of African children in the first year and the influence of maternal behavior," *Journal of Social Psychology* 47 (1958): 185–95.

9–12   Daniel G. Freedman, *Human Infancy: An Evolutionary Perspective* (Hillsdale, N.J.: Lawrence Erlbaum, 1974).

12–14   James Tanner, *Education and Physical Growth* (London: University of London Press, 1961).

19–33   C. Super and S. Harkness, "The infant's niche in rural Kenya and America," in *Cross-Cultural Research at Issue*, ed. L. L. Adler (New York: Academic Press, 1982), 47–55.

101:1–6 P. R. Zelazo, N. A. Zelazo, and S. Kolb, " 'Walking' in the newborn," *Science* 176 (1972): 314–15.

7–9 Clark, "Vestibular stimulation's influence on motor development."

16–40 Melvin J. Konner, "Infancy among the Kalahari Desert San," in *Culture and Infancy: Variations in the Human Experience*, eds. P. Leiderman, S. Tulkin, and A. Rosenfeld (New York: Academic Press, 1977), 287–328.

102:1–2 Ibid.

8–12 H. Kaplan and H. Dove, "Infant development among the Ache of eastern Paraguay," *Developmental Psychology* 23 (1987): 190–98.

18–21 Ann Bigelow and Monica Watson, "The relation between walking and changes in play with objects." Paper presented at International Conference on Infant Studies, Paris, 1994.

24–29 J. J. Campos and B. I. Bertenthal, "The importance of self-produced locomotion in infancy," *Infant Mental Health Journal* 5 (1984): 160–71.

31–35 C. E. Granrud and A. Yonas, "Infants' sensitivity to depth cue of shading," *Perception and Psychophysics* 37 (1985): 415–19.

103:15–16 P. H. Leiderman, B. Babu, J. Kaglia et al., "African infant precocity and some social influences during the first year," *Nature* 242 (1973): 247–49.

6. Sensory Nourishment

104:11–16 Richard Selzer, "Travels in Rhineland," in *Confessions of a Knife* (New York: William Morrow, 1979).

24–31 Carolyn C. Goren, Merrill Sarty, and Paul Wu, "Visual following and pattern discrimination of face-like stimuli by newborn infants," *Pediatrics* 56, no. 4 (1975): 544–49.

105:6–9 Aidan Macfarlane, "Olfaction in the development of social preferences in the human neonate," in *Parent-Infant Interaction*, ed. M. Hofer (Amsterdam: Elsevier, 1975).

9–10 R. H. Porter, J. Cernoch, and F. J. McLaughlin, "Maternal recognition of neonates through olfactory cues," *Physiology and Behavior* 30 (1985): 151–54.

11–13 R. H. Vallardi, J. Porter, and J. Winberg, "Does the newborn find the nipple by smell?" *Lancet* 344 (1994): 989–90.

23–25 A. J. DeCasper and M. J. Spence, "Prenatal maternal speech influences newborns' perception of speech sounds," *Infant Behavior and Development* 9 (1986): 133–150.

40 A. Janniruberto and E. Tajani, "Ultrasonographic study of fetal movements," *Seminars in Perinatology* 5, no. 2 (1981).

106:1–2 Ibid.

5–12 Peter Hepper, "An examination of fetal learning before and after birth," *Irish Journal of Psychology* 12, no. 2 (1991): 95–107.

15–19 Cited in Thomas Verny, *The Secret Life of the Unborn Child* (New York: Summit Books, 1981), 23.

35–38 Yvonne Brackbill, "Continuous stimulation and arousal level in infancy: effects of stimulus intensity and stress," *Child Development* 46 (1975): 364–69.

108:4–7   Ashley Montagu, *Touching: The Human Significance of the Skin* (New York: Harper & Row, 1986).

12–15   Porter, "Maternal recognition of neonates through olfactory cues."

15–18   M. Kaitz, A. Eidelman, P. Lapidot et al., "Postpartum women can recognize their infants by touch," *Pediatric Research* 25 (1989): 14A.

18–20   M. Kaitz, S. Shiri, S. Danziger et al., "Fathers can also recognize their newborns by touch," *Infant Behavior & Development* 17 (1994): 205–207.

21–23   Lee Salk, "Mother's heartbeat as an imprinting stimulus," *Transactions of the New York Academy of Sciences* 3 (1962): 165–67.

27–40   H. J. Ginsburg, S. Fling, M. L. Hope et al., "Maternal holding preferences: a consequence of newborn head-turning response," *Child Development* 50 (1979): 280–81.

109:3–12   For a review of sex differences, see Anne Moir and David Jessel, *Brain Sex* (New York: Carol Publishing Group, 1991).

16–22   Helen Fisher, *Anatomy of Love* (New York: Fawcett Columbine, 1992).

24–40   D. McGuinness and K. H. Pribram, "The origin of sensory bias in the development of gender differences in perception and cognition," in *Cognitive Growth and Development*, ed. M. Bortner (New York: Brunner/Mazel, 1979).

110:25–30   M. Rosenzweig, E. Bennett, and M. Diamond, "Brain changes in response to experience," *Scientific American* 226 (1972): 22–29.

32–35   Richard M. Restak, *The Infant Mind* (Garden City, N.Y.: Doubleday, 1986).

111:4–6   Fisher, *Anatomy of Love*, 28.

6–11   D. R. Kenshalo, ed., *The Skin Senses* (Springfield, Ill.: Charles C. Thomas, 1968).

7. CONTAINER CRAZY

115:11–15   Anaïs Nin, quoted in Mary Lawrence, *Mother and Child* (New York: Balance House, 1975): 198.

116:34–37   Margaret Mead, *Sex and Temperament in Three Primitive Societies* (New York: William Morrow, 1935): 40–41.

117:2–9   K. Kaye and A. J. Wells, "Mothers' jiggling and the burst-pause pattern in neonatal feeding," *Infant Behavior and Development* 3 (1980): 29–46.

118:10–15   Sandra Edwards, "Babes in arms," *OT Week* (22 June 1989), 19.

19–26   Patricia Wilbarger, "Planning an adequate 'sensory diet'—application of sensory processing theory during the first year of life," *Zero to Three* V, no. 1 (September 1984), 12.

33–37   Patricia Wilbarger and Patti Oetter, "Sensory defensiveness and related social/emotional and neurological disorders." Workshop given in Panama City, Fla. (January 1994).

119:11–23   Stephanie Day, "Mother-infant activities as providers of sensory stimulation," *American Journal of Occupational Therapy* 36, no. 9 (1982): 579–85.

24–26   A. H. Parmalee, H. R. Schulz, and M. A. Disbrow, "Sleep patterns of the newborn," *Journal of Pediatrics* 58 (1961): 241–50.

29–32   M. Richards and J. Bernal, "An observational study of mother-infant interaction," in *Ethological Studies of Child Behavior*, ed. N. G. Blurton Jones (New York: Cambridge University Press, 1972).

30–32   F. Rebelsky, and G. Abeles, "Infancy in Holland and the United States." Boston University, 1973, unpublished manuscript.

32–34   Tiffany Field, Jeff Harding, Barbara Soliday et al., "Touching in infant, toddler, and preschool nurseries," *Early Child Development and Care* 98 (1994): 113–20.

34–36   Urs Hunzikar and Ronald G. Barr, "Increased carrying reduces infant crying: A randomized controlled trial," *Pediatrics* 77 (1986): 641–48.

38–40   Melvin J. Konner, "Infancy among the Kalahari Desert San," in *Culture and Infancy: Variations in the Human Experience*, eds. P. Leiderman, S. Tulkin, and A. Rosenfeld (New York: Academic Press, 1977), 287–328.

120:1–7   Ibid.

28–30   Harriet Rheingold, "The measurement of maternal care," *Child Development* 31 (1960): 565–75.

33–40   Mary Kay Floeter and William Greenough, "Cerebellar plasticity: modification of Purkinje cell structure by differential rearing in monkeys," *Science* 206 (1979): 227–29.

121:1–9   Ibid.

26–33   Barbara Ayres, "Effects of infant carrying practices on rhythm in music," *Ethos* 1, no. 4 (1973): 387–404.

34–36   Colin McPhee, "Children and music in Bali," *Childhood in Contemporary Cultures*, eds. M. Mead and M. Wolfenstein (Chicago: University of Chicago Press, 1955), 70–99.

122:35–39   Itzhak Bentov, *Stalking the Wild Pendulum* (New York: E. P. Dutton, 1977).

123:20–23   T. B. Brazelton, E. Z. Tronick, L. Adamson, et al., "Early mother-infant reciprocity," in *Parent-Infant Interaction*, CIBA Foundation Symposium (Elsevier, Oxford, 1975), 33.

28–30   W. S. Condon and L. W. Sander, "Synchrony demonstrated between movements of the neonate and adult speech," *Child Development* 45 (1974): 456–62.

30–32   Daniel Stern, "A microanalysis of mother-infant interaction: behavior regulating social contact between a mother and her three-and-one-half-month-old twins," *Journal of the American Academy of Child Psychiatry* 10 (1971): 501–17.

35–39   Barry M. Lester, "There's more to crying than meets the ear," in *Infant Crying*, eds. Barry M. Lester and C. F. Zachariah Boukydis (New York: Plenum Press, 1985), 7.

124:1–3   Ibid.

8. Sensory Overkill

125:24–40   Barbara Fajardo and Daniel G. Freedman, "Maternal rhythmicity in three American cultures," in *Culture and Early Interactions*, eds. T. M. Field, A. M. Sostek, P. Vietze, and P. H. Leiderman (Hillsdale, N.J.: Lawrence Erlbaum, 1981): 133–47.

126:1–5   Ibid.

25–27   John W. Callaghan, "A comparison of Anglo, Hopi and Navajo mothers and infants," *Culture and Early Interactions* (1981): 115–31.

34–40   Fajardo and Freedman, "Maternal rhythmicity in three American cultures."

127:1–2   Ibid.

5–8   W. A. Caudill and H. Weinstein, "Maternal care and infant behavior in Japan and America," *Psychiatry* 32 (1969): 12–43.

12–14   C. Kluckhohn, "Some aspects of Navaho infancy and early childhood," in

Readings in Child Development, eds. W. E. Martin and C. B. Stendler (New York: Harcourt, Brace, & World, 1954): 181.

129:13–18   Daniel Stern, *The First Relationship: Infant and Mother* (Cambridge: Harvard University Press, 1977).

21–23   Martin Seligman, *The Optimistic Child* (New York: Houghton Mifflin, 1985).

24–31   M. Lewis, S. M. Alessandri, and M. W. Sullivan, "Violation of expectancy, loss of control, and anger expressions in young infants," *Developmental Psychology* 26 (1990): 745–51.

34–38   Melvin Konner, *Childhood* (Boston: Little, Brown and Company, 1991), 65.

130:26–29   Jayne M. Singer and Jeffrey W. Fagen, "Negative affect, emotional expression, and forgetting in young infants," *Developmental Psychology* 28, no. 1 (1992): 48–57.

40   T. Berry Brazelton and Bert G. Cramer, *The Earliest Relationship* (Reading, Mass.: Addison-Wesley, 1990).

131:1–6   Ibid.

23–26   Lina Zahr, "Premature infant responses to noise control by earmuffs: effects on behavioral and physiological measures." Paper presented at the International Conference on Infant Studies, Paris, 1994.

33–40   Cited in Steven Halpern, *Sound Health* (San Francisco: Harper & Row, 1985).

133:3–8   Patricia Wilbarger and Patti Oetter, "Sensory defensiveness and related social/emotional and neurological disorders." Workshop given in Panama City, Fla., January, 1994.

23–26   B. M. Knickerbocker, *A Holistic Approach to the Treatment of Learning Disorders* (Thorofare, N.J.: C. B. Slack, 1980).

36–39   Patricia Wilbarger and Julia Wilbarger, "Sensory affective disorders beyond tactile defensiveness." Lecture given in Milwaukee, Wis., 1988.

134:8–11   Patricia Wilbarger and Julia Wilbarger, *Sensory Defensiveness in Children Ages 2–12: An Intervention Guide for Parents and Other Caretakers* (Santa Barbara, Calif.: Avanti Educational Programs, 1991).

14–16   See Jean Ayres, *Sensory Integration and the Child* (Los Angeles: Western Psychological Services, 1979).

135:5–7   Personal communication with Patricia Wilbarger, May 1997 (Miami, FL).

23–26   Andrew N. Meltzoff and R. W. Borton, "Intermodal matching by human neonates," *Nature* 282 (1979): 403–404.

34–36   D. Sinclair, *Mechanisms of Cutaneous Stimulation* (London: Oxford University Press, 1981).

136:3–5   See Jean A. Ayres, "Interrelationships among perceptual-motor function in children," *American Journal of Occupational Therapy* 20 (1966): 68–71.

37–40   Peter A. Gorski, Lee Huntington, and David J. Lewkowicz, "Handling preterm infants in hospitals: stimulating controversy about timing stimulation," *Pediatric Round Table* 13, ed. Nina Guzenhauser (Skillman, N.J.: Johnson & Johnson Baby Products Company, 1987).

138:1–2   Ibid.

6–7   G. A. DeGangi and S. I. Greenspan, "The development of sensory functions in infants," *Physical & Occupational Therapy in Pediatrics* 8, no. 4 (1988): 21–33.

14–16   J. Kagan, J. S. Reznick, N. Snidman et al., "Inhibited and uninhibited types of children," *Child Development* 60 (1989), 2212–25.

21–23   J. Kagan, J. S. Reznick, and N. Snidman, "Biological basis of childhood shyness," *Science* 240 (1988): 167–71.

27–40   Jerome Kagan, *Galen's Prophecy* (New York: Basic Books, 1994).

139:1–9   Ibid.

140:12–18 "Q & A Behavior," *Parents* (November 1994), 54.

141:35–37 J. S. Chisholm, "Biology, culture, and the development of temperament," in *The Cultural Context of Infancy*, vol. 1, ed. J. K. Nugent, B. M. Lester, and T. B. Brazelton (Norwood, N.J.: Ablex, 1989), 341–64.

142:10–14 Cited in Peter D. Kramer, *Listening to Prozac* (New York: Viking, 1993).

9. THE BODY FORBIDDEN

143:40   Desmond Morris, *Intimate Behavior* (New York: Random House, 1971), 32.

144:1   Ibid.

9–17   Noelle Oxenhandler, "The eros of parenthood," *The New Yorker* (19 February 1996): 47–49.

19–22   Michel Odent, *Entering the World* (New York: Marion Boyers, 1984), 29.

24–29   John B. Watson, *The Psychological Care of the Infant and Child* (New York: W. W. Norton, 1928), 43–44.

30–35   Ann Hulbert, "Dr. Spock's baby," *The New Yorker* (20 May 1996): 83.

145:4–8   Irenäus Eibl-Eibesfeldt, *Human Ethology* (New York: Aldine de Gruyter, 1989), 215.

26–28   Helen Fisher, *Anatomy of Love* (New York: Fawcett Columbine, 1992).

33–39   Quoted in Esther Davidowitz, "The breast-feeding taboo," *Redbook* (July 1992): 114.

146:25–31 Vidal S. Clay, "The effect of culture on mother-child tactile communication." Ph.D. diss., Teachers College, Columbia University, 1966.

147:6–18   Robert Crooks and Karla Baur, *Our Sexuality* (Redwood City, Calif.: Benjamin/Cummings Publishing, 1990), 482.

30–34   John Money and Margaret Lamacz, "Genital examination and exposure experienced as nosocomial sexual abuse in childhood," *Journal of Nervous & Mental Disease* 175, no. 12 (1987).

37–39   Richard A. Gardner, "Exposing children to parental nudity," *Medical Aspects of Human Sexuality* 9, no. 6 (1975): 99–100.

148:3–6   Margaret Mead, *Male and Female* (New York: William Morrow, 1949/1967), 83–84.

22–25   John Money and Patricia Tucker, *Sexual Signatures* (Boston: Little, Brown and Company, 1975).

149:3–8   Robert Lawlor, *Voices of the First Day* (Rochester, Vt.: Inner Traditions, 1991), 171.

16–20   Money, *Sexual Signatures*.

26–40   Robin Lewis and Louis Janda, "The relationship between adult sexual adjustment and childhood experiences regarding exposure to nudity, sleeping in the parental bed, and parental attitudes towards sexuality," *Archives of Sexual Behavior* 17 (1988): 349–62.

150:1–2   Ibid.

11–15   M. Hoyt, "Children's accidental exposure to parental coitus," *Medical Aspects of Human Sexuality* 1 (1982): 64–65.

34–40   Department of Labor, Children's Bureau, *Infant Care* (Washington, D.C.: Government Printing Office, 1914–51).

151:1–5   Ibid.

14–20   Rene A. Spitz, "Autoeroticism: Some empirical findings and hypotheses on three of its manifestations in the first year of life," *The Psychological Study of the Child*, vols. 3, 4 (New York: International University Press, 1949).

26–27   N. Newton and M. Newton, "Psychologic aspects of lactation," *New England Journal of Medicine* 277 (1967): 1179–88.

27–28   Floyd Martinson, "The sex education of young children," in *Sex Education in the Eighties*, ed. Lorna Brown (New York: Plenum Press, 1981).

31–37   Michael Lewis and Jerome Kagan, "Studies in attention," *Merrill-Palmer Quarterly* 2 (1965): 95–127.

152:1–4   A. Kinsey, W. Pomeroy, and C. Martin, *Sexual Behavior in the Human Male* (Philadelphia: Saunders, 1948).

153:9–15   As They Grow, *Parents* (April 1995): 66.

31–34   Sigmund Freud, *The Three Contributions to the Theory of Sex*, A. A. Brill, trans. (New York: Nervous and Mental Disease Monograph, 1905 [1948]).

154:2–5   Margaret Mead, *Childhood in Contemporary Cultures* (Chicago: University of Chicago Press, 1955), 27.

6–11   Stephen Suomi and Harry F. Harlow, "Play," *Natural History Magazine*, (December 1971).

29–37   Martinson, "Sex education of young children," 52.

155:19–22   Ashley Montagu, opening remarks, Touch Research Institute Symposium, Miami, Fla. May 1993.

23–28   S. M. Jourard, "An exploratory study of body accessibility," *British Journal of Social and Clinical Psychology* 5 (1966): 221–31.

156:8–11   Jules Henry, *Jungle People: A Kaingang tribe of the Highlands of Brazil* (New York: Vintage Books, 1964).

14–20   Melanie Thernstrom, "Diary of a murder," *The New Yorker* (3 June: 1996): 62–71.

32–34   Ashley Montagu, *Touching: The Human Significance of the Skin* (New York: Harper & Row, 1986), 357.

39   Edward T. Hall, *The Hidden Dimension* (New York: Anchor Books, 1966).

157:1–4   Ibid.

5–15   B. Connolly and R. Anderson, *First Contact: New Guinea Highlands Encounter the Outside World* (New York: Viking Penguin, 1987).

17–21   Julius Fast, *Body Language* (New York: M. Evans 1970).

158:11–16   Dean Tong, *Don't Blame Me, Daddy: False Accusations of Child Sexual Abuse; A Hidden National Tragedy* (Norfolk, Va.: Hampton Roads, 1992), v.

32–36   Sandra J. Weiss, "Parental touch and the child's body image," in *The Many Facets of Touch*, Pediatric Round Table 10, ed. C. C. Brown (Skillman, N.J.: Johnson & Johnson Baby Products Co., 1984).

39–40   Adam Gopnik, "Wonderland," *The New Yorker* (9 October 1995): 82–90.

159:1–10   Ibid.

12–16   Marion C. Hyson, Linda C. Whitehead, and Catherine M. Prudhoe, "Influences on attitudes towards physical affection between adults and children," *Early Childhood Research Quarterly* 3 (1988): 55–75.

20–22   Richard A. Gardner, *Sex Abuse Hysteria, Salem Witch Trials Revisited* (Cresskill, N.J.: Creative Therapeutics, 1991).

28–39   Davidowitz, "The Breast-Feeding Taboo."

160:7–11   Niles Newton, "Interrelationships between sexual responsiveness, birth, and breast feeding," in *Contemporary Sexual Behavior: Critical Issues in the 1970s*, ed. Joseph Zubin and John Money (Baltimore: Johns Hopkins University Press, 1973): 77–98.

14–24 Alice Rossi, "Maternalism, sexuality, and the new feminism," in *Contemporary Sexual Behavior*: 145–74.

25–26 W. J. Masters and V. E. Johnson, *Human Sexual Response* (Boston: Little, Brown, 1966).

26–28 R. E. Sears, E. Maccoby, H. Lewin, *Patterns of Child Rearing* (Evanston, Ill.: Row, Peterson, 1957).

29–32 Robin Fox, *The Red Lamp of Incest* (Notre Dame, Ind.: University of Notre Dame Press, 1983).

34–37 Rossi, "Maternalism, sexuality, and the new feminism."

161:1–5 Margaret Mead and Niles Newton, "Cultural patterning of perinatal behavior," in *Childbearing: Its Social and Psychological Aspects*, eds. S. A. Richardson and A. F. Guttmacher (Baltimore: Williams & Wilkins, 1967): 142–244. Niles Newton, "The effect of psychological environment on childbirth: combined cross-cultural and experimental approach," *Journal of Cross-Cultural Psychology* 1, no. 1 (1970): 85–90.

6–17 Newton, "Interrelationships between sexual responsiveness, birth, and breast feeding," 78.

19–21 Eibl-Eibesfeldt, *Human Ethology*.

21–24 Kathryn Harrison, "Sharing life," *Parenting* (February 1996): 95.

24–31 Freud, *The Three Contributions to the Theory of Sex*.

10. Breast or Bottle?

163:39–40 For benefits of breastfeeding, see, for a review, M. S. Eiger and S. W. Olds, *The Complete Book of Breastfeeding* (New York: Workman Bantam, 1987).

164:1–10 Ibid.

2–3 M. R. Forman, B. I. Graubard, H. J. Hoffman et al., "The Pima infant feeding study: breast feeding and gastroenteritis in the first year of life," *American Journal of Epidemiology* 119, no. 3 (1984): 335–49.

5–9 M. H. Labbock and G. E. Hendershot, "Does breastfeeding protect against malocclusion? An analysis of the 1981 Child Health supplement to the National Health Interview Survey," *American Journal of Preventive Medicine* 3, no. 4 (1987).

11–15 A. Lucas, R. Morley, T. J. Cole et al., "Breast milk and subsequent intelligence quotient in children born preterm," *Lancet* 339 (1992): 261–64.

29–36 Jean Liedloff, *The Continuum Concept* (Reading, Mass.: Addison-Wesley, 1977), 56.

38–40 Frank E. Hytten and Isabella Leitch, *The Physiology of Pregnancy* (Oxford: Blackwell, 1971).

165:12–17 R. St. Barbe Baker, *Kabongo* (New York: A. S. Barnes, 1955), 18.

166:4–10 Ronald G. Barr and Marjorie F. Elias, "Nursing interval and maternal responsivity: effect on early infant crying," *Pediatrics* 81 (1988): 529–36.

15–23 N. G. Blurton Jones, "Comparative aspects of mother-child contact," in *Ethological Studies of Child Behavior*, ed. N. Blurton Jones (Cambridge: Cambridge University Press, 1972): 305–28.

27–35 Melvin J. Konner, "Aspects of the developmental ethology of a foraging people," in *Ethological Studies of Child Behaviour*, 285–304.

36–40   S. Boyd Eaton, Marjorie Shostak, and Melvin J. Konner, *The Paleolithic Prescription: A Guide to Diet and Exercise and a Design for Living* (New York: Harper & Row, 1988).

167:6–14   Melvin J. Konner and Carol Worthman, "Nursing frequency, gonadal function and birth spacing among !Kung hunter-gatherers," *Science* 207 (1980): 788–91.

168:13–16   M. DeCarvalho, S. Robertson, A. Friedman et al., "Effect of frequent breastfeeding on early milk production and infant weight gain," *Pediatrics* 72 (1983): 307–16.

170:2–8   Dept. of Labor, *Infant Care* (Washington, D.C.: Government Printing Office, 1963), 16.

14–18   Niles Newton, "The fetus ejection reflex revisited," *Birth* 14 (1987): 106–108.

34–37   Anne Wright, Sydney Rice, and Susan Wells, "Changing hospital practices to increase the duration of breastfeeding," *Pediatrics* 97, no. 5 (1996): 669–75.

171:2–4   D. Rafael, "Effects of supportive behavior on lactation." Paper presented at the meeting of the American Anthropological Assoc., New York, November, 1971.

11. Co-Sleeping Taboos

173:20–33   T. Berry Brazelton, *Touchpoints* (Reading, Mass.: Addison-Wesley, 1992), 123.

35–40   Richard Ferber, *Solve Your Child's Sleep Problems* (New York: Simon & Schuster, 1985), 62.

174:1–2   Ibid.

29–34   H. Barry III and L. M. Paxson, "Infancy and early childhood. Cross-cultural codes 2," *Ethnology* 10 (1971): 446–508.

35–36   Margaret Mead and F. C. Macgregor, *Growth and Culture* (New York: G. P. Putnam, 1951).

175:3–4   Gilda A. Morelli, Barbara Rogoff, David Oppenheim, and Denise Goldsmith, "Cultural variations in infants' sleeping arrangements: questions of independence," *Developmental Psychology* 28, no. 4 (1992): 604–13.

25–30   John Bowlby, *Attachment and Loss: Vol. 2 Separation*, (New York: Basic Books, 1973).

176:12–20   Jean Liedloff, *The Continuum Concept* (Reading, Mass.: Addison-Wesley, 1977), 55.

178:17–18   Chisato Kawasaki, J. Kevin Nugent, and Hiroko Miyashita, "The cultural organization of infants' sleep," *Children's Environments* 11, no. 2 special issue, "Environments of birth and infancy," (1994): 135–41.

21–23   J. C. Moloney, "Thumbsucking," *Child and Family* 6 (1967): 29–30.

36–40   R. St. Barbe Baker, *Kabongo* (New York: A. S. Barnes, 1955), 18.

179:24–25   William C. Dement, *Some Must Watch While Some Must Sleep* (New York: Norton, 1978).

38–39   William Sears, *Nighttime Parenting* (Franklin Park, Ill.: La Leche League, 1984).

180:12–20   Heather Paul, *Parents* (January 1995): 60.

27–31   James McKenna, "Researching the sudden infant death syndrome (SIDS),"

Monograph, New Liberal Arts Series (Stony Brook, N.Y.: Research Foundation of the State University of New York, 1991).

181:7–8   T. Berry Brazelton, *Infants and Mothers* (New York: Delta/Seymour Lawrence, 1983), 8.

17–19   T. Berry Brazelton, "Parent-infant cosleeping revisited," *Ab Initio* 2, no. 1 (1990).

22–25   Ferber, *Solve Your Child's Sleep Problems.*

26–31   Jean-Louis Flandrin, *Families in Former Times: Kinship, Household and Sexuality* (Cambridge: Cambridge University Press, 1979).

32–35   Lawrence Stone, *The Family, Sex and Marriage in England, 1500–1800* (New York: Harper and Row, 1977).

182:4–10   W. A. Caudill and H. Weinstein, "Maternal care and infant behavior in Japan and America," *Psychiatry* 32 (1969): 12–43.

19–22   Sears, *Nighttime Parenting.*

183:13–18   A. Wolf and B. Lozoff, "Object attachment, thumbsucking, and the passage to sleep," *Journal of the American Academy of Child & Adolescent Psychiatry* 4, no. 28 (1989): 292.

32–36   Steven Tulkin, "Childrearing attitudes and mother-child interaction in the first year of life," *Merrill Palmer Quarterly* 19, no. 2 (1973): 95–106.

184:4–16   Susan Abbott, "Holding on and pushing away: Comparative perspectives on an Eastern Kentucky child-rearing practice," *Ethos* 20, no. 1 (March 1992): 33–65.

28–31   James McKenna, "The all-American infant: at odds with its evolution?" Paper presented at 5th International Congress of the Pre and Peri-Natal Psychology Assoc. of North America, 18–21 July 1991, Atlanta, Ga.

32–38   McKenna, "Researching the sudden infant death syndrome," *Sleep* 16, no. 3.

185:5–10   Ibid.

10–11   M. B. Sterman, "Relationship of intrauterine fetal activity to maternal sleep stage," *Experimental Neurology* 19 (1967): 98–106.

16–19   J. McKenna, E. B. Thoman, T. F. Anders et al., "Infant-parent co-sleeping in an evolutionary perspective: Implications for understanding infant sleep development and the sudden infant death syndrome," *Sleep* 16 (1993): 263–282.

29–39   Ibid.

186:8–10   McKenna, "Researching the sudden infant death syndrome."

10–16   E. B. Thoman and S. E. Graham, "Self-regulation of stimulation by premature infants," *Pediatrics* 78, no. 5 (1986): 855–60.

187:7–13   McKenna, "Researching the sudden infant death syndrome."

27–33   C. Richard, S. S. Mosko, J. J. McKenna, and S. Drummond, "Sleeping position, orientation and proximity in bedsharing infants and mothers," *Sleep* 19, no. 9 (1996): 685–90.

36–38   Toshiaki Hashimoto, Kyoichi Hiura, Shoichi Endo et al., "Postural effects on behavioral states of newborn infants—a sleep polygraphic study," *Brain and Development* 5 (1983): 286–91.

188:3–7   A. N. Stanton, "Overheating and cot death," *Lancet* (1984): ii; 199–201.

35–40   Sarah Mosko, Christopher Richard, James McKenna, and Sean Drummond, "Infant sleep architecture during bedsharing and possible implications for SIDS," *Sleep* 19, no. 9 (1996): 677–84.

189:6–10   McKenna, "Researching the Sudden Infant Death Syndrome."

11–14   James J. McKenna, "The potential benefits of infant-parent cosleeping in relation to SIDS prevention: overview and critique of epidemiological bed sharing studies," in *Sudden Infant Death Syndrome: New Trends in the Nineties*, ed. T. O. Rognum (Oslo: Scandinavian University Press, 1995): 256–65.

14–18   Personal communication with Gene Anderson, April 1997.

37–39   McKenna et al., "Infant-parent co-sleeping in an evolutionary perspective."

190:1–2   Ibid.

9–11   James J. McKenna, Sarah S. Mosko, and Christopher A. Richard, "Bedsharing promotes breast feeding," *Pediatrics*, in press.

18–24   Melvin Konner and Charles M. Super, "Sudden infant death syndrome: an anthropological hypothesis," in *The Role of Culture in Developmental Disorder*, ed. Charles M. Super (London: Academic Press, 1987)

12. CRYBABIES

192:27–30   Marc Weissbluth, *Crybabies* (New York: Berkley Books, 1984), viii.

193:19–21   Irven DeVore and Melvin J. Konner, "Infancy in hunter-gatherer life: an ethological perspective," in *Ethology and Psychiatry*, ed. N. White (Toronto: University of Toronto Press, 1974), 113–41.

17–22   Ronald G. Barr, Melvin J. Konner, Roger Bakeman, and Lauren Adamson, "Crying in !Kung San infants: a test of the cultural specificity hypothesis," *Developmental Medicine and Child Neurology* 33 (1991): 601–10.

37–40   R. N. Emde, R. J. Harmon, D. R. Metcalf et al., "Stress and neonatal sleep," *Psychosomatic Medicine* 33 (1971): 491–97.

194:6–13   Jeffrey W. Fagen, Phyllis S. Ohr et al., "The effect of crying on long-term memory in infancy," *Child Development* 56 (1985): 1584–92.

22–29   Wenda R. Trevathan, *Human Birth: An Evolutionary Perspective* (New York: Aldine de Gruyter, 1987).

195:19–29   P. H. Wolff, "The natural history of crying and other vocalizations in infancy," in *Determinants of Infant Behavior IV*, ed. B. M. Foss (London: Methuen, 1969).

31–34   Evelyn B. Thoman and Sue Browder, *Born Dancing* (New York: Harper & Row, 1987).

197:3–4   A. F. Korner, H. C. Kraemer, M. E. Haffner, and E. B. Thoman, "Characteristics of crying and noncrying activity of full-term neonates," *Child Development* 45 (1974): 946–58.

5–7   J. F. Bernal, "Crying during the first ten days of life and maternal responses," *Developmental Medicine in Child Neurology* 14 (1972): 362–72. Sylvia M. Bell and Mary D. Ainsworth, "Infant crying and maternal responsiveness," *Child Development* 43 (1972): 1171–90.

16–21   Melvin J. Konner, "Aspects of the developmental ethology of a foraging people," in *Ethological Studies of Child Behaviour*, ed. N. G. Blurton Jones (Cambridge: Cambridge University Press, 1972), 285–304.

30–32   Cited in Amelia D. Auckett, *Baby Massage* (New York: Newmarket Press, 1982).

198:10–16   C. A. Aldrich, C. Sing, and C. Knop, "The crying of newly born babies," *Journal of Pediatrics* 27 (1945): 89–96.

16–39   T. Berry Brazelton, "Crying in infancy," *Pediatrics* 29 (1962): 581.

199:2–4   Ronald G. Barr and Marjories F. Elias, "Nursing interval and maternal responsivity: effect on early infant crying," *Pediatrics* 81 (1988): 529–36.

14–25   Urs A. Hunziker and Ronald G. Barr, "Increased carrying reduces infant crying: a randomized controlled trial," *Pediatrics* 77 (1986): 641–48.

200:27–40   See Sandra Weiss, "The language of touch," *Nursing Research* 28, no. 2 (1979): 76–80.

32–34   Frank A. Geldard, "Body english," *Psychology Today* (December 1968): 44.

201:9–11   Cited in Beulah Warren, "Early evening 'colic': another point of view," *Australian Association for Infant Mental Health Newsletter* (Autumn 1989).

33–37   Weissbluth, *Crybabies*, viii.

202:11–18   Ibid.

21–27   Liv Ullmann, *Changing* (New York: Alfred A. Knopf, 1977), 230.

30–31   D. R. Kenshalo, ed., *The Skin Senses* (Springfield, Ill.: Charles C. Thomas, 1968).

203:3–4   Weissbluth, *Crybabies*.

10–27   Bruce Taubman, "Clinical trial of the treatment of colic by modification of parent-infant interaction," *Pediatrics* 74 (1984): 998.

204:16–18   F. L. Porter, R. H. Miller, and R. E. Marshall, "Neonatal pain cries: effect of circumcision on acoustic features and perceived urgency," *Child Development* 57 (1986): 790–802.

24–25   J. Lind, V. Vuorenskoski, and O. Wasz-Hockert, "The effect of cry stimulus on the temperature of the lactating breast primipara," in *Psychosomatic Medicine in Obstetrics and Gynecology*, ed. N. Morris (Karger, 1972).

205:35–39   T. Berry Brazelton, "Implications of infant development among the Mayan Indians of Mexico," in *Culture and Infancy*, eds. P. Leiderman, S. Tulkin, and A. Rosenfeld (New York: Academic Press, 1977): 287–328.

206:10–29   Ibid.

207:19–20   J. C. Moloney, "Thumbsucking," *Child and Family* 6 (1967): 29–30.

208:4–6   Robert Lawlor, *Voices of the First Day* (Rochester, Vt.: Inner Traditions, 1991).

18–21   Leigh Minturn and William W. Lambert, *Mothers of Six Cultures* (New York: John Wiley, 1964).

38–40   Bell and Ainsworth, "Infant crying and maternal responsiveness."

209:1–7   Ibid.

13. THE SELF-RELIANT SUPERMOM

213:19–23   Erik Erikson, *Insight and Responsibility* (New York: W. W. Norton, 1964).

214:20–22   S. W. Olds, "Interview with Margaret Mead, New York, Dec. 20, 1977," in *A Child's World*, eds. D. E. Papalia and S. W. Olds (New York: McGraw-Hill, 1993), 248.

215:20–24   Leigh Minturn and William W. Lambert. *Mothers of Six Cultures* (New York: John Wiley & Sons, 1964), 211.

30–40   Robert Coles, "Touching and being touched," Public Broadcasting Corporation, *The Dial* (December 1980): 26–30.

216:15–24   E. Z. Tronick, S. Winn, and G. A. Morelli, "Multiple caretaking in the context of human evolution: why don't the Efe know the Western prescription for child care?" in *The Psychobiology of Attachment and Separation*, eds. M. Reite and T. Field (Orlando: Academic Press, 1985), 293–322.

217:1–17   Selma Fraiberg, *Every Child's Birthright: In Defense of Mothering* (New York: Basic Books, 1977), 78.

36–39   S. W. Olds, "Interview with Margaret Mead, New York, Dec. 20, 1977."

218:28–29   M. Kotelchuck, "The infant's relationship to the father: experimental evidence," in *The Role of the Father in Child Development*, ed. M. Lamb (New York: Wiley, 1981).

19–31   H. Parker and S. Parker, "Father-daughter sexual child abuse; an emerging perspective," *American Journal of Orthopsychiatry* 56 (1986): 531–49.

219:13–32   Sharon W. Tiffany, *Women, Work, and Motherhood* (Englewood Cliffs, N.J.: Prentice-Hall, 1982).

220:18–26   Ibid.

222:7–12   S. G. Timmer, J. Eccles, and K. O'Brien, "How families use time," *ISR Newsletter*, University of Michigan (Winter 1985–1986): 83.

15–22   S. Boyd Eaton, Marjorie Shostak, and Melvin J. Konner, *The Paleolithic Prescription: A Guide to Diet and Exercise and a Design for Living* (New York: Harper & Row, 1988).

32–40   Melford E. Spiro, *Children of the Kibbutz* (Cambridge: Harvard University Press, 1975), 111.

223:8–20   Daniel Goleman. " 'Expert' baby found to teach others," *New York Times* (21 July 1993): 10:3, section C.

24–34   For a general review, see Ross D. Parke, *Fatherhood*, The Developing Child Series (Cambridge: Harvard University Press, 1996).

224:17–23   Margaret Mead, *Blackberry Winter: My Earlier Years* (New York: Pocket Books, 1975), 293.

225:18–21   Zero to Three/National Center for Clinical Infant Programs, "Heart Start: The Emotional Foundations of School Readiness" (Arlington, Va., 1993).

29–32   Tiffany Field, Jeff Harding, Barbara Soliday et al., "Touching in infant, toddler, and preschool nurseries," *Early Child Development and Care* 98 (1994): 113–20.

226:22–27   Sandra Scarr, *Mother Care Other Care* (New York: Basic Books, 1984).

27–35   *Zero to Three*, 1993.

227:10–12   Tiffany Field, "Quality infant day-care and grade school behavior and performance," *Child Development* 62 (1991): 863–70.

14–16   Alison Clarke-Stewart, "Consequences of child care for children's development," in *Child Care in the 1990s: Trends and Consequences*, ed. A. Booth (Hillsdale, N.J.: Erlbaum, 1992).

21–24   Jay Belsky, "Infant day care: a cause for concern," *Zero to Three*/National Center for Clinical Infant Programs 6 (September 1986): 1–7.

28–32   Alan Sroufe, "A developmental perspective on day care," *Early Childhood Research Quarterly* 3 (1988): 283–91.

32–40   NICHD Early Child Care Research Network, "The effects of infant child care on infant-mother attachment security: results of the NICHD study of early child care," in *Child Development*, in press.

228:1–16   C. A. Stifter, C. M. Coulehan, and M. Fish, "Linking employment to attachment: The mediating effects of maternal separation anxiety and interactive behavior," *Child Development* 64 (1993): 1451–60.

20–22   Carollee Howes, Carol Rodning, Darlene C. Galluzzo et al., "Attachment and child care: relationships with mother and caregiver," *Early Childhood Research Quarterly* 3 (1988): 403–16.

30–34   D. C. Farran and C. T. Ramey, "Infant day care and attachment behavior towards mothers and teachers," *Child Development* 48 (1977): 1112–16.

14. FINISHING TOUCHES

231:3–8   T. Berry Brazelton, *Infants and Mothers* (New York: Delta/Seymour Lawrence, 1983), xxv.

233:19–24   Dale M. Stack and Darwin W. Muir, "Adult tactile stimulation during face-to-face interactions modulates five-month-olds' affect and attention," *Child Development* 63 (1992): 1509–25.

234:8–9   Allan Bloom, *The Closing of the American Mind* (New York: Simon & Schuster, 1987).

Resource Guide

Touch

BOOKS

Susan S. Cohen, *The Magic of Touch* (New York: Harper & Row, 1987).
Jean Liedloff, *The Continuum Concept* (Reading, Mass.: Addison-Wesley, 1977).
Ashley Montagu, *Touching: The Human Significance of the Skin* (New York: Harper & Row, 1986).
Desmond Morris, *Intimate Behavior* (New York: Random House, 1971).

Birthing

BOOKS

Robbie E. Davis-Floyd, *Birth as an American Rite of Passage* (Berkeley: University of California Press, 1992).
Marshall H. Klaus and Phyllis Klaus, *Mothering the Mother: How a Doula Can Help You Have a Shorter, Easier, Healthier Birth* (Reading, Mass.: Addison-Wesley, 1993).
Frederick LeBoyer, *Birth Without Violence* (New York: Alfred A. Knopf, 1975).
Jessica Mitford, *The American Way of Birth* (New York: E. P. Dutton, 1992).
Lennart Nilsson, *A Child Is Born* (New York: Dell, 1977).
Michel Odent, *Birth Reborn* (New York: Pantheon Books, 1984).

ASSOCIATIONS

For more information contact:
International Childbirth Education Association
P.O. Box 20048
Minneapolis, MN 55420
(612) 854-8660

Postpartum Education for Parents (PEP)
P.O. Box 6154
Santa Barbara, CA 93160
(805) 564-3888

For information on: *doulas*
National Association of Childbirth Assistants
(800) 868-6222
Doulas of North America
1100 23rd Avenue East
Seattle, WA 98112

Newborn Care

BOOKS

T. Berry Brazelton, *Infants and Mothers* (New York: Delta/Seymour Lawrence, 1983).
T. Berry Brazelton and Bert G. Cramer, *The Earliest Relationship* (Reading, Mass.: Addison-Wesley, 1990).
Marshall H. Klaus and Phyllis Klaus, *The Amazing Newborn* (Reading, Mass.: Addison-Wesley, 1985).
Marshall H. Klaus, John H. Kennell, and Phyllis Klaus, *Bonding* (Reading, Mass.: Addison-Wesley, 1995).
Susan Ludington-Hoe and S. K. Golant, *Kangaroo Care. The Best You Can Do to Help Your Preterm Infant* (New York: Bantam Books, 1993).

ASSOCIATIONS

For more information on *kangaroo care*, contact:
Dr. Gene Anderson
Case Western Reserve University
School of Nursing
10900 Euclid Avenue
Cleveland, Ohio 44106-4904

Parent-Infant Relationship

BOOKS

John Bowlby, *Attachment & Loss: Attachment, vol. 1* (New York: Basic Books, 1969).
John Bowlby, *A Secure Base* (New York: Basic Books, 1988).
T. Berry Brazelton, *On Becoming a Family* (New York: Delta/Seymour Lawrence, 1981).
Robert Karen, *Becoming Attached* (New York: Warner Books, 1994).
Kyle Pruett, *The Nurturing Father* (New York: Warner Books, 1987).
Daniel Stern, *The First Relationship: Infant and Mother* (Cambridge: Harvard University Press, 1977).
Evelyn B. Thoman and Sue Browder, *Born Dancing* (New York: Harper & Row 1987).

ASSOCIATIONS

For information on infant mental health counselors, contact:
National Center for Clinical Infant Programs
733 15th Street NW, Suite 912
Washington, D.C. 20005
(202) 347-0308

Baby Massage

BOOKS

Amelia D. Auckett, *Baby Massage* (New York: Newmarket Press, 1982).
Vimala Schneider, *Infant Massage: A Handbook for Loving Parents* (New York: Bantam, 1982).

ASSOCIATIONS

For more information contact:
International Association of Infant Massage Instructors
P.O. Box 16103
Portland, OR 97216

Sensory Stimulation

BOOKS & ARTICLES

"Baby Carrier Basics," *Parents* (August 1996): 23–27.
Susan Ludington-Hoe, *How to Have a Smarter Baby* (New York: Bantam Books, 1985).
Daniel Stern, *Diary of a Baby: What Your Child Sees, Feels, and Experiences* (New York: Basic Books, 1990).

ASSOCIATIONS

For information on *sensory defensiveness* contact:
Avanti Educational Programs
642 Island View Drive
Santa Barbara, CA 93109
(805) 962-8233

American Occupational Therapy Association (AOTA)
1383 Piccard Drive
Rockville, MD 20850-4375

Sensory Integration International
1602 Cabrillo Avenue
Torrance, CA 90501-2819
(310) 320-9987

Breastfeeding

BOOKS

Nancy Dana and Anne Price, *Working Woman's Guide to Breastfeeding* (New York: Meadowbrook Press, 1987).
Marvin Eiger and Sally Wendko Olds, *The Complete Book of Breastfeeding* (New York: Workman; Bantam, 1987).
La Leche League International, *The Womanly Art of Breastfeeding* (New York: Plume/ Penguin, 1991).

ASSOCIATIONS

For more information, contact:
La Leche League International
1400 N. Meacham Road
Schaumberg, IL 60187
(800) 525-3243

Nursing Mothers Council
P.O. Box 50063
Palo Alto, CA 94303
(415) 326-2395

International Lactation Consultants Association
201 Brown Avenue
Evanston, IL 60202
(708) 260-8874

Sleep

BOOKS & ARTICLES

William Sears, *Nighttime Parenting* (Franklin Park, Ill.: La Leche League, 1984).
Tine Thevinin, *The Family Bed: An Age-Old Concept in Childrearing* (Wayne, N.J.: Avery, 1976).

SIDS:
James McKenna, "Sudden infant death syndrome (SIDS): Making sense of current research," *Mothering* (Winter 1996): 74–80.
William Sears, *SIDS: A Parent's Guide to Understanding and Preventing Sudden Infant Death Syndrome* (New York: Little, Brown, 1996).

ASSOCIATIONS

For more information on SIDS risk reduction and "Back to Sleep" campaign call:
• (800) 505-CRIB
• National Sudden Infant Death Syndrome Resource Center
  (703) 821-8955
• The Sudden Infant Death Syndrome Alliance
  (800) 221-SIDS

Crying

BOOKS

Sandra Jones, *Crying Baby, Sleepless Nights* (New York: Warner Books, 1983).
William Sears, *Keys to Calming the Fussy Baby* (New York: Barron's, 1991).
Marc Weissbluth, *Crybabies* (New York: Berkley Books, 1984).

Child Care and Support

BOOKS

Judith Berezin, *The Complete Guide to Choosing Childcare* (New York: Random House, 1990).

Sandra Scarr, *Mother Care Other Care* (New York: Basic Books, 1984).

Lin Yeiser, *Nannies, Au Pairs, Mothers' Helpers, Caregivers: The Complete Guide to Home Child Care* (New York: Random House, 1987).

Edward Zigler and Mary Lang, *Child Care Choices* (New York: Free Press, 1991).

ASSOCIATIONS

For more information, contact:
The Childcare Action Campaign
330 Seventh Avenue, 17th Floor
New York, NY 10001
(212) 239-0138

National Association for the Education of Young Children (NAEYC)
1509 16th Street, NW
Washington, DC 20036-1426
(800) 424-2460 or (202) 232-8777

For information on *family support* contact:
Family Focus
310 S. Peoria Street, Suite 401
Chicago, IL 60607-3534
(312) 421-5200

Family Resource Coalition
200 S. Michigan Avenue, Suite 1520
Chicago, IL 60604
(312) 341-0900

Index

and rejecting mother, 69
and sexual arousal, 159–61
and sensuality, 159–60
in Sweden, 169–70
and turn-taking, 117
breastfeeding frequency, 166–69, 232
and crying, 196, 198–99
and SIDS, 190
breast pump, 168
Brenneman, Dr. J., 16
Brott, Boris, 106
Burnt by the Sun (film), 158

calming, infant. *See* relaxation; soothing;
self-soothing.
Canada, 187, 199
Care and Feeding of Children, The (Holt), 14
caregivers
father as, 218, 223
and infant day care, 225–30
multiple, 216–18, 223–30
Carmichael, Stokely, 71
Carroll, Lewis (Charles Dodgson), 158–59
carrying (holding)
advantages of, 97, 102–3
vs. baby carriage, 115–16
and contingent behavior, 129–30
cultures, vs. Western, 119–20
difficulty of, 47–48, 97–98
importance of, 232–33
infant's need for, 41–53, 93
and later musical taste, 121–22
left-sided, 108
methods of, 98–99
and playing, 101–2
and prevention of colic, 202
and prevention of indigestion, 164
and reduction of crying, 196, 199, 207
and sensory defensiveness, 141
and sensory stimulation, 111
and vertigo, 49
and vestibular stimulation, 92
and walking, 99, 101
Caucasians, 50–51, 82, 100
Central Africa, 122
Charles, Prince of Wales, 155
child abuse, 38, 69, 70, 71–72, 74, 81
and behavior patterns, 78–79
and crying, 194
and lack of maternal support, 88–89
sexual abuse hysteria, 157–60
child care, 213, 215, 221–30
China, 49, 50, 51, 83
circumcision, 194, 204

Clay, Vidal, 83, 146
Coles, Robert, 215
colic, 38, 138, 201–3, 207
Common Folks (Slone), 184
Conroy, Pat, 143
cortisol, 29, 31–33, 38–39, 78, 138, 139
co-sleeping, 172–91
and breathing, 186, 189–90
and decrease of SIDS, 186–90
and fear of suffocation, 180–81
and heart rate, 186
and incest, 181
in Japan, 84
with newborn, 32
and prevention of crying, 179
and security, 178
and sensory exchanges, 184
taboos, 8, 173–74, 232
and temperature regulation, 184–85
and vestibular stimulation, 189–90
cradle, 97
cradleboard or papoose, 51
crawling, 7, 28, 57, 69, 99, 101, 102, 128,
132, 176, 217, 222
reflex, 30, 105
crib, 51–52, 97, 119
Crittenden, Patricia, 63–65, 67–69, 78, 88
Crooks, Robert, 147
crying
and anxious mothers, 66–67, 200–1
and body temperature, 45
and carrying, 93
and colic, 201–3
and contingent behavior, 203
delayed response to, 14, 193–209, 232
effect of swaddling on, 49, 50
effect on parent of, 194
and feeding, 166, 168–69
and human evolution, 194
and K-care, 35
and learning, 194
and newborn, 30–32, 41–43
and parental history, 75–76
and prevention during co-sleeping, 190
and rocking, 91
and separation, 193, 196
and sleeping alone, 173
and sucking, 45–46
types of, 195
Crybabies (Weissbluth), 202
cuddling, 4, 5, 14, 29, 53, 55, 69, 74, 127,
140. *See also* non-cuddlers.
reflex, 29